Advance Praise for
Stress For Success

"Hanson offers every manager a sustainable competitive advantage, and their families are winners too."
- Ray Smith, CEO, MacMillan Bloedel Limited

"A must for all interested in the future of their business and their body. Invigorating and enlightening. Beware, it could change your lifestyle."
- J. Blanton Belk, Founder and President, Up With People, Inc.

"Dr. Hanson's section on jet lag . . . should be required reading for all frequent fliers."
- Rhys T. Eyton
  Chairman and CEO, Canadian Airlines

"In this age of global competition, deregulation, and international corporate takeovers, people have never been more concerned about stress on the job. Dr. Hanson's prescription is refreshingly positive, and eminently practical."
- Michael Sanderson, CEO, Merrill Lynch Canada Inc.

On *The Joy of Stress*

"Dr. Hanson . . . has rare perceptions of the human psyche, as well as the body, and a merry sense of humor."
- Publishers Weekly

"The JOY OF STRESS forces you to take a long, hard look at just what it is you're doing in your own life that's helping or hurting you. It also gives practical, no-nonsense advice on how to avoid dangerous habits and cultivate good ones."
- West Coast Review of Books

"Instead of strategies which emphasize avoidance of all sources of stress, Hanson offers ways to manage the sources of stress."
- Chicago Tribune

"The revised second edition sports Hanson's now familiar brand of simple common sense mingled with humour."
- The Toronto Sun

On Dr. Peter Hanson,
the Stress Doctor:

"We greatly appreciate the time and effort you extended for your participation as a speaker. Thank you for doing a fantastic job and making the program such a success."

- G. Carey Hauenstein, CLU, President-elect, 1989 Million Dollar Round Table
- I.B. Meisel, CLU, Divisional Vice President, 1988 Annual Meeting Division

"Peter, I could go on at length discussing your value to a corporate group concerned about motivation, stress management, self improvement, balance of lifestyle, etc. I could use a variety of adjectives to describe your strong, but very easy style of presentation which integrates serious facts with humour and warmth, in a most professional manner. However, I'll sum it up by saying 'YOU'RE SUPER!' I would 'stress' your worth to anyone who expressed interest in an exceptional speaker for their seminar or corporate meeting."

- Barbara Lee Cohen, Executive Vice President, Gershman & Company

"Your speech was very well-received as being informative, motivating, appropriate and entertaining. And judging from the new popularity of water in the cafeteria, I know your book is being read carefully by many of us."

- W.J. Buchan, Business Area Director, Telecommunications, IBM Canada

"Your presentation on THE JOY OF STRESS was one of the highlights of our Wellness Week programme and generated a lot of interest with Crown Lifers."
- Elliot A. Williamson, M.B., Ch.,B., F.C.F.P., Medical Director, Crown Life

"Dr. Hanson's seminar was incredibly informative and his books and tapes were a most popular feature during break time. I received a great deal of positive feed-back from those fortunate enough to have participated in his presentation and many of Dr. Hanson's 'buzz-words' were included in conversation for the duration of the conference."
- Roberta M. Creber, President, Direct Sellers Association

"Your informative and entertaining talk on 'THE JOY OF STRESS' was a resounding success. My only regret is that our full agenda for the afternoon session prevented us from having a question and answer period. From the numerous comments I have received since your talk, I can only assume that a large percentage of the audience headed for the nearest bookstore to buy your book!"
- Val Peever, Advertising Manager, Print Production, Canadian Tire Corporation Limited.

STRESS *for*
SUCCESS

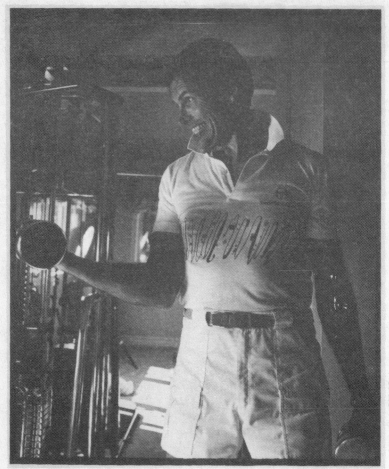

Peter G. Hanson, M.D.

STRESS *for* SUCCESS

Thriving On Stress At Work

Pan Books London, Sydney and Auckland

First published in Canada in 1989 by Collins Publishers, Toronto
This edition first published in Great Britain in 1989 by
Pan Books Ltd, Cavaye Place, London SW10 9PG

9 8 7 6 5 4 3 2 1

ISBN 0 330 30687 1

Printed and bound in Great Britain by
Richard Clay Ltd, Bungay, Suffolk

To my wife, Sharilyn, and our children,
Kimberley, 7
Trevor, 5
Kelly, newborn

CONTENTS

PREFACE

Stress — it goes with the territory; it comes with the job. By definition, stress is the adaptation of our bodies and minds to change. In a world where it seems the only constant left in the workplace is change, it comes as no surprise that work has become universally stressful. Stress has been blamed for costing the North American economy $200 billion per year. (In fact some major car companies pay as much for mismanaged stress as for the steel they use.) Similar high costs are reported in virtually all of the industrial world, making stress appear to be public enemy number one in the global economy. In terms of our health, stress is related to 80% of all illnesses. In medical problems as diverse as heart attacks, ulcers, and infections, stress is implicated in the deaths of millions around the world each day.

On the other hand, *stress is also the key to excellence*. Assignments that have no time frame usually take forever, and the results are usually of poorer quality than assignments with definite deadlines.

Students maximize their learning curves with the stress of an upcoming exam. Athletes set world records only with the stress of stiff competition. Entrepreneurs and "intrapreneurs" (entrepreneurs within a large corporation) can only achieve their greatest profits and productivity with the stress of knowing there's always the potential of falling flat on their faces. When governments or bureaucracies protect workers from individual acclaim or failure, those workers lose their competitive edge, causing whole companies or even countries to decline. When the elderly encounter stress, they often rise to the challenge with youthful vigor. When they are denied stress in a boring, idle retirement, they are soon dead or senile.

Stress, however, does not actually *cause* excellence, nor does it actually *cause* illness or financial losses. In fact, stress is neutral until it lands on a person. What that person has chosen to do about past stresses, and what the person chooses to do in response to the present stress, will determine the outcome. Not all air traffic controllers need to suffer ulcers or die of early heart attacks. Not all of us can, like Olympic athletes, set world records in front of a huge audience. In other words, a given stress does not produce the same results in every individual. As I have seen in my own office, and as has been consistently reported by health authorities around the world, the majority of stress-related illnesses, injuries, and early deaths are completely preventable.

The appalling tragedy of stress-related medical problems is on a scale even grander than that of lemmings following each other over a cliff to their deaths. Our collective response to the carnage has been to gather our resources at the bottom of the cliff and perform some heroic and truly newsworthy rescues. However, we are forgetting that the simplest way to stop the carnage is to focus on the top of the cliff, trying to help people change their direction before they reach the edge. Too often, simple prevention has been demeaned in comparison to the glamor of expensive high-technology rescues such as heart transplants and laser surgery. The financial costs of this prevention-ignoring, high-tech approach are not matched by any overall improvement in general health levels, or even much of an increase in life expectancy. It has become clear that we must become far more aware of low-tech preventative measures, which are in fact far more effective.

Meanwhile, back up at the top of the cliff, the passive followers of bad habits are keeping their heads down, their eyes blinkered, and their mouths cursing all the wrong enemies. Smokers who cause their own lung cancer usually blame their bosses or their work for making them smoke. Executives or sales representatives who suffer job burnout point their accusing fingers at the customer, the company, or the competition. Alcoholics who cause their own cancer of the pancreas, liver, or stomach — or who develop bleeding ulcers — rarely blame themselves for drinking. They all have outside excuses such as a stressful job or even the loss of the job, which they claim drove them to drink. Most heart attack victims think they were innocent victims of the demon stress, and that their Type A hostility, lack of exercise, slothful time management habits, inadequate relaxation skills, fatty diet, and smoking had nothing to do with their illness.

The simple fact is that the answers are within the grasp of each individual. Each of us, as a manager of his or her own Department of One, has the power to break out of the lemming herd and turn away from the precipice that awaits the incompetent stress-handler. As we shall see, the tools are simple, the sacrifices few, and the rewards rich.

To begin, we should get to know our alleged "enemy." Stress is simply the adaptation of our bodies and minds to change; and change, as we have noted, is about the only constant left in the workplace. Stresses come in every form and every intensity, and can range from the chronic to the acute. Stress can and often does surprise us in ambush, rather like a huge boulder falling across our path. Although the inert rock itself is neutral, the nature of the person ambushed is not. For the unprepared victim, the obstacle is a stumbling block. For the prepared victor, it is but a stepping stone.

In *The Joy of Stress*, I showed you how to harness the stress in your life to give yourself greater health and personal satisfaction. In this book I will show you how to actively choose to have the stress of your work life bring you conquest instead of carnage. As a side effect of your learning to use stress energy to your benefit, everyone wins. Your business (whether in the private or public sector) can have happier employees and reap greater profits. You can create new solutions, ideas, and directions, and gain long-term stability. The public will benefit from better-quality goods and services, and dramatic improvements in safety.

In a sailboat, the prepared can navigate through storms that would capsize the unaware. Similarly, the difference between failure and success in handling work stress is the difference between passive and active luck. Success depends not so much on how you set the sails, but on how you rig the odds.

Chapter 1

STRESS AND THE WORKING WORLD

DO YOU HAVE ANY STRESS IN YOUR JOB?

If your answer to this question is a resounding *yes*, then welcome to the modern workplace. Stress levels, as determined by patient questionnaires, are rising alarmingly, and are having a major impact on the health of businesses and individuals. In my fifteen years of family practice, where 80% of all patient visits were traceable to poorly-managed stress, the vast majority of this stress originated in the workplace. My practice was in the commuter town of Newmarket, Ontario, and provided me with a unique window through which to see the effects of stress in a cross-section of vocations. My patients' workplaces were in the surrounding farmlands, on the main streets in nearby small towns, or in the heart of Toronto's international financial district.

By getting to know the whole family of the worker, I learned a lot more about each of my 4,000 patients than would the specialist who treated a single disease or organ system. I delivered their babies, and made housecalls on their children and their grandparents. I gave them physical examinations, preventative counseling, and treatments for illnesses and injuries in my office. When necessary, I treated more serious health breakdowns in the emergency ward, operating room, or hospital bed. However, the reality of active practice was not at all as I had envisioned as a starry-eyed medical student. I was not at all the heroic medical figure who helped innocent victims of fate or bad luck. It was to my great frustration that most of the health problems I saw, from the trivial to the tragic, never needed to happen. As long as people feel no different than they did in the ''good old days,'' they feel immune to the effects of their bad habits, and many of my attempts at preventative counseling fell on deaf ears. Once one of these unnecessary disasters did strike a patient, there was finally an interest sparked on the subject of prevention. However, when they sought my recommendations for available resource material to read, most were confused by the plethora of books written in the medical jargon.

The Joy of Stress was written to give each patient some knowledge of what was happening inside his or her body in times of stress, and to provide each with the realization that the simple controls necessary to defend the body were within easy reach. However, patients and readers wanted to know more about how to handle the specific stresses of their jobs, and so the demand for this book began to grow. Research was through a wide variety of sources. I learned from the traditional medical literature, through the experiences of my patients, from audiences in person or on talk shows, and, most importantly, on a personal level.

In the tumultuous years since I took the bold step of mortgaging our house (with my wife Sharilyn's willing support) to self-publish 27,000 copies of *The Joy of Stress*, I came to know even more about stress than can be gleaned from any book or classroom. This was a particularly outrageous first printing in a country with such a sparsely-spread population (fewer than 20 million anglophones in an area roughly the size of Russia); in this country a national bestseller is a book that sells a mere 5,000 copies. Within one week of the copies' arrival into our basement in February 1985, every major bookseller in the country turned it down, because I was self-published, and unknown. My wife then drove me around to all the small independent stores, with books in the trunk, and our two toddlers asleep in the back seat, while I would run inside to try and place a few copies on consignment. Knowing that we were going to self-publish from the outset, any sane adviser would have thought us mad to put ourselves under such stress. But stress was my secret ally. Without the fear of failure, as would have been the case if I had been given a rich inheritance or a government grant, the motivation to achieve success would have been less. But, knowing that stress was the missing key to excellence, I used the opportunity to learn as much about the business as possible. I spoke to authors, customers, marketing experts, bookstore managers, and, most importantly, the kids that work in the front lines in the booksellers. I interviewed many, and selected but a few to be on my team; the best editor, the most skilled artist, and the most effective promotional specialist I could find. At the same time, I was a lot more careful about the writing style, content, and packaging knowing that one false step would mean a fall without a safety net. All of these risks are shared by any who borrow against their homes or life's savings to start up a small business, and indeed are common to all who share the entrepreneurial spirit.

Thus it was that I put my own theories to the ultimate test: a stress book that was (intentionally) born out of stress. After two months of encouraging sales in the independent stores, our national chains reluctantly gave the book a brief trial. On June 2, 1985, the impossible happened, and *The Joy of Stress* appeared on the national bestseller list, at number 10. By the end of the summer, it had risen to number 1, bumping *Iacocca* off the top spot. It stayed in that position for a further eleven weeks, and on the list for a total of sixty-nine consecutive weeks. Sales soared to record levels, both in Canada (where sales have passed 200,000 and continue at the rate of 1,000 per week after four years) and around the world, proving to the skeptics that stress, after all, can be the best ally in the workplace — if it is correctly managed.

Since the book was released, I began to do extensive speaking engagement with corporations, associations of professionals or independent business operators, and government departments in Europe, the United States, Canada, Australia, and New Zealand. Audiences have ranged in size from ten to five thousand people at a time, and before each address extensive research into the stresses facing the audiences was undertaken. As a result, I had the good fortune to broaden my patient base to encompass the stresses of people in all lines of work, all around the world. When it comes to stress, the whole world agrees, work is the cause of most of it. Stress at work can manifest itself in a number of ways:

- too much work, as is often the case around the time of a merger or acquisition, or with the self-employed.
- too little work, as in the case of a plant closing or lay-off.
- poor direction at work, as seen with those working for a bad boss.
- the right job, but pursued with workaholic fervor, leading to eventual breakdown of health, spirit, or personal relationships.
- the good job, but too little time to constantly update one's technological skills to stay ahead of the ever-changing competition.
- the special pressures of women in the workplace, and, in particular, of single parents.
- the exhausting problems of travel on the job, and the arduous task of digging out from under the "in" basket after one returns.
- the inability to relax, or to focus on outside activities during off-work hours.
- the growing presence of substance abuse in the workplace.

Workers today have never been more frustrated. If they do their job badly, their company will probably be taken over by a foreign conglomerate. If they do their job well, their company will definitely be taken over by a foreign conglomerate. Authors, lecturers, dieticians, psychologists, medical researchers, surgeons, homepaths, hypnotists, televangelists, vitamin hucksters and charlatans are falling all over themselves to sell their solutions to the confused public. But it falls to the low-tech family doctor to help an individual patient see his or her stresses in the context of the whole body, and to sort out the good advice from the bad. It is my mission to bring my perspectives, observations, and specific remedies for handling stress at work to each of you, as I did for my individual patients, in a practical and entertaining form. The stress you face at work will not go away, but if you follow my action tips you will be able to use that stress to bring out your own excellence. Those of you who think you have no stress at work may not need this book, but you do need to see your doctor — chances are you are either suffering a delusion or, if you truly don't have any stress, are moribund. For the rest of you who recognize stress as a permanent companion at work, read on.

WORKPLACE STRESS — AN "EQUAL OPPORTUNITY" OPPONENT

Stress is not limited to any one level in an organization. Although typically we have assumed all the heart attack candidates come from the executive ranks, it is now known that middle and lower levels have their own unique problems, making stress an "equal opportunity" opponent.

STRESS AT THE TOP

George is a Chief Executive Officer. He has an incredible level of responsibility — to the shareholders, to the board of directors, to the thousands of employees, and to his customers. However, George has trained for years for this job, and is happier having this level of stress than doing anything else, including retiring.

In spite of the rich trappings that come with his job, George has considerable handicaps unique to his station. In particular, being a CEO is lonely. As he was ascending the corporate ladder,

George had a large and vigorous group of peers with whom he could socialize (both at the office and on weekends). He never had to look too far to find a friendly opponent for a game of tennis, or a sympathetic ear when the going got tough. But now that George has made it to the top, he is all alone. About the only other people who could truly understand and share the levels of stress he faces are other CEOs, and they are all too busy to meet with each other.

The problem of loneliness for high-level executives is beginning to be addressed by formal international groups such as the Young Presidents' Organization and Australia's Executive Connection. But the need to share experiences and gain insights into how others are facing their challenges has far exceeded the capacities of such structured meetings. Thus many CEOs around the world are also turning to informal local luncheon meetings such as those started by Ceco's Erwin E. Schulze in Oakbrook, Illinois. Schulze now has good network ties with his neighboring peers in MacDonald's, Nalco Chemical, Interlake Corporation, Federal Signal, Spiegel, Waste Management Inc., and Centel. These ties provide great mutual benefit.

Other CEOs get to know each other at diverse functions, including charity or university boards, or even at the local golf course. But the principle is the same all over the world, even at this high level of success: no person can achieve maximum potential unless he or she is managing stress well. We all need the support and understanding of those around us to be our best.

STRESS IN THE MIDDLE

Robin is a medical doctor, having graduated at the age of 25. Now 40, she is still doing exactly the same work as is being done by graduating interns and residents. In fact, Robin is doing exactly the same work as she will be doing for the next three decades. As is the case in many professions, such as dentistry, accountacy, and law, the medical profession offers few transfers, promotions, or department changes such as are seen in the corporate world.

The same often applies to people involved in small family retail businesses. After a couple of decades of doing the same work, a sense of monotony can easily set in. When one looks ahead to more decades without change, a sense of desperation can even contribute to a midlife crisis.

In larger businesses, people in the mid-levels have a different handicap. They are given most of the responsibility, but have none of the control — a combination known to have a high correlation with heart disease. Most victims of corporate downsizing are from the middle ranks; now that computer terminals can keep upper management in direct contact with the plant floor, there is less need for supervisory personnel. In the civil service, a worldwide trend towards drastic cost cutting has placed severe budgetary restraints on workers. These limitations, when added to the increasing public demand for services and the normal red tape of bureaucracy, can prove extremely frustrating for mid-level personnel.

One of the most effective ways for individuals "caught in the middle" to deal with their stresses is to continue upgrading their skills, even if they have to do it on their own. The encouraging fact is that, although the major companies have been shedding jobs, people are turning to small entrepreneurial jobs in unprecedented numbers. The results are very encouraging for anyone who feels trapped in a large organization. Although the hours are long for a small business owner, and the financial commitment is high, the success ratio has never been better. More new wealth is being created by small businesses than by big ones.

STRESS AT THE BOTTOM

Although workers at the bottom of the ladder usually don't have heavy responsibilities, they face the challenges of mind-numbing boredom and union-management antipathy, as well as the frustration of feeling out of step with the public's perception of economic success. Noting that not one television family has a lifestyle as meager as their own, such people face a great temptation to overspend on credit cards, or to waste significant portions of the weekly paycheck on losing lottery tickets. Having no surplus cash left after basic living expenses are covered further adds to the difficulties of coping with stress at the bottom of the ladder.

THE STRESS OF STARTING A NEW JOB

With the high levels of employee turnover, the obvious corollary is that large numbers of people are having to face the challenge of starting a new job. As we recall from our first day in school, the stress of being in unfamiliar surroundings, with the resultant loss of personal identity, is traumatic enough to remain forever etched in our memories. Starting a new job can be even more stressful than starting school. The newcomer is completely unknown, sees no recognizable faces, and will undoubtedly be subaverage in proficiency and speed for the first few days. Office politics may play an additional part in the pressure. For example, the predecessor may have been very outgoing and popular, leaving large shoes to fill. On the other hand, the predecessor may have been a terrible manager, having left a residue of animosity that will be directed at the newcomer.

Without doubt, starting a new job is difficult. However, in order to balance our fears, we must also look for the opportunities and retain positive images of them. New responsibilities, new environments, and new challenges will all expand the horizons of our known potential. In addition, once we start to feel more familiar with our roles, new friendships will help us enjoy our new positions.

THE STRESS OF ENDING A JOB

One of the major stresses of the workplace, for both managers and lower-level personnel, is that of having to fire an employee, or being the person who is fired. While managers are taught to understand and appreciate that a fast, clean break is best for all parties, it is often very difficult to do, and must be handled in a humane manner, without anger.

Many instructional brochures have been written to help both the employer and the soon-to-be ex-employee. These should be read by the manager before the event, and given to the employee at the time of severance, so that he or she will have understanding and guidance to think coherently about how to make a positive step into the future. The wise manager should keep in mind that he or she is letting the worker go *for a good reason, and that it's probably better for both parties*.

The guilt that a manager feels and, in a number of cases, the feeling of failure that they were not able to motivate or encourage productivity within the worker can add a lot to their stress level. Having to act upon their decision and face the rest of the company during the ensuing days (especially if the worker was popular), can be debilitating.

On the side of the ex-employee, the anger, insecurity and aloneness that one experiences on being let go, not to mention the shame of having to admit one's failure to family and friends, can lead to severe health problems if the situation is not immediately faced. If you should be let go from your work, the first and probably best thing to do is allow yourself a sense of relief. Chances are you saw it coming and a part of you is glad. Most employees who adopt a positive attitude to this type of change are honestly able to look back and say that it was the best thing that could have happened.

THREE MAJOR CHANGES CONTRIBUTING TO TODAY'S WORKPLACE STRESS

People have worked, often under considerable stresses, since the beginning of time. However, since the beginning of *our* time, three major changes have contributed to the enormous role that stress plays in our working lives.

1. THE NATURE OF WORK HAS CHANGED

Originally, people's work was largely agricultural. Early human beings were hunters and gatherers, with all their automatic stress reflexes programmed for the brilliant "fight or flight" responses to primitive stresses.

As time went on, work became more diversified. In the last two centuries, the Industrial Revolution created a radically different new working reality, one for which the original "fight and flight" reflexes became less adequate. Rural agricultural workers were drawn to new urban factories. Instead of measuring the passage of time by the seasons, people began measuring it by the millisecond. Workers, suddenly out of their natural element, needed to be molded to work in harmony with their assembly line machinery. Thus it was that a system of education was developed to teach the masses uniform, rote regurgitation of behavior and facts. Through such education, people became better adapted to face uniform industrial stresses.

About the year 1970 we entered the Information Age. This presents each of us with a completely different set of challenges, rendering both our reflex and memorized stress responses less than adequate. Though challenging, these stresses can still be overcome by the aware individual. Unfortunately many people are not aware of the control they can exert over modern stresses, and as a result are falling needlessly by the wayside.

Many people are still relying too heavily on obsolete "fight or flight" weapons to fight new stresses such as time pressures, stock market fluctuations, traffic buildups, and computer breakdowns. The results, as in historical fields of battle, are a new kind of carnage, every bit as deadly and just as preventable. Heart attacks, lung cancers, stomach ulcers, burnouts, accidents, suicides: the list goes on to include virtually every organ system in the body, including the immune defences. Mismanaged stress can adversely affect the prognosis of virtually every disease, which is why it is viewed as the biggest public health threat in the world today.

The racing heart, the soaring blood pressure, and the thickened bloodstream that helped early humans survive primitive battles can now cause heart attacks and strokes as we moderns sit behind our computer terminals. Even when we override the basal brainstem "fight or flight" reflexes, we often do so by using another outdated weapon, the retentive side of the brain, to regurgitate standard memorized data from past learning. Although this weapon was effective during the Industrial Age, when many workers ideally memorized their jobs, it has proved to be a disastrous way of dealing with our radically changed modern problems.

Today's technological stresses were made possible only by people using the creative side of the brain. Thus, it should come as no surprise that the coping methods for these new stresses are also going to have to come from the brain's creative hemisphere.

The new victors over stress are no longer necessarily the physically strong or those with the highest marks in school. Rather, they are the self-starters, the entrepreneurs, the risk takers, the adaptable, and the innovative. Those who use their stress for success are aware of their primitive reflexes, and of the shortcomings of relying only on memorized data. They are able to balance these factors with a well-developed sense of creativity.

WEAPONS OF THE NEW VICTORS OVER STRESS

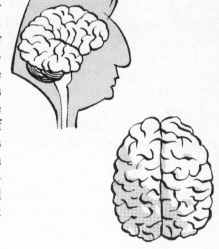

One type of weapon is seldom enough to win a war. The same is true in our bodies. The successful conquest of the stresses we now face at work requires that we understand the strengths and limitations of each of these three levels of defence and use them in concert to encourage victory, prevent disaster, and cultivate excellence at work.

2. THE NATURE OF THE PLACE OF WORK HAS CHANGED

As we in our Western societies become more committed to the Information Age, we leave the Industrial era farther behind us. Many of the easy-to-learn "grunt" jobs have been exported to less developed countries or eliminated altogether by technology. Tasks formerly requiring brute force on the factory floor can now be done by a microchip in a quiet office, or with a small home computer.

Even lower-level jobs, such as being a short-order cook or a secretary, have enjoyed the fruits of technology. Yet the stresses have not been eased as greater pressure is exerted on people to leave aside certain mechanical skills and learn to operate complex electronic equipment. Also, the frustration of not having any, or very little, decision-making responsibility can put additional stress on the worker.

We have witnessed the beginnings of a new de-urbanization trend, in which people have the ability to work in smaller centers, with flexible work hours. Our capacity to move people and information around the country and around the globe has brought about a tremendous decentralization of the workplace. Portable phones and facsimile machines have meant that conferences between departments, companies, or customers can take place even if one is in the middle of a traffic jam, out on a sailboat, or on the other side of the world.

Businesses and government agencies now have the ability to set up components of their activities wherever the economies of raw materials, available labor, and markets dictate. In today's business world, regional and national boundaries are blurring as the workplace and marketplace become more global. As a consequence, new stresses are quickly being brought into the lives of modern workers.

3. THE NATURE OF PEOPLE IN THE WORKPLACE HAS CHANGED

Our current demographics reflect the strong influences of three main "baby" groups. In graphic terms, these represent two hills and a valley.

1. The post-World War I baby boomers — born from 1919-1930, who are now poised to enter the ranks of the retired.

2. The post-World War II baby boomers — born from 1945-1965 (in Europe the boom went on until 1970), who are entering or in their peak working years. In the countries that fought in the war, this group represents about a third of the total population. However, these "boomers" were the first group to grow up in the infancy of birth control (if you'll pardon the oxymoron), and have not replaced their ranks with the traditional number of children. This then leads us to the last group. . . .

3. The baby bust generation — born since 1965 or, more to the point, born after the beginning of mass use of birth control pills by women of childbearing age. For the first time in history, women had reliable control over their reproductive systems, allowing them to choose the size and timing of their family, while still enjoying a normal sex life. As a result, most chose to have far fewer and later pregnancies, which became evident as the classrooms of the 1970s (built to handle ever-increasing numbers of children) were largely empty.

With over 10 million fewer teenagers in North America today than a decade ago, the pool of applicants to fill new jobs has declined dramatically. The shortage of teenaged labor is so acute in many areas that senior citizens are starting to fill jobs traditionally held by adolescents.

The significance to the corporate world of these three groups is of vital importance. The post-World War I boomers are collecting their gold watches and leaving the management of businesses to their post-World War II counterparts. Although the Information Age has made many menial jobs obsolete, there has never been a greater demand for creative, entrepreneurial talent to drive today's working world into the future.

However, when the post-World War II baby boomers try to find young people to fill the vacancies left by retirees, they are confronted by the slim pickings of their own baby bust.

Until recently, it was possible to run a corporation in the traditional military style. Managers would drive their corporation on a permanent forced march until someone dropped, then shout "Next," and carry on. This was possible only because of the seemingly endless pool of cheap labor and the uncomplicated nature of many jobs. As we have seen, though, the pool of new workers has dramatically dried up. To make matters worse, modern jobs requiring the key skills of creativity and entrepreneurship take many years to learn. Replacement workers, if one can find them, now take a major investment (of years and resources) to bring them up to speed.

Also, with the changing of the workplace to involve more sedentary information and service jobs, the criterion of physical "perfection" is frankly ridiculous. This revelation is beginning to dawn on recruiters for all kinds of businesses. An applicant who fulfils the job criteria, but by a fluke of war, accident, or genetics, lacks a full inventory of efficiently working human parts should not be overlooked.

It is no longer unusual to see braces, wheelchairs, or crutches in the office, on the plant floor, in the board room, or for that matter on the ski hill. The biggest handicap these people face is the rest of the population's perception of them. One must always remember that the man who held perhpas the world's most difficult job for longer than any of his successors was confined (albeit covertly) to a wheelchair. Franklin D. Roosevelt, showed the world that a disability should not inhibit anyone from assuming his or her own rightful place in history.

For the first time in history, success at work depends not primarily on capital and discipline, but on the fitness and motivation of each individual in the company. From now on, the winning managers will be those who help their employees win — keeping them well trained, committed to a mission, and, above all, healthy.

THE DAYCARE CRISIS

Current studies show that the number of children under six whose mothers work is over 8 million in the U.S. and is expected to be over 12 million by 1990. Statistics are proportionately similar in Canada, Great Britain, Australia, New Zealand, and most other Western nations. Thus the demand for daycare has never been greater. However, post-birth-control demographics have left us with a scarcity of teenagers to fill positions as childcare workers, nannies, or babysitters. The only other pool of potential help is at the age of retirement, where many no longer have the affinity for the job.

Daycare facilities, once thought of with derision by (male) corporate planners, are now seen as the best way for a corporation to attract and keep topnotch female staff. With women comprising fully half the graduates of America's three top business schools — Harvard, Yale, and Stanford — corporate recruiters are realizing that it takes more than just a couple of free tickets to the ballgame to attract and keep the best talent. As a result, the question of daycare has come out into the mainstream.

However, the pace of change is agonizingly slow, probably because most major corporations are still run by men. Of the 44,000 mid-to-large size companies in the U.S., only a paltry 2,500 offer help with employees' childcare needs. Nevertheless the numbers are almost four times what they were four years ago, and show every sign of continuing to rise. The main problem is the initial expense, as well as the reluctance of senior male staff to take note of what all the fuss is about.

It can cost a family $3,000 to $15,000 for childcare per year, with the average being closer to the former figure. Many companies, such as Procter and Gamble and American Can, are now offering a menu of benefits to allow employees to select those most helpful to their situation. Thus, instead of chosing a benefit of more holiday time per year, many employees are choosing to have daycare assistance in the form of subsidies or, ultimately, in the form of in-house or near-house daycare centers.

OFFICE DAYCARE IN ACTION

Many organizations have in-house daycare centers. I have been in offices of publishers where a number of children are crawling and playing in one corner of the office, without a designated babysitter on staff. Supervision of the kids is a pooled responsibility, and the system seems to work well. I have also toured many facilities where one or two qualified childcare workers are allotted a designated section of the office, well out of the way of the normal distractions of the working world.

When Wang Computer's chairman, Dr. An Wang, received a note from a female employee who was leaving because she could not find quality daycare, he initiated a company-sponsored program. The result: a one-story, semicircular building a mile down the road from Wang Laboratories. It houses 24 classrooms, a cafeteria, and a gymnasium where, from 6:30 a.m. to 6:00 p.m., 80 fulltime caregivers look after 280 preschoolers. Parents pay up to $100 per week, and the company picks up the difference in operating costs. Wang is happy to do so because it means his workers' minds are freed to be on their work. Indeed his employee absentee rates have plummeted, and his ability to recruit and retain talented employees has surged.

Other companies including Merck and Co. and Campbell Soup Co. have established similar centers. Companies such as 3M have even experimented with at-home nursing services for sick children of employees. However, there is still considerable resistance among the vast majority of corporations.

Such companies fear excess liability costs, and point out that the government should be offering some assistance in the form of taxbreaks or matching grants. Some interesting pilot projects are demonstrating that this can work. In California in 1985, BankAmerica Foundation, Pacific Telesis Group, Mervyn's Department Stores (a division of Dayton Hudson), and 22 other corporations worked with state and local agencies to split the tab on a $700,000 pilot project. State resource and referral agencies were helped to train new and existing daycare providers, who would then be licenced. In addition to initial training, there are even counsellors whom providers can call if they have a problem on the job. With the initial good success, funding has more than doubled, and 3,000 new spaces were created for children in 1988. The daycare is all based in local communities, which seems to be the employees' preference.

Companies such as American Express and IBM are working to increase the supply of community-based daycare nationwide. Although corporations resist the idea of having to pay for the construction of new buildings to house daycare, they seem to be quite willing to work with governments to fund the expansion of services.

In other Western countries, there is some degree of legislation to assure workers of leave for pregnancy or a child's illness, and some sponsorship of childcare (such as a comprehensive program in Sweden). In many countries a blend of private and government expertise is seen to provide the most hopeful solution. However, knowing the incredible inefficiencies of government-run organizations, it would seem wise to continue to have at least some private input into the running of any daycare system. Literally thousands of private child care centers are operating efficient, profitable operations but, knowing the possibilities for private greed, it would seem wise to have at least some government licencing and quality control. A system left completely up to private supervision is open to abuses. Perhaps the California project is an encouraging prototype for other countries to consider.

Chapter 2

STRESS AND THE DEPARTMENT OF ONE

ARE YOU TAKING CARE OF YOURSELF?

Because I have looked after thousands of patients in over 15 years of family medical practice and now speak to over 100 international organizations, associations, and Fortune 500 companies each year, I enjoy a unique window from which to view the health of the modern worker. Considering the diversity of jobs, cultures, climates, and economies that I have visited, one might expect a great variety of unique problems.

Remarkably, the opposite is true. Callers to radio phone-in shows tend to ask me the same questions in Perth, Australia as in Perth, Scotland, and these questions reflect those asked by my patients in Newmarket, Ontario. Discussions with audiences before and after my speeches confirm that work stresses in the computer age are now global among all industrialized nations.

Not only are the stresses much the same from one country to the next, but so too are the inappropriate responses to these stresses. This is primarily because most people are not aware of their *real* full-time job. The importance of whatever else we do as a career pales in comparison with the importance of our most important job. No matter how competent we might be at managing a vocation, we can never maximize lifetime earnings, happiness, health, and longevity without turning that same competent attention to the job that needs it most. That job, which is unpaid and is shared by each one of us, forms the basis for:

Hanson's
1ST
Law of Stress at Work
Each of us is a personnel manager of a department of one.

Most people who are running their "department" poorly are fully aware, in at least an elementary way, of the dangers of this poor management. The delusion comes when they think they will be somehow granted personal immunity from all risks.

Thus it is that smokers continue to poison themselves (and, of course, others around them) while thinking that heart attacks, cancers, and chest infections happen only to other smokers. Alcoholics and drug abusers kid themselves that they are not addicts because they could stop any time. Workaholics tell themselves that they are working for the future of their spouses and children, with whom they have left themselves no time to spend. Obese, out of shape "couch potatoes" convince themselves of their immunity from danger because they don't feel any different now than when they used to play active sports in school.

Although we all have good intentions, such as our New Year's resolutions, often the first item to be jettisoned when the working day becomes overcharged is the time we have set aside for ourselves, whether that time was to exercise, rest, or read to our children. Rather than taking ourselves for granted, we should be running our bodies with all the competence we devote to external objects in our work. Our lives, our jobs, and our loved ones depend on how well we keep:

Hanson's
Golden
Rule *of Stress*
Defence

Do unto yourself as you are doing unto others.

Most of us are considerate of others around us, and would never expect a store clerk apprentice, or babysitter to work without remission. And yet many of us push ourselves mercilessly, taking no breaks, allowing ourselves only enough time to eat on the run, and taking work home (or talking shop in our sparetime, which is the same). Thus we are effectively doing unpaid overtime.

We punish our bodies with inappropriate diets, cigarettes, or drugs. Slave uprisings have occurred with less provocation, yet we recklessly underestimate our own mortality. If we treated ourselves to the same consideration we extend to employees, family members, pets, and even our cars, we would benefit greatly.

For those who, like a callous slavedriver, choose to ignore their bodies' needs, the early signs of poor self-management are many. They include decreasing productivity, sinking morale, declining judgment, and increasing mistakes. The results to the individual are accidents, illnesses, divorces, debt, and usually a shortened life.

The results to the individual's business are increased absenteeism, employee turnover, computer crime, rising costs, falling sales, and increased chances of bankruptcy. Studies now indicate that 80% of all industrial accidents are caused by badly managed stress. Coincidentally, it turns out that the same number (80%) of patients seen in a family doctor's office are also there for reasons related to stress — reasons which could have all been avoided with competent stress management.

SIGNS INDICATING THAT STRESS IS OVERWHELMING YOUR DEFENCES

We are all under stress all the time, but we need to know when the stress is overwhelming our defences, preferably long before problems erupt. Fortunately, there are three early-warning lines of defence to tell us whether we are losing the battle with stress — physical sensations, feedback from others, and medical checkups.

PHYSICAL SENSATIONS

Physical sensations are subjective, and are often not accurate stress-effect indicators. However, they are still important. Mismanaged stress can destroy our defence mechanisms and thus affect virtually every disease and every part of our bodies.

Head and neck:
- Job burnout.
- Anxiety (excessive hostility, nervous habits such as nail biting or clearing the throat too frequently).
- Inability to concentrate.

- Insomnia.
- Fatigue.
- Depression; feelings of poor self worth.
- Headaches, including migraine and tension varieties.

Chest:
- Spasms of the bronchial tree, literally squeezing the breath out of you. This is the same mechanism that triggers asthma, and in some cases can be quite painful.
- "Globus Hystericus," a severe spasm in the upper throat muscles, making it virtually impossible to swallow. Usually noticed after acute stress, if one tries to eat or drink. Though quite harmless, it is extremely painful and frightening at the time.
- Heartburn.
- Rapid pulse, felt either in the throat or over the apex of the heart.
- Heaviness or pain in the chest. Both could be symptoms of a heart attack. Heart pains can also radiate up to the chin, into either shouldertip, or down the left arm, and can even occur in one of these areas with little or no pain in the chest. In general, pains such as these that get worse with exercise but disappear with rest should be investigated at once by a doctor.

Stomach:
- Change of appetite and, with it, a change of body weight. Under stress, most people lose interest in food and thus lose weight, but some react by nibbling all day long and gain massive amounts of weight.
- Increased use of alcohol and drugs.
- Intestinal distress. Some people become constipated, while others have diarrhea. Most experience some bloating and discomfort after a meal.

Urino-genital tract:
- Urinary frequency.
- Impotence in males.
- Decreased libido in females.

General signs:
- Unexplained frequent illnesses, such as sore throats that last all winter and fevers with every flu virus that is going around the office.
- Flare-ups of skin disorders such as acne, psoriasis, and other rashes.
- Exacerbations of existing diseases such as arthritis, infections, or even cancers.

One should never ignore any of the above symptoms. However, an important caveat with the list is that all or none of these signs may be present in an individual under stress. I have seen many cases brought into the emergency room where the patient's first warning of an impending heart attack was his or her last breath.

FEEDBACK

At home, this is usually pretty obvious when a child asks, ''Why does Daddy (or Mommy) never seem to be listening when I'm talking?'' Your friends might note that your shotmaking on the golf course has gone to blazes, or that your baseball pitch has turned from a bullet into a powder puff. They may comment that your conversation seems distant, as if you are preoccupied. Your secretary may note that you are making mistakes that are unusual for you, from missing the wastebasket at close range, to losing letters or documents and forgetting appointments. A coworker may comment that it is not like you to lose so much of your equipment.

Rather than react to such feedback with hostility and rejection, it is best to treat it as valuable intelligence, and a vital warning signal in your stress defence. Without being aware of how well (or poorly) you are doing in your battle with stress, it is impossible to effectively defend yourself.

MEDICAL CHECKUPS

Inside our bodies, many physical and chemical changes occur, which can warn us of high stress levels long before something breaks down. It is only by having a checkup by your doctor that these changes will be detected, because virtually all of them have no symptoms that you would be aware of until it is too late. Relevant tests include those for high blood pressure, high blood levels of sugar, cholesterols, triglycerides, and catecholamines such as adrenaline and cortisol.

The stomach can silently bleed, warning of an impending ulcer. If one is under chronic stress, decreased levels of circulating antibodies may be detected, as many reduced levels of the killer white cells that protect us from invading infections. The lymph glands may shrink drastically, making one more vulnerable to infections or existing cancers. The heart may suddenly start beating irrationally, or the airways can go into silent asthmatic spasms. Thus a full medical history and physical exam, combined with blood, urine, and stool test — as well as noninvasive tests such as the EKG and lung function tests where indicated — may give you your only advance warning of impending crisis.

STRESS AND THE SINGLE PARENT

Once, the single parent could be assumed to be female, but now the courts are taking a less prejudiced view towards child custody. Thus, both men and women who are raising children find themselves sharing similar concerns. In most big cities, real estate costs have escalated to the point where lower-income groups are out the mainstream of "middle class" neighborhood life. This means that it is becoming harder and harder to find neighbors to do the low-paying jobs of childcare. Companies are slowly but surely taking more notice of the childcare crisis now that single parents of both sexes are taking more sick-days to tend to their kids, and are distracted with worry about their children during times of illness. In any event, there is no question that a worker having his or her mind distracted by concern over the health and well-being of their offspring will be less able to perform to the best of their ability against the stresses of work.

The average single working parent, on average, spends approximately 21 additional hours per week ''working'' — that is, not having any personal time in which to unwind from his or her stress.

STRESS AND THE SINGLE PERSON

It is known that married people live longer than singles (although pessimists complain it only seems longer). It also appears that married people have better stress-coping skills at work. No doubt this is partly due to the fact that singles return home to an empty house or apartment, and have no one at hand to help talk them down after a tough day. To be sure, this does not mean that singles are all to be patronized or pitied, as many have worked at building and maintaining a supportive group of friends with whom they can share the highs and lows. However, those who find it difficult to cultivate such relationships often tend to end up with a ''main friend'' with whom they spend much of their ''free'' time, or, ultimately, spend considerable time alone. By protecting themselves from the latter option, many choose to prolong a relationship of convenience that in fact prevents either partner from meeting suitable romantic partners.

From talking to my patients, it seems that men appear have a somewhat easier time of single life than their female counterparts. In part, this difference is sociological, based on exposure to sports. One woman who stood at the top of her class in the Western Business School, raised the point that men are used to playing team sports, where they lay down their bodies to block for a team-mate, even if that person might be someone they normally would never get along with. Thus it seems that men revert back to this peer-camaraderie a little easier than women, and even though the single man might be no more successful in meeting friends of the opposite sex, at least men tend to be less lonely.

I have had a number of patients comment that stereotypes also work against women. This is particularly true if men are raised to feel that they must always be the mainstay of the relationship. Many men are intimidated by a woman who is economically their peer, or their superior in the workplace. With the hours spent in traffic added to the long hours of work, singles definitely have to be a little more creative organizing their spare time to best help them cope with the stresses they face at work.

HARNESSING STRESS TO ACHIEVE SUCCESS

In spite of the simplicity of the three levels of stress warnings, in practice they usually go unheeded. People put up with physical ailments, although perhaps resorting to some form of non-prescription medication. Most of us ignore the feedback of our peers and family or, worse yet, react to it with hostility. The vast majority of people at risk for stress-related illnesses do not seek preventative medical investigation. Heart attack victims often postpone coming in to seek help until the third or fourth day of their chest heaviness, and many do not survive even that long. People with family histories of early heart attacks avoid having their cholesterol levels tested, as if by ignoring the problem they could make it disappear. The obese, the smokers, and the out-of-shape — particularly males — assiduously avoid seeing the doctor for the same reasons.

The challenge is not the impossible task of eliminating all stress. Rather it is the eminently possible task of learning how to manage our personal responses to stress. Those who choose to do this right can thrive on stress and harness its energy as a supercharger to achieve excellence, happiness, and long life. Those who choose to do it wrong, by ignoring the needs of their own bodies and by blaming the stresses instead of their own responses to them, may find those same stresses predictably bringing about business and personal disasters.

It is my mission to help you stop the carnage — to use the existing stress in your life to bring out the best in yourself, in just the same way that world-class athletes use the stress of their competitions to break records. Thankfully this can all be achieved without stoic sacrifice or misery. By taking an active, informed role in managing the stresses in your own Department of One, as well as encouraging your colleagues to do the same, you will note that your morale, humor, and health will improve, along with your productivity and competitiveness. The stakes couldn't be higher in any poker game. Your job, your family, and even your own life depend on you to competently play your cards. Although you will not avoid all the stresses you will at least avoid most of the dangers. It is my sincere hope that each of you, as you continue reading this book, will learn to use *Stress for Success*.

Chapter 3

THE EXTREMES OF STRESS

STRESS LEVELS DEPEND ON CONTROL AND PREDICTABILITY

The levels of stress that people face at work fill the spectrum from boredom to panic. In between, most people can cope well with their stress levels. It is at the two extremes that health problems are most likely to arise.

There are numerous lists that rate the most stressful jobs in the world, and there is some argument about which are the worst. However, in reviewing them, some common factors emerge that make a job hard to cope with. Given a particular level of pressure on the job, how that job will be perceived by an individual worker depends on whether he or she has any control over the outcome.

I have spoken with many of my colleagues who attend professional racing car drivers at Mosport and the Molson Indy in Toronto, and they tell me it is very common for a driver's pulse to be higher when he's in a pit stop than when he is slipstreaming at speeds of up to 200 mph. The difference is that when the driver is in the pit, he is not in control of the outcome of the pit stop. He must depend on his crew to save those precious seconds which could mean the difference between winning or placing in a race.

Even within groups of people who lack an executive's control over what happens in a work situation, the degree of stress-related medical problems varies tremendously depending on the reliability of the stresses happening when they are expected. For example, during World War II, there was a rise of 50% in the incidence of people developing stomach ulcers in central London during the nightly bombing blitzes. However, out in the surrounding suburbs, where people were uncertain whether bombs would hit their area on any given night, the rate of ulcers soared by 300%. Even though central Londoners were harder hit by bombs, the fact that the stress could at least be counted on reduced its bad effects. Results are similar for people living in current trouble spots, such as Beirut.

Because of the importance of control and certainty, executives tend to do better than middle management or lower ranks when a particular stress strikes. Thus, for those companies that think stress management courses are only for executives, I would remind them of the simple facts. *Stress affects all workers, and the ones most often affected are the middle managers and lower-level employees.* Therefore these people should definitely be included in your plans to bring stress management education into the workplace. For those of you who are not working for bosses benevolent enough to introduce stress management education, it is critically important for you to take control of your own Department of One and make yourself even more bulletproof than the boss.

STRESS LEVELS DEPEND ON APTITUDE

The most stressful job in the world is one for which you have no aptitude, and one that you hate. As we have seen, the real question is not "What kind of stress does this person have?" but, "What kind of person does this stress have?" If a person has a high energy level, is a self-starter, enjoys risks, and deals well with the public, then the job of running a busy restaurant might be just ideal. The same person, working in a backroom office, might end up having insomnia, chest pains, and headaches, and be a most inefficient and unproductive worker, because a solitary office job simply doesn't suit his or her temperament. Studies of manual laborers in a match factory in India compared high performers with low performers. Both did the same repetitive job of stuffing matches into the inner sleeve of a matchbox, and then sliding the sleeve into the outer box and placing it on a tray. Maybe a help wanted column would describe this job as "technical initiator of the two-step pre-ignition phase in the energy industry." I would describe the job as a roaring bore. Oddly enough, the high performers in the match factory had the highest rates of subjective health complaints, as well as mental health problems such as depression and anxiety. High performers also had the highest rates of absenteeism. It appears from these studies that, when we take peak performers and place them in a job that has too little stress for their capabilities, they react with more stress-related illness than their lower-achieving coworkers.

The reverse holds true as well. A person with a low energy level, a long attention span, and a dislike of risks, might feel very comfortable performing repetitive tasks. Such a person might develop chest pains, headaches, or insomnia when thrust into an entrepreneur's role.

No matter what level of stress you face in your job, you will benefit from comparing your experiences with those of workers who face the extremes of stress. Let's first examine those with high-stress jobs, and then those with boring, repetitive, low-stress jobs.

HIGH-STRESS JOBS AND THEIR SPECIAL PROBLEMS

High-stress jobs and the people who handle them well, offer valuable insights and lessons.

DO YOU HAVE ONE OF THESE HIGH-STRESS JOBS?

- air traffic controller
- armed forces personnel
- competitive athletes
- construction worker who walks the high steel in all weather
- customer service/complaint officer
- dental technician/health aide
- emergency room health personnel
- flight attendant
- fighter pilot
- inner-city school teacher
- journalist
- medical intern (I can vouch for that one)
- military or police explosives expert
- miner
- negotiators in labor-management disputes
- oil well firefighter (such as the famous Red Adair)
- police officer
- professional racers aboard cars, boats, or skis
- secretary/computer operator
- stockbroker
- urban bus driver
- waiter/waitress

In high-stress jobs, the people who handle themselves well do not waste their time trying to eliminate stress (although they are careful to eliminate unnecessary hazards and mistakes). Time and effort are spent preparing for stresses, rehearsing for them and, most importantly, developing ways to use job stress to help achieve peak levels of performance.

Preparation for very sensitive high-stress jobs, such as many in the military, begins with the selection process itself. Applicants are carefully screened for the appropriate aptitudes, skills, background training, and experiences. Then some form of barricade or initiation test is placed in their way. In the case of young adults entering the military, this barricade might be in the form of "boot camp," as well as the years of serving in the trenches before assuming greater responsibilities.

Although many returning Vietnam War veterans found difficulty (verging on discrimination) in gaining re-entry into the American business community, others did not encounter such prejudice. Businessman Ross Perot (who risked his life to rescue two of his EDS executives from Teheran), felt that officers who conducted themselves well in battle would be well qualified to handle the high stresses of the business world. He built his EDS empire around a diverse group of nonconformists with seemingly nothing in common. However, all were self-starters; all knew how to handle themselves when the going got tough; and most were veterans of the Vietnamese War.

WHO SAYS CIVIL SERVICE JOBS ARE EASY?

Although the public image of a civil service job is one of secure routine verging on boredom, many of the most dangerous, colorful, and highly stressed jobs in the world are included among government occupations. Obvious examples include air traffic controllers, antiterrorist commandos, and front-line fighter pilots. Thousands more shoulder their high-risk jobs in anonymity.

For example, the crews who scramble around underneath jets during catapult launchings on an aircraft carrier risk their lives during every shift, with a "danger pay" supplement of just pennies per hour.

SOME LOW-STRESS JOBS

- Assembly-line worker
- Cleaning staff
- Lighthouse attendant
- Night watchman
- Receptionist in a toll booth
- Winter worker in Antarctica
- Efficiency spotter in post office
- Swiss Navy consultant, antisubmarine division

LOW-STRESS JOBS AND THEIR SPECIAL PROBLEMS

Low-stress, low-responsibility jobs carry unique problems of their own. Where the level of stress involved is literally all an individual can handle, then problems may not occur. For most people, though, low-stress jobs involve a tremendous disparity between childhood expectations of what work would be like, and the stark realities.

The way most employees handle an undemanding job is to relegate it to a subordinate position in their lives. While on the job, they often occupy their minds by thinking about and discussing other interests ranging from world affairs to sports, cooking, philosophy, and religion. As soon as the whistle blows, signifying the end of their shift, they rush off to their ball park or to do work around the house, and they will then display sustained enthusiasm and energy that their supervisors would never have believed possible.

We all need to feel committed to a mission. If a mission is not forthcoming on the job, it is human nature to seek a mission in one's off-work hours. Some people, who have high levels of stress in their personal lives and a strong sense of mission — for example, single parents — may prefer a low-stress job as something of a change from their otherwise hectic lives. A low-stress job does not always represent a problem that needs a solution.

A few years ago, management at one of General Electric's radio assembly plants in New York State noted that the women who were performing some of the simple, repetitive steps at their assembly stations did not have much variety in their work. Management tried to bring in a system of job rotation, in which the women in this section would all learn each other's jobs, thus breaking the monotony. They expected the workers to be delighted, but the result was the opposite. The women all indicated that they had a great deal of stress in their busy personal lives. They looked forward to a familiar, unthinking job as a way to rest their minds, and to enjoy a bit of peace and quiet. By making them take on the stresses of new challenges, management was simply making their lives unhappy.

For some workers, however — who have the potential to do more challenging jobs but don't for reasons of interrupted education, poor self-image, or simply living in a one-industry town — the stress of having too little stress on the job can produce a number of problems. These include less sense of personal self-worth and job satisfaction, greater absenteeism rate, somatic complaints (for example, backaches, headaches), increased boredom and falling asleep on the job, and a greater tendency towards substance abuse. When such a worker is understimulated for more than a few years, his or her expectations start to resemble the limitations of the job, and energy levels and prospects for escape into a new career decline.

WINTER WORKER IN ANTARCTICA

One of the most boring spots on this earth to hold a job is on the continent of Antarctica during the nine-month winter. Although virtually all 800 human inhabitants of the continent are well educated and carefully selected for the rigors of life in this hostile environment, the actual incidence of illness related to job stress, or rather the lack of it, is remarkable.

For those of us who have occasionally wished we could do away with all our stresses, it is instructive to see what happens to others who have tried it. The key feature of work in the Antarctic winter is the months of permanent darkness. Even when light returns in the spring, the air is so cold that almost all one's time is spent inside small huts. Thomas J. Maugh II graphically described the situation in *The Los Angeles Times*, September 28, 1987. When the Antarctic worker does venture outside, Maugh points out, the work itself is not exactly enough to occupy the busy mind, unless you consider counting penguins, chiseling ice, or timing how many seconds your earlobes can withstand frostbite to be among life's great challenges.

By the end of a few months of this, many develop "big eye," a wide-eyed stare caused by pure boredom and by constantly focusing on nearby objects. In the middle of a meal, the bored worker will lose the concept. His or her spoon will pause halfway along its voyage from plate to palate, until the person snaps out of the trancelike state. The popular wish to avoid all distractions to enable one to accomplish a great deal is here shown to be a fool's dream. A worker's attention span tends to shrink to that of a horsefly, with great attention paid to trivialities and little attention left for the original project.

The list of health problems related to the absence of stress among Antarctic workers is remarkable. Fistfights are common. One Australian cook chased a diesel mechanic with a meat cleaver for three hours before both got tired, drunk, and reconciled (in that order). A Russian scientist is said to have committed murder with an axe after his opponent beat him in a game of chess (one of the first known sports injuries in the history of the game). The taking of what can only be described as stupid risks also increases as the boredom drones on. The interesting thing to note is that these same people thrust together in a siege or with a common mission (stress) would have gotten along much better.

In 1982, three British scientists died when they fell into a crevasse while exploring the forbidden sea ice; their ennui-bred adventurism has not been an isolated event. Many others are known to have perished in the same ways, literally dying for the lack of stress.

It is worth remembering how desperate people become for stress when none is available. We should reflect on this before we categorically think of stress as a negative element in our lives.

THE DREADED COMBOS — JOBS WITH HIGH AND LOW STRESSES

A third important category in the discussion of stress extremes at work is jobs that involve both ends of the spectrum, vacillating from mundane to panicstricken from one day to the next, or even from one minute to the next.

JOBS WITH ALTERNATING STRESS LEVELS

- All swing shifts, especially in which workers change shifts every two weeks or less.
- Anaesthesiologist. (In Canada and Commonwealth countries, we call them anaesthetists. Both terms are terrible tongue twisters, so feel free to do as we family practitioners do, and just call them gas-passers.)
- Crane operator
- Airline pilot
- Firefighter
- Forest ranger
- Astronaut

As can be seen with people living in war zones or in boring labor camps, the human spirit can adapt to almost any extreme of stress levels at work. However, when the external stress swings from one extreme to another, the adaptation capacity is burned out much more quickly. The effect would be something like that of living in a peaceful New England fishing village for all the even numbered days of the month, and being instantly transported to downtown Beirut on all the odd days.

An interesting side of the job description of the astronaut is the aspect of boredom. Although the astronaut's job is considered by earthlings as one of the most glamorous possible, the truth is that the initial moments of high stress, such as seen on blastoff and re-entry, are interspersed with incredible periods of boredom. In December 1982, Soviet cosmonauts Anatoli Berezevoi and Valentin Lebedev risked a very hazardous night landing during a blizzard rather than extend their 211-day mission another week. In a rare display of candor, Soviet authorities admitted that the reason both cosmonauts wanted to come home was that they were bored to death by the cramped quarters, absence of gravity, repetitive routines on the job, and each other's constant company. In other words, the cause of their symptoms was a direct result of too little stress on the job.

This phenomenon obviously concerns NASA officials, who are planning spacestation trips of six months' duration in the coming decade, and a three-year trip to Mars soon after that. If the problems are not resolved, officials have images of the Mars astronauts at each other's throats all the way home. Scientists are hoping to select more compatible groups by sending carloads of them off for extended tenting holidays together. The apparent theory here is that, if potential crews of astronauts can tolerate three months of vacation in a pup tent and a Subaru, they should be ready for anything.

For those who hold "schizophrenic" jobs of this sort, there is no reason to expect undue problems as long as the job suits the personality and as long as the person keeps himself or herself physically and mentally in shape for it. Studies of firefighters show that heart rates typically escalate dramatically for the first two minutes after the alarm sounds and return to normal levels thereafter. However, in workers who are out of cardiovascular shape, pulse recovery is slower and in fact tends to stay high throughout the rest of the emergency. Thus the risk of an untimely heart attack is greater.

Studies of young sailors show that, when they are awakened from sleep at 3:00 a.m., their ability to perform their routine manual tasks is dreadful for about the first 15 minutes after they wake up. Jobs with emergency calls can prove dangerous during that first quarter hour of the mid-sleep alarm. Obstetricians are at the greatest danger of having a car crash enroute to the delivery suite during this period, and firefighters are more likely to have accidents during the first 15 minutes after being awakened.

When people are awakened in the early part of the night, their reaction time is impaired. However, when they are awakened in the latter part of sleep, coordination is severely impaired. With chronic sleep deprivation, the other stresses of work are harder to cope with.

SHIFT WORK — SPECIAL PROBLEMS, SPECIAL REMEDIES

The number of workers who go through shift changes may seem small to the average person, but in reality it is surprisingly high. Consider the following facts about the North American workplace.

- One out of thirty workers does night shifts.
- One out of five does evenings, all nights, or split shifts.
- Ten million workers are on the job at 3 a.m. on any given night of the week in the United States alone.

As with the traveler, it can take a worker as long as one day per hour of time shift to become acclimatized. Thus starting a two-week shift means that the worker will have up to eight days of decreased mental alertness, drowsiness, indigestion, and reduced well-being. This puts the worker at high risk to make errors, either by falling asleep on the job, or by wearily resorting to old habits from another job that might cause disasters on this one. Even when adapted to a new schedule, there is still a periodicity to the sleep-awake cycle that makes us all prone to dozing off between midnight and 7 a.m., and between 1 p.m. and 4 p.m. if we do not have enough stimulation (stress) to keep us going through those hours. The records of workers' compensation claims for accidents on the job show a decided increase among shift workers, especially in the initial phases of a new shift when they have not yet had time to adapt.

Typically, after a substandard performance on the first week of a new shift, the worker then has one good week. However, in the typical two-week shift cycle, the worker next finds himself or herself on a different shift, and another bad first week is about to begin. This schizophrenic existence from night to day shifts, and from good to bad work, is very detrimental to employee morale if left unmanaged. It can also be hard on a marriage. Police officers' spouses, when questioned about the hardships of their spouses' vocations, quote the shift work hours as even more worrying than the physical dangers. It is known, however, that married shift workers have an easier time adapting to and handling their stresses than their single colleagues.

AN INTERN'S LIFE IS NOT AN EASY ONE

Continual, frequent shift changes can give people the equivalent of a permanent jet lag. This leads to a reduction in the body's immune system, with increased incidences of illness, accidents, and simple mental errors, sometimes costing millions of dollars, or putting lives at risk.

A classic example of this is the sleep deprivation of medical interns, which leads to frequent mistakes. A week has only 168 hours in it, and interns are often awake and working for 120 of those hours, for months at a time. This job probably has the longest (and most ridiculous) shift in the world. Happily, in many hospitals, there has been an outbreak of rationality among those responsible for staffing, and interns are finally being given a chance to find a little rest.

The optimum length of time to leave someone on night shifts before rotating him or her back to day shifts is as long as possible, but no less than four weeks. However, the practicality of shift scheduling must take into account personal realities, such as trying to have some semblance of family and social life with the majority of the population, which runs on the normal day shift.

In addition, the nature of many jobs necessitates employees working at all times of the day, so shift work will never disappear. Given the inevitability of changing shifts, managers and all affected employees should be aware of the latest techniques to make the best of the situation.

MEDICAL TIPS TO COPE WITH SHIFT WORK

- Fight the "shift lag" with the jet lag recommendations, discussed in chapter 9.
- Sleep at the same time each day if possible, and don't be afraid to take a catnap before you start your shift if you were unable to have a long sleep during the day. It's better to take that nap at home than on the job.
- Install blackout curtains in your bedroom, and keep them drawn when you are sleeping during the day. As with jet lag, light can be a powerful weapon, alerting our chemical wakeup alarms. Keep an extra bright desk light at your work station if the

general lighting is dim, and use sunlight or room light to wake you up at home when you want to force yourself back onto a night-sleeping routine. If you are working the afternoon shift (from about 4:00 p.m. until midnight), try to sleep as soon as you get home. Then use the sunlight to help keep you awake during the day.

- Use physical activity to stimulate you when you wish to wake up. Exercise can invigorate. Instead of starting your day only with the sedentary pursuit of breakfast, television, or the newspaper, try spending some of the time increasing your alertness. Invigorating aerobics or brisk calisthenics can prove stimulating, especially if they can be combined with a bit of fresh air. If your building has stairs, climb them. If the building has too many stairs for this to be physically advisable, then get off the elevator at the wrong floor and climb up or down the rest of the way. If your work station has been ergometrically designed like the cockpit of an airplane, so that everything is at your fingertips, then try to modify it. If you are alone at night in a big office, put your phone on a nearby desk so that you cannot reach it without standing up and walking a few paces.
- Lively music can keep you up, and soothing music can help you rest. (See chapter 10)
- A cool shower can stimulate, so take one before you start your shift. A long warm bath can relax, so take one after work or before you sleep.
- A gripping adventure on the television screen or a brisk murder novel can wake one up thoroughly before a shift starts.
- A relaxation tape (see chapter 10, the *Stress for Success* Power Nap) can render one unconscious for a last-minute nap before starting work. The tape can also be used to help you sleep at home when household noises distract.
- An agitation tape (such as the *Stress for Success* alertness tape for shift workers) can also be lifesaving. It comes with distracting scenarios, designed to fit into a coffee break or even to be used as background stimulation while working or driving.

It also includes an invigorating 10-minute wake-up exercise session.

• Colors can make a difference; control them wherever you can. Decorating your work area, or one of your rooms at home, in bright vibrant colors can make you feel more alert in these spots. Cool, soothing colors can do the opposite, so these colors are better suited to the bedroom. If you have your own office, the colors you choose can influence the desired mood. In a waiting room, restful colors are best. In your own work station you will probably benefit from bolder colors, or at least bright sunlight when available.

If your own work situation has not been specifically discussed, but has high or low stress or a combination of these, then all the foregoing comments can still be applied. Although the extremes of stress may not be entirely in your control, these insights can make a real difference in the final outcome with respect to your health and your performance.

PROBLEMS UNIQUE TO WOMEN
SHOULD SHE OR SHOULDN'T SHE?
Today, North American figures show that female professionals outnumber men in 51% of the workplace, with similar figures shown for business and trade school graduates. Many married men find they enjoy much greater freedom to take a few career risks, knowing their wives are earning money. Thus the old macho attitude, ''No wife of mine is ever going to work for a living,'' has largely been eclipsed.

Normally, one adapts to change by simply learning new rules to replace the old ones. However, when the old rules for being a good mother are inculcated into a girl's mind from earliest childhood, they can prove difficult to eradicate. Mothers, grandmothers, and even their mothers before them were all taught basically the same set of "shoulds," which formed the basis for their work ethic. The list was long and formidable. Fortunately, enlightened parents are no longer forcing stereotypes on their offspring. However, for many the trap has already been set. Career women have told me that, even in the midst of their highly charged workdays, they still have pangs when they hear echoes of maternal voices reciting parts of the catechism of a traditional mother's "shoulds:"

- You should get married; I was married at your age.
- You should follow your husband wherever his career takes him.
- You should have children; all my friends are grandmothers already.
- You should stay home and look after your husband and children.
- You should stay married for the sake of the children, even if the relationship has broken down.
- You should take every holiday with the kids.
- You should keep the house spotless; you never know when someone might pop in.
- You should make three meals a day; we never used to eat in restaurants all the time.
- You should put everyone else before yourself. Remember, a mother's work is never done.

There is no question that guilt is the gift that keeps on giving. But when it comes to someone else's "shoulds," even your own mother's, the best medical advice I can give is: "Decide on your own shoulds." Don't try to cope with modern stresses using an obsolete agenda. Make up your own list of shoulds based on your current realities of time and priority.

PITFALLS FACING WOMEN IN THE WORKPLACE

Traditionally, stress-related health problems have been considered a masculine phenomenon. Heart attacks, stomach ulcers, burnout, and strokes were all considered diseases of men in the workplace, and indeed are the reasons why elderly widows out-number widowers by almost five to one. However, with the equal responsibilities women are taking at work now, they are also being exposed to at least equal amounts of stress. If anything, in fact, stress levels faced by career women can be considerably greater than those levels imposed on men.

While women are being given equal hiring opportunities and equal rates of promotion to the middle management levels, they seem to encounter a "glass ceiling" preventing their climb up the corporate ladder. In other words, they have been granted equal access, but not equal ascent. In fact, only 2% of top manage-ment in North America's major corporations is female. This figure reflects a modest advance of women in selected fields such as financial services, telecommunications, retailing, advertising, pub-lic relations, and publishing.

GOOD MANAGEMENT POTENTIAL

If I'm assertive,
I'm seen as aggressive.
If I'm aggressive,
I'm a bitch.
I won't be promoted.
Let's try it again.
If I'm nonassertive,
I'm seen as a patsy.
If I'm a patsy,
I won't be promoted.
Let's try it once more.
If I'm very careful,
I can go unnoticed.
If I'm unnoticed,
No one will know
I want to be promoted.
Any suggestions?

Natasha Josefowitz in *Is This Where I Was Going?*

Women are expected to make greater personal sacrifices than men, especially as regards their family lives. More than 40% of female executives are unmarried (single, separated or divorced), and over half are childless. On the other hand, most male executives have a nice comfy family to come home to: 99% are married and 95% have children. This situation can mean frustration for talented, ambitious and experienced women, as they lack the same kind of sympathy and understanding that married men find so readily at home.

Job burnout, which is most likely to hit after one's progress up the ladder is blocked, thus strikes women about a decade before it hits men. As a result of the high stress level being skewed towards women, many are faced with critical career choices, and some are opting to quit the corporation entirely. As an illustration, one out of four women graduates of the Harvard Business School class of 1976 has already quit the managerial workforce and Canadian statistics are very similar. However, this does not mean that such women have accepted defeat.

More and more women are setting out on their own. Women are now starting small businesses at triple the rate of men. Happily, these businesses seem to thrive on their good management, and the women in them do not face the traditional male-imposed ceilings on their incomes or achievements. Many of the ranks of the newest millionaires have come through this route, which only goes to underline the folly of corporations that deny this kind of talent room to grow. It is estimated that, by the year 2000, half of all sole proprietorships will probably be owned by women. Whether success is measured in gaining wealth, control over one's working life, or simply the satisfaction of a job well done, the new breed of career woman is proving that she can do very nicely in spite of men's traditional rules.

Women have a big problem in the traditional workplace that men don't have: men. Women are victims of most of the sexual harrassment in the workplace. Sexual harrassment is an abuse of power and, since men still hold most of the power within corporations, they do most of the harrassing. Although not as badly at risk as female slaves and servants were in the last century, working women are still being subjected to considerable abuse. If they reject the advances of their bosses, they could see their career advancement ended, their workload increased, or their jobs terminated. Recent studies show that as many as 40% of women experience some form of sexual harrassment during their careers. (Sexual harrassment is here being taken to mean "unwelcome sexual advances, requests for sexual favors, and other verbal or physical conduct of a sexual nature.")

Most sexual harrassment goes unreported, because of fear or embarrassment. However, starting with a landmark case in 1976, in which Diane Williams was found the victim of sexual harrassment by her boss in the U.S. Justice Department, courts have been seeing a twofold increase in reported cases since 1981.

As we have noted, even high levels of stress do not need to be equated with heart attacks, mental breakdowns, ulcers, and other stress-induced illnesses. If women continue to manage their stresses better than men, then they could continue to dominate the longevity sweepstakes. Sadly, however, this is not what is happening. Women are turning out to be every bit as incompetent in running their own Departments of One as men are, and the results are just as wasteful and just as tragic. Alcoholism and cigarette smoking used to be largely men's problems, but now women have adopted them as their own, even surpassing men in numbers. In addition, women tend to take more tranquilizers and pain pills than men. (See chapters 14 and 15 on substance abuse.)

Career women are being caught in the same time management trap as men, and are finding it hard to fit exercise into their schedules. As a result of business lunches or snack food on the run, women are consuming more cholesterol and less fiber than their ancestors did. Type A "hurry sickness" sees more women reacting to neutral cues as if they were life-threatening attacks. For example, Type A women are just as aggressive as their male counterparts in traffic, and respond to the simple changing of a traffic light with the same outpouring of adrenaline, clenching of muscles, and mighty screech of rubber. Women executives are every bit as likely to be seduced by the attractions of workaholism as their male counterparts, and just as likely to bear the brunt of their children's manipulative behavior when they are not spending enough time at home.

Even financially, where working women should have seen some advances, all is not rosy. Overall expenditures on credit cards and the low rate of personal savings show that workers in North America and, to a lesser extent, other Western nationals, are on a spending binge that eats up almost all their disposable income. In other words, all the destructive stress management choices that have nurtured anxieties and health breakdowns in the traditionally male workplace are now being chosen by women as well.

The deadly consequences of these choices mean that women will be unlikely to retain their majority in the over-70 age group. It is now apparent that the reason most of the elderly are women is simply because their men didn't give themselves a chance to die of natural causes. Women, on the other hand, worked in the home, where they were usually in more control of the stresses around them, and in control of the time frame in which to get jobs done.

However, those days are gone forever, and a whole new set of deadly traps lies waiting for the woman who mismanages her stress. In tomorrow's news, we might well be reading about a 41-year-old well-dressed workaholic — over-extended at the bank, mortgage company and on all credit cards, smoking heavily, and abusing drugs and alcohol — who feels a sudden chest heaviness while on an overseas phone call at the office. The rest of the obituary would read as it has always done, except that the victim could very well be a woman.

Chapter 4

THE MODERN HIGH-TECH WORK ENVIRONMENT

TECHNOLOGY — A MIXED BLESSING

Technology is changing our lives and our stresses at an incredible pace today. Almost half of today's work force in the Western world is linked to electronic work stations, from Japan to Germany, and from Canada to Australia. Current studies predict that, within five years, most people who own a telephone will also own a computer terminal.

Galloping technology is having a profound influence on the workplace, as well as on personal health, motivation, and productivity. Senior managers find themselves doing their own typing on laptop computers in crowded airplanes and commuter trains. Middle managers see a dramatic change in their roles, as less supervisory personnel is required to run informational businesses. Labor sees threats to its traditional power base, as many union jobs are being replaced with non-union information jobs.

Modern computers and software should make our lives less stressful. In reality, for workers who see their in-baskets overflowing with endless printouts, or those who find their word processor key strokes counted by heartless monitors, the computer itself is seen as a major source of stress. Craig Brod has called this new condition *technostress*, which he defines as the unpleasant condition resulting when the balance between people and computers is violated.

In reality, since any stress is neutral until it lands on a person, the term *technostress* should refer only to the adaptation of people to machines. However, for the sake of clarity, and because the vast majority of personal encounters with technology at work and in our personal lives have been less than optimal, I will use the word *technostress* to mean only the negative results of that adaptation.

Of course, some very positive results occur when technology, like any other stressor, is managed well. Computerized robots can handle toxic or "hot" radioactive elements. They can even remove a bomb left in a crowded shopping center. When these jobs used to be done by human hands, the subjects risked delayed cancers or immediate trauma.

Computers aboard satellites are helping to save lives at sea. Most boats, even small craft, that sail into open waters are equipped with the latest navigational radio sets. Satellite communications then enable these vessels to pinpoint their location, almost to the exact wave, and to make for safe harbor when a hurricane approaches.

In the field of modern medicine, computerized ultrasound machines can detect a heart defect in an unborn fetus and alert pediatric heart surgeons to stand by the delivery to save the baby's life. Arterial lasers can blast away cholesterol deposits on the walls of coronary arteries, literally giving life back to the near-dead.

THE RETENTION HELMET APPROACH — INAPPROPRIATE IN TODAY'S WORLD

However, as we have seen, technological victories have not been without their negative impact. Early futurists predicted that modern life would be a pure "pushbutton" utopia. They didn't allow for the resistance of the human spirit when pushed too hard by the winds of change. We all like to feel comfortable in our routines — to take the same route to work each day, to see the same familiar faces and tasks waiting when we get there, and to collapse into the same easy chair after the day is done.

Although routines in themselves are harmless, the inertia they cultivate can interfere with our ability to cope with new stresses. Unless we actively fight back, there is a natural human tendency to divide our lives into two discrete periods: our "learning years" and our "earning years." The former period ends, many think, when the latter begins. Rather than the graduate's mortarboard turning into a thinking cap, it can easily become a retention helmet.

In the days before the information explosion, many job skills, once retained in the memory as a student or apprentice, needed no revisions for the rest of the person's working career. Unfortunately the "retention helmet" approach is becoming less and less appropriate in our rapidly changing society — both to dealing with the workplace and to relating to the younger generation.

"Son, when I was a young lad we used to walk 10 miles to school, run home at recess to pluck the chickens, and be back in class before the bell rang."

Maybe you're faced with relearning your job when a computer arrives on your desk. Instead of seeing huge obstacles and only minuscule benefits, try turning your mental binoculars around and reversing the proportions. Effective adaptation can take place only if the image of achievement far outweighs the image of inconveniences and embarrassments. Visualize how proud you will feel after you have mastered the challenge and are fluent in working with your new keyboard. Imagine, five years from now, someone asking you if you would ever give up these changes and go back to doing things the old way. Picture yourself feeling so comfortable with the new technology that you would give a sincere no.

Not very long ago, telephone numbers all had quaint alphabetical prefixes such as BUtterfield 8, and our phones all had charming operators at the other end of each long distance call. When that system changed to direct dial calls around the country and around the world, some adults were quite anxious about having to relearn skills for the new technology. How could they ever remember anyone's phone number?

In the overall scheme of things, I would suggest that the current resistance to computers will be looked upon by future generations as similarly unwarranted. It is to be hoped that we will all achieve an improved perspective on computers, using them as an aid to processing data, thoughts, and communications — and not as a substitute for low-technology interpersonal skills.

TECHNOSTRESS MANAGEMENT FOR THOSE WHO DIDN'T EVEN KNOW THEY WERE TECHNOSTRESSED

Although the trend is certainly for the computer to be as common as the calculator on every desk, half the Western world's population still does not personally operate a computer terminal at work or at home. These people often assume that technostress can do them no harm. However, nothing could be farther from the truth.

As well as affecting employees and management in technologically sophisticated companies, technostress can affect all who are users of today's many high-tech gadgets. Have you ever been stuck in an elevator, frustrated by reading the complex instructions for the new office photocopier, or driven to distraction when your microwave remote-control garage door opens the door only a third of the way? For all who can identify with any of the above frustrations, and who daily experience countless others, there are two simple rules to minimize the negative effects of technostress.

Hanson's Anti-Technostress Rule
#1 Ask yourself — Do I really need this?"

More than at any time in the history of our species, we are facing exploding levels of computerization and complication in our lives. Some of this seems beyond human control; for example, never being able to get through on the fax number because the system is programmed to the wrong mode. Offended by such a machine, many people naturally demand some satisfaction. Often a harmless oath, perhaps accompanied by a stiff thump, will satisfy our base urge for revenge.

On occasion, sterner punishments have been meted out. Recently, after watching an automated bank teller eat two of his credit cards, a Florida man fired six rounds from his .32 caliber pistol into the mouth of the omnivorous machine. In such a case, it may appear that justice was served, but the victory was a hollow one. Childish retaliations against technology are doomed, and are wasteful of our limited time on this planet.

Of course, a lot of the technostress we encounter is self-inflicted by our unbridled love of gadgets. With an array of office machines and household tools that would make the original James Bond seem a technological peasant, the average worker has invited a host of unnecessary mechanical inconveniences and breakdowns into his or her life to add to the overall levels of technostress.

Hanson's Anti-Stress Rule
#2 *If you need it, keep the instructions.*

With the rising technology in the workplace many people have suffered additional stress from their insecurity of having to use high-tech machines.

How many of us have experienced incredible frustration when we found ourselves unable to exit from a computer program, only to find that in our haste we had merely overlooked one simple step? By keeping the manual handy, and referring to it as needed, our stress levels would not have been pushed so hard.

Our offices and homes are filled with gadgets, most of which come with their own sets of clever instructions. However, statistics show that such instructions are rarely ever read, and even more rarely followed. I have done thousands of house calls in my career as a family doctor. In most cases, the patients are found sitting or lying in front of their television sets in their living rooms or bedrooms. As is reflected in current statistics, most of these televisions are attached to VCRs. A statistic that is not reflected, however, is that most of these video processors had their digital clocks blinking "12:00 Sunday." If you really do need that burglar alarm system, word processor, or voice-activated telephone dialer in the first place, then you will definitely need to know how to fix it when it "breaks down." Expensive and time-wasting service calls can usually be avoided by taking a quick look at the instructions.

TECHNOSTRESS AND THE BUSINESS OWNER OR MANAGER

With the ability to turn sand into silicon chips came a tide of technological change that washed over the whole business world. A job market that was capital intensive became idea intensive. Competition was no longer limited to select members of the establishment who had a lot of wealth, but was thrown wide open to creative minds from every part of the social stratum, in every part of the world and of any age.

For example, in 1975 a skinny 19-year-old boy dropped out of Harvard to design software for the Altair, the original hobbyist's computer. He never finished his schoolwork, but his company, which he called Microsoft, started a revolution. In March 1987, at the age of 31, Bill Gates became the youngest person ever to make a billion dollars in any business.

Young, inventive minds on every continent came up with other new computer ideas that have been quickly transposed into the workplace all around the world. Apart from a few traditional labor-intensive crafts and services, almost every job, from farming to manufacturing, from national giants to "Mom and Pop" stores, has felt the impact of this universal computerized "arms" race.

Companies that chose to ignore the new technology found themselves being out-gunned by their global competitors. Survival became a matter of adaptation. However, with many people wearing retention helmets and resisting relearning, it has been a complicated adaptation. In most jobs and in most companies, old ways of doing business have become prescriptions for bankruptcy.

Instead of taking scheduled breaks in a workshift, a computer operator's work routine may well require pacing around spontaneously — thinking out loud — trying to foster creative thinking to get the job done. One of the most significant changes in the role of today's managers seems to be a form of operative schizophrenia. On one hand, new business conditions mean that some employees must be let go as their jobs are replaced by technology. The manager is in a firing mode. On the other hand, new workstyles demand new skills. When these skills are available in young graduates but not in the fired employees, then the manager may find himself or herself in a hiring mode.

It has always been a difficult task for a manager to fire people, but in the past there was always a sense of the whole company sharing austerity in adversity. Today, by contrast, many people are being fired while lavish budgets are simultaneously wooing younger recruits for different jobs in the same department. This has increased the strain on managers and, of course, on employees. It's also not easy for the newly-hired workers having to overcome the antipathy of the remaining employees (who for their own part feel relief at not yet being fired, as well as anxiety about possibly being replaced). How well the interpersonal as well as technological stresses are managed will make a difference of not just a few dollars and cents per share, but sometimes the difference between the company's survival or death.

INTRODUCING NEW TECHNOLOGY INTO THE WORKPLACE

The introduction of computer technology into the workplace is usually management's idea (hardly ever the idea of labor unions). Thus the story of how to prevent debilitating technostress should begin with managers. As in the home renovation business, it is wise to adhere to the old "factor of two" rule when changing an office over to a new computer system: No matter what your computer sales representative estimates, the costs will be double and the benefits will be half.

THE PRE-SELL PHASE

When the decision has been made to modernize a company's technology, it is in management's best interest to involve the rank-and-file users at the outset. This could be called the *pre-sell* phase. Management should make all staff members aware of the larger picture. This might include: what the local and foreign competition are planning, and the importance of computerization to future efficiency, profitability, and viability of the company and thus the future security of all jobs in the company. The pre-sell phase is an ideal time to reinstill the sense of a shared corporate mission.

The critical pre-sell phase communication can come in a number of ways, such as through a corporate newsletter, on bulletin boards, or in speeches from the chief executive officer (either in person or, if scale does not permit, via videotape). Ultimately small groups of potential computer users meeting with their appropriate managers and a representative of the computer company can help customize the technology to the tasks at hand. At this stage, it is critical to have a computer expert present, lest the others just waste their time pooling technological ignorance.

The company benefits from such sessions by avoiding expensive technological overkill. The employees benefit by hearing answers to their questions and having input into the kinds of change that will affect them directly. The computer company benefits by having more satisfied customers. "Hands on" demonstration models of proposed work stations set up as early as possible before general installation day will offer a good "stress rehearsal" for the theater of the real. In these and similar ways, a great deal of the initial fear response to computers can be painlessly trained out of people.

THE OPERATIONAL PHASE

The next phase is the actual operation of the machines, once all are on line. It is important that routine workloads are dropped to allow time for the learning curve of the new computer "pilots" to come up to speed. If the original justification for bringing new machines into the workplace was correctly thought through, allowing for the "factor of two" rule, then there should be enough payback within the next few quarters to make up for initial productivity losses.

As always, interpersonal relations are important. When measurements are taken of rates of key strokes per day for each worker, then the users should be praised for good performances rather than only berated for poor ones. Regular feedback from the users will also be helpful in identifying and fixing bugs in the system. People should be encouraged to establish new buddy systems (such as an older person teaming up with a younger, more computer-literate colleague). Allowances should be made for unstructured breaks so that people in difficulties can ask questions freely as they arise. Designated troubleshooters should be identified for each work area. Successful implementation of such steps will reduce the stress levels of startup dramatically.

THE POST-GRADUATE PHASE

Once people feel comfortable with the technology — when the answer to the question, "Would you ever give up your computer to go back to the old way of doing things?" is a resounding, "No!" — then the third, or post-graduate, phase is reached. Rather than relaxing to a state of overconfidence, it is important that each user have the attitude of a perennial student. Management can encourage this by paying the tuition for employee upgrades as more sophistication enters the system.

Frequent fun rewards such as recognition lunches, small trophies, or other ideas from the staff suggestion box have all proven well worth the effort in maintaining good team levels of morale and productivity. Managers can also help by not over-using technology.

Sheila, a highly-overworked secretary for a brokerage house in San Francisco, told me that her boss routinely made her retype small changes of phrasing in his letters at least five or six times, just because he thought changes were "free" on her word processor. He would dictate without much thought, read the print-out version, and then change a metaphor or two. When he received the next printout, he would again change a few words. It took Sheila twice as long to produce a letter as it had when she had typed it with her old typewriter and when her boss gave the letter a bit more thought while he was dictating it.

Feedback from regular small meeting groups can help eliminate a lot of costly abuses such as this, and keep tempers and blood pressures from rising unduly.

FIGHT HIGH-TECH WITH HIGH-TOUCH

If you spend long hours at a computer terminal, find ways to increase contacts with other people. For example, eat lunches with others, not alone in front of the keyboard. The life of the computer operator is inherently lonely. Rather than compound that loneliness by exercising one's theoretical franchise to live on a remote mountain top, working on a computer hooked up to a satellite dish, a more social approach to the computer age is developing. The revitalization of large- and medium-sized cities around the world is testimony to the strength of the need many of us feel to be with others, in spite of the obvious drawbacks of traffic and overcrowding.

SOME TECHNOSTRESS NIGHTMARES OF A MANAGER

Even with excellent planning and consideration there are bound to be problems, and managers must be prepared to expect some opposition and take human error in their stride. Several examples of management problems are outlined below.

POORLY COORDINATED COMPUTERIZATION

In June 1985, Consumers Distributing, a major catalog retail chain in Canada, shut down its distribution center for three weeks to reopen with a simpler computerized system for receiving and distributing products. When the chain reopened, there was a major problem, which turned out to be one of the worst ever in the industry, costing over $50 million in lost sales.

Consumers Distributing's central warehouse could receive normally, but could process and ship out only 10 or 12 truckloads per day instead of the normal 30. Soon the 620,000 square foot warehouse was jammed to the rafters, and goods spilled over into additional rented space of over 350,000 square feet. This disaster lasted until October 1985, when the new owners sent in Les McPhail to straighten things out.

After a crash course of four days of deliberation with the management team, which McPhail divided into eight small groups, a new and simpler plan emerged, using suggestions from all levels involved. After 10 days of implementing the new plan, the Consumers Distributing warehouse was able to ship out 71 truckloads per day, almost double the previous best. Today the company is still using the same system that was born out of the meetings in the middle of incredible technostress. Consumers Distributing has been able to keep its handling costs to the same levels as they were back in 1984, which represents a significant improvement of efficiency.

McPhail, as a good boss should, gives the credit to the entire group working on the problem, and notes that all now take even greater pride in their work, having been so much a part of saving their jobs from technostress. McPhail notes that the disaster occurred not because of computerization of the system by the original management, but because new programs were implemented prematurely in the rush to reduce labor costs and increase efficiency.

This was a classic example of poorly coordinated computerization almost destroying a company from within. It would behoove other bosses to consider the scenario, making sure not to make similar mistakes.

SECURITY THREATS

With the computerization of the workplace, great efforts have been made to design systems to be "user-friendly." Unfortunately, as we have begun to witness, the systems are also a little too "abuser-friendly." They offer a tremendous potential for sabotage and theft by competitors, disgruntled employees, or simply by young pranksters with a home computer and a modem. Even the most sophisticated security system has not been fully effective, as witnessed by recent cases of teenagers gaining access to central files from NATO, NASA, and the United States Defense Department.

One Miami employee who was given notice of dismissal spent his last days at the office jiggering the company's complex computer records. He managed to change the entry code word so that nobody could gain access to the system for the next six weeks. This caper cost the company hundreds of thousands of dollars. Other potential threats include espionage and the malicious planting of a computer "virus," which causes whole records of companies or governments to erase themselves over time.

Once computers have been introduced into the workplace, attention and resources must be directed at keeping all security systems as tamperproof as possible. But the battle to maintain computer security is not entirely one of hardware and software. Most computer crime is not carried on by outsiders, but by disgruntled employees. Thus, one of the best preventions is to get back to some good old-fashioned, low-technology interpersonal skills to make people feel like the important corporate assets they are.

The key to the billion-dollar success of Ross Perot's Electronic Data Systems company was not so much in its technology, but in the way people (both employees and customers) were treated. By creating a corporate culture that fostered high levels of loyalty and ethics, Perot demonstrated that low-technology human considerations can overcome a lot of technostress.

INCREASING WORKLOAD

In the old days, one could delay a non-urgent request an extra day or two by simply placing it on the bottom of the pile or telling inquirers that it must be still "in the mail." Today, with facsimile machines and computer modems, people expect instant responses to even non-urgent needs. If a company's high-tech machinery includes a corporate plane, then it will often be expected that long distance meetings will take place in person, all over the country, instead of over the phone.

This has telescoped the workload into a greater density, making a mockery of the push-button "easy worklife" that computers were supposed to have brought. Instead of enjoying extra spare-time because technology can cut the work time in half, what happens is that the deadlines are often telescoped. Workload quotas and expectations are expanded, placing the workers under even more stress.

TECHNOSTRESS AND THE WELL-BEING OF EMPLOYEES

The technological revolution has redistributed levels of stress in the workplace. Many jobs that formerly involved high stress levels, such as burning the midnight oil to do year-end inventory checks, can now be done in minutes, with less stress, thanks to computers. Jobs that were formerly considered to have little stress, such as routine typing, now involve much more stress because of computers.

A recent study by the National Institute of Occupational Safety and Health showed that computerized clerical workers suffered higher levels of stress-related complaints than any other occupational group, including air traffic controllers. Worker's compensation claims for computer-related stress form the fastest growing category of illnesses in the workplace.

The human cost of the poorly planned march towards technological utopia has been significant, and can affect any part of the body. Although much highly publicized research has been done into the possible harmful effects of sitting in front of Video Display Terminals, especially for pregnant women, scientists have so far failed to turn up any significant health risks. However, a host of other complaints relate directly to the computerized work environment.

COMPUTER-RELATED EYESTRAIN

Polls of computer workers show that eyestrain is a concern in more than half of all cases. To a certain extent, eyestrain is an inherent part of running today's computers, because of the need for users to focus continuously on screens at such close range. This problem is currently being addressed through the development of better screens and voice-activated artificial intelligence. But for the moment eyestrain is common on today's equipment.

After prolonged sessions in front of a green display screen, a worker may notice phantom red letters for the first few minutes when casting his or her gaze onto a blank white wall or ceiling. If the original screen was amber, then the phantom letters will be blue-green.

In many cases, this phenomenon can be quite alarming. Fortunately, the color reversal effect, also called the McCollough Effect, is a normal part of the way vision works.

Action tip for eyestrain: Routinely break your gaze away from the screen to focus on something in the distance. This can help the tense eye muscles relax and lessen the strain.

COMPUTER-RELATED HEADACHES

Headaches are one of the more common complaints of the computer worker. Although sometimes caused by eyestrain (see above), most often these headaches are due to tension involving muscles of the temples, upper neck, and base of the skull.

Action tips for headaches:
- A great number of moderate headaches are successfully treated by rest and/or mild pain killers such as aspirin or acetaminophen.
- In many cases simple massage and relaxation techniques can be helpful in prevention of further attacks. Holding a fingertip on the source of the most pain and pressing very hard into the offending muscle for up to a minute can often abort a headache in its early stages. This technique, known as acupressure, is well known to any competent massage or Shiatsu therapist. (See chapter 10)
- Check the furniture. See if the height of your computer screen is at a level that allows you to read it without stretching or retracting your neck. Your head weighs about 25 pounds. If it spends all day tilted and craned to see a screen that is awkwardly located, this can easily cause neck pains or headaches. Other headaches can occur because of having a chair at the wrong height or having no armrests when sitting for protracted periods. This situation means that the full weight of the arms pulls down on the shoulders, causing great tension at the shoulder-tip and base of the skull. Spasms often radiate up into the head, causing considerable pains.
- Periodic breaks in the routine to stand up and do some simple neck, shoulder and arm stretching exercises can help.
- Some headaches, including migraines, can be triggered by poor lighting, including fluorescent bulbs that strobe or flicker with the alternating electrical current, lights that are too dim for the

workspace, or light that is too bright. In these cases, the appropriate lighting corrections will provide real medical benefits.

- At the end of the day, if a headache has persisted, then some well-proven relaxation techniques such as a hot bath, meditation, prayer, or the *Stress for Success* Power Nap tape could well be curative.
- If your headache persists in spite of the above, then I strongly suggest you see your doctor.

ARMS AND THE COMPUTER WORKER

A Japanese survey of over 16 million workers showed that computer workers and assembly line workers are prone to shoulder and arm pains. The authors called the condition the *occupational cervicobrachial syndrome*. It is probably a result of holding the arms in an anatomically unnatural position in front of the body for extended periods of time.

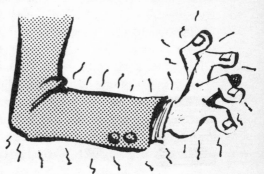

THE SWIVEL-CHAIR POTATO

Like his first cousin, the television addict, the full-time computer operator runs a significant risk of turning into a swivel-chair potato. With the loss of time perspective, it becomes all too easy to neglect physical exercise. This can lead to poor cardiovascular tone, varicose veins, obesity, constipation, hemorrhoids, and backache, as well as decreased mental alertness. As important as the furnishing surrounding the computer terminal are the time and space for a little office exercise. (See chapter 13 on physical fitness.)

Studies have shown that VDT workers suffer higher levels of stress than control groups who do not use these machines. Elevated levels of stress hormones stay high for longer periods after work than for non-VDT workers. This underlines the importance of low-tech activities in one's sparetime.

MENTAL HEALTH SIDE EFFECTS OF TECHNOSTRESS

The signs of mental burnout from technostress can come in the form of an increased error rate when working on the computer. Frequently, because of such constant association with machinery, technostressed workers lose many of their interpersonal skills. Constant associations tend to have a merging effect on our personalities. If we spend most of our time with comedians, we will tend to be funnier. Constantly associating with happy people, we will be more positive.

However, if we spend most of our time with a computer terminal (especially one that tattles on us every time we leave to go to the washroom or spend too long on the phone), there is a strong tendency for us to become more impatient with the imperfections of human relationships. This can lead to significant mental trauma, ranging from mild insomnia and anxieties to more severe manifestations.

I have seen technostress trigger an acute anxiety attack complete with sweating, pallor, hyperventilation, and collapse. I have also seen it cause a chronic burnout, with fatigue, depression, loss of time sense, impotence, and slow erosion of the patient's social and family life.

In any case where symptoms persist, it is wise to seek medical help. In my office, I have generally gone beyond the question of what sort of complaints the patient has, and ask the person to walk me through a typical day in his or her week. In addition to asking about the technological and interpersonal (such as with a supervisor) stresses, I have always sought to obtain a picture of the patient's mental defences.

Great insights are gained by noting how well patients manage their time. It is important to allow for exercise and distraction breaks when necessary or, even better, before necessary. Rather than reaching for a pill it is better to solve mental manifestations of technostress by trying harmless remedies such as relaxation techniques, yoga, or a simple change of routine. Many studies have shown that having a pet such as a dog or cat can help ease anxieties as soon as one goes home.

If these simple measures are not enough to improve job-related mental symptoms such as depression, anxiety, insomnia, and apathy, then it may be appropriate to escalate the treatment to include a professional psychological or psychiatric assessment. In some cases, it may even be necessary to resort to hospitalization and/or medications such as antidepressants and tranquilizers. If all else fails and the job stresses are intractable, quitting the job entirely may be the solution.

Chapter 5

LEADERSHIP AND THE BAD BOSS SYNDROME

EFFECTS OF BAD BOSSING

By a massive popular vote, the leading cause of stress at work is the bad boss. But before we dust off the golden turkey award, it would be wise to reflect on how many bosses are actually out there. In most organizations everyone in the company except the chief executive officer *has* a boss, or has the potential to become a boss, even if that means you are instructing an apprentice or a student who is at the company for a short time on a work orientation program.

As we have seen, in terms of making our own choices in response to stress, even the very lowest person on the work ladder is still a boss — a boss of his or her own Department of One. Thus, while a lot of people complain of having a bad boss, the corollary is that most of us *are* bad bosses — if not of others, then at least of ourselves. Although the advice that follows will extremely relevant to dealing with bad bosses, remember to reflect also on how the advice might be appropriate to you personally as well.

The damage that a bad boss does is sometimes far more widespread than is seen at the time. In the course of my speaking engagements, I have met literally hundreds of employees who have asked my advice on how to manage their managers, because they recognize that they are not contributing their personal best efforts under their current bosses. In my medical practice I have seen the effects on the health of workers who must suffer a bad boss. The results in human terms can be quite significant.

With the ultimate control, as well as knowledge of the bigger picture, the boss escapes the highest levels of stress at work, but can still be a powerful stress carrier. In just the same way that a child who is humiliated by a bully comes home and yells at a younger sibling, a boss can transfer anxieties and stresses to employees without ever letting them know the reasons behind the negative behavior.

When an employee is frustrated all day by the boss, these frustrations tend to get transferred along to innocent bystanders, rather like one of those dreadful chain letters. One of my patients transferred his frustrations into an injury. After a particularly testy day with his boss, he had a few too many drinks with his TGIF (Thank God It's Friday) coworkers, and punched a likeness of the boss's face that was tacked on the barroom wall. Unfortunately, the boss's nose was positioned directly over a supporting beam for the building, and the fist came out rather the worse for the encounter — with three broken bones.

I have, unfortunately, seen more drastic repercussions, ranging from demoralization and loss of self worth, to burnout of virtually any organ system in the body. In the brain, this burnout takes the form of fatigue, insomnia, anxiety, depression, or obsessive behavior. Aggression can be triggered, causing such tragedies as wife and child beating, or even mass murders during a sudden wild shooting spree. Bad bosses are even the motivation for some suicides. In the stomach or heart, the results of a bad boss are often seen in ulcers or heart attacks. The body system most commonly affected (after the obvious mental declines in morale) is the immune system. When I have a patient who is working for a bad boss, I can often tell by his or her response to disease. First of all, when one is under stress, one has a diminished immune response to disease, and thus gets sick more readily, and is slower to physically recover. When a worker finally becomes ill enough to call the doctor, there is a distinct difference in response, depending on what kind of boss is awaiting the particular patient back at work. A bad boss can also adversely affect mental stamina. Many who have a bad boss are such incredibly astute diagnosticians that they are able to take time off from work several days *before* any symptoms actually develop. They also exhibit a remarkable concern about contaminating their fellow workers. "So what do you say, Doc? Let's sign me off for a couple of weeks of rest." I must say I am amazed how often these notices of impending illness occur during the fishing season or during fine weather, and how rare they are during the rainy months or when the boss is away on holidays.

On the far less frequent occasions when a worker who does have a good boss gets sick, he or she seldom comes to see me before trying to fight off the disease for several days independently. Once treatment has begun, they are most anxious to return to work, even sooner than suggested.

ON YOUR MARK, GET SICK . . . .

The only one who can stay calm through this kind of working day is the boss. Only the boss knows the goals and directions of activity, which he changes whenever he feels like it. The employees become so confused they don't know whether to fill in forms or wind their watches. No wonder the stress makes some of them ill. There are many varieties of bad bosses, running the gammut from twits to thieves. Let's look at some common traits of bad bosses.

SIXTEEN COMMON TRAITS OF BAD BOSSES

1. FUZZIFIES GOALS

This can be particularly distressful because staff are never quite sure what they should be doing. When a newcomer arrives on the job, no training or ground rules are given and the results expected of the person's activity are never clearly explained. A classic case was of a man who tried to make a point of delaying his exit until at least 10 minutes after the boss had walked past his desk on the way home. After his six-week performance evaluation, he was surprised to learn that his boss had transferred him out of the department. When the employee demanded to know what he had done wrong, the boss's secretary revealed that the boss refused to tolerate anyone who couldn't get his or her work finished by the end of the day, as he assumed that those who took longer were inefficient. Although the assumption may have had some grounding in logic, the fact that the employee did not know whether he was expected to go home late or early made such a criterion meaningless. Thus any incompetence involved in this story was that of the boss, not of the confused employee. Yet it was the employee who suffered.

2. CAN'T DELEGATE

This can be critical to an organization, because employees are not allowed to develop the responsibilities and confidence levels that come only with being given full credit or blame for outcomes. If a boss is always butting in and making corrections, or doublechecking everything before it is sent out, then the worker can never grow. The corollary is that the boss doesn't grow either, being too busy running around trying to do everyone else's work.

3. WASTES YOUR DAY WITH MEETINGS

Often, this occurs when the boss is in over his or her head and can't get anything done alone. In this case everything is delegated, but without leadership. Office energy is spent. However, rather like a bunch of puppies tugging on the corners of a blanket, much heat and activity are generated, but no forward motion is detected.

4. HAS POOR ETHICS

The boss spends hours trying to fiddle his or her expense accounts, and then expects this fine example to encourage loyalty and honesty among staff. What usually happens is that, when bosses behave in unscrupulous ways, their employees extrapolate that a little white-collar crime would not be out of character within the company. Although such crimes may be just a series of minor incidents, such as using the office photocopier for personal needs, they may also escalate into something more serious such as full-fledged computer crime, which could easily bring the company to its knees. When employees see the boss bend the rules, some will soon follow suit. Bad bosses beware: your employees' revenge could be far more ruthless than you could ever be.

5. PLAYS POLITICS

The bad boss picks out a favorite for the fast track, often based on no evidence of superior performance. The office toady, the slick operator, the chairperson's son, or the girl with the great legs might be the lucky one. When a "boss's pet" is chosen as the rising star in an office and others who could do a better job are passed over, then morale and performance decline, and stress at work rises.

6. DENIES YOUR PERSONAL LIFE

The boss then expects you to work overtime to get your work done. Usually the bad boss expects all employees to be workaholics because the boss, as a result of a major ego problem, is more comfortable at work than at home. Typically, the bad boss often phones you at home, or even pages you in restaurants or on the golf course, in order to satisfy personal neurotic inadequacies.

7. NEVER SAYS A WORD WHEN YOU DO SOMETHING RIGHT

A bad boss assumes that, when you do your job well — even when you do something especially well — it is simply what you are paid to do and is not worthy of even a passing compliment. If anything of a positive nature is said, it is usually so long after the fact — such as at the annual performance review — that even the worker can scarcely remember the incident.

8. ALWAYS SPEAKS UP WHEN YOU MAKE A MISTAKE

This, in combination with the above trait, is what is popularly referred to as the "seagull" school of management. According to this method, the boss occasionally flies out from behind the executive desk, makes verbal deposits all over everyone in the department, and then flies back to roost behind closed doors. The "firings will continue until morale improves" motto would fit this kind of a boss.

9. ALWAYS PLAYS IT "BY THE BOOK"

This kind of bad boss must stick by the rules, or all is lost. Thus there is no room for improvisation on the job, and no place for suggestions from lower levels in the organization. If someone doesn't have the same credentials as the boss, preferably from the same school, then he or she has no opinion worth considering.

Whenever a problem or crisis arises, the workers are supposed to respond only in the standard fashion. When this fails, the worker is held responsible for the failure, but does not have the power to modify the responses as circumstances dictate.

10. WORKS IN SPLENDOR

The bad boss often believes in letting the hired help work in squalor with antiquated equipment and drab furnishings. Meanwhile, the boss has plush carpets so deep that a gopher could hide in them, and a collection of expensive office memorabilia that would make even a defrocked televangelist blush. Most importantly, the boss has a door, which is always closed unless the boss is out. Which brings us to:

11. HAS A CLOSED DOOR POLICY

Anyone with a great suggestion for saving the company money, or an idea for boosting sales, runs into the "Berlin Wall" when trying to pass the word up to the boss. The bad boss believes he or she is regal; the employees are lackeys. Assuming the worker can get past the layers of managerial check-points set up by the bad boss, he or she will still have to gain access to the inner sanctum. There, further impediments await in the form of the personal secretary, who stiffly states that the boss is in a meeting and therefore cannot be disturbed.

12. NEVER LISTENS TO THE EMPLOYEES' AND CUSTOMERS' COMPLAINTS

However, he or she will gladly accept the credit for any compliments.

13. ALWAYS IMPOSES CHANGES FROM THE TOP DOWN

The bad boss refuses to consult with the workers who spend their lives perfecting their particular job skills. The boss is in charge here. Therefore, with the advice of outside consultants, he or she is the one best qualified to tell workers how to make changes.

14. THINKS ALL CONTINUING STAFF EDUCATION IS A WASTE OF MONEY

This goes for all training courses, as well as educational books and tapes for staff. Employees all went to school, so why bother teaching them more? The bad boss worries that a junior will become more skilled, threatening his or her position. The bad boss ignores all the benefits, like keeping up with the competition, that added staff education can bring.

15. LOVES TO PUSH PEOPLE TO BE WORKAHOLICS

(See chapter 6.) Such a boss lives by the motto that people are a cost, not a resource. His or her idea of creative planning for future corporate growth is to push people until they drop and then shout, "Next!"

16. PAYS LITTLE ATTENTION TO DETAIL

Believes in the credo, "Let's do it right the second time." The main objective with this boss is to clear off all projects from the in-basket, even if they are sent to the wrong person or wrong department. After all, it will eventually get done by somebody. And, for the moment, it's not his/her problem.

PUTTING A BAD BOSS INTO PERSPECTIVE

In terms of direct effects on the staff's health, a bad boss is at the top of the list in potential stress hazards. In financial terms, the bad boss robs the company of potential productivity and sales, which causes decreased performance and profits in large bureaucracies, and bankruptcies in small businesses. In personal terms, a bad boss can squelch one's thirst for more challenges and smother a budding career. As we all know, it's hard to soar like an eagle if you're working for a turkey.

If you decide to speak to your boss directly in an attempt to change his or her management techniques, handle it carefully. Ask for a personal appointment and then make your pitch. This will require all of your speechmaking skills (see chapter 8) to control your emotions under stress, and to use the stress to help you to think on your feet. If you don't, you will be forever wishing you had said something else at the time. As in the case of speechmaking, read your audience, not your speech. Don't beat around the bush. Even if your boss is a twit, he or she will still be on a time schedule, so don't waste your whole appointment on smalltalk.

Start with a concise statement, in language and lingo your boss will understand. Document your claims and proposals with graphs, charts, customer complaints, competitors' sales figures, and so on. Remember to read your audience. Stop before your boss stops your speech; know when you are pushing him or her too far.

Some of your communication with a bad boss may be more appropriate to do in writing. Always keep copies of such memos. That way, there will at least be a record of your opinions, or of your being directed against your better judgment to do something that you know is wrong, unwise, or wasteful.

Another possibility is that you are blaming your boss for things beyond his/her control. If you're bored or insecure, or always feel that you're overworked, these factors can push your stress level. But are they your boss's fault? You must consider carefully whether it is your boss or your job, or possibly, something outside your workplace that is the cause.

WHAT MAKES A BOSS BAD?

Bad bosses are people too, with their own fears, feelings, strengths, and weaknesses. Sometimes the pompous ones are basically shy and insecure. The ones who yell at people and unduly assert their aggression may be having significant family problems. Bosses with personal health problems may take these out on the staff. Still other bosses may be nice people who are simply in over their heads, and have absolutely no aptitude for their jobs.

By realizing that human frailties often underlie even the most objectionable qualities of bad bosses, employees can be in a better position to deal with them, and to judge whether the situation is temporary or hopeless. This may help them decide whether to stick it out or to quit the job.

Even though a bad boss counts on the inertia of the human spirit, you can break free of the intangible bonds that bind. Also beware of some of the tangible bonds. Whatver you do, don't lock yourself into an enormous mortgage, or you will not have the option of cooling off in another job at a reduced salary. There is a shortage of skilled labor, and a tremendous shortage of versatile labor (people who will accept a total change in career direction when circumstances dictate). Even if you end up with a different bad boss, at least the change will be refreshing. Remember that the average worker will have between four and six complete job changes in the course of a working lifetime, so you don't need to be caught in the ''one company, for better or for worse'' trap for your whole career.

In today's information society, we have never had more options in the form of starting new businesses, or moving to areas of sustained new growth in smaller businesses. Remember, the Fortune 500 giants may be downsizing, but many of the little companies are upsizing. Unemployment figures show that, when employees do leave a company, they usually find a new job within six weeks (or more if they are picky). Corporate "headhunters" may be an excellent resource to help you determine how saleable your attributes and skills are. Many excellent schools and correspondence courses offer training for new skills to supplement your old ones, to hope you get an even better position than the one you left behind.

As soon as you recognize that your boss is a terminal jackass, consider using the opportunity to make yourself as saleable as possible. Rather than imagining huge obstacles that will block your escape, view the known dangers of doing nothing in their proper perspective. If you stay working for a bad boss, your finances may plateau, your family life may suffer, your morale and skills may decline, or your health may suddenly fail. Any one of these realities is a far greater obstacle than the fear of having to break into a new group of friends at a new office, or having to go through a few weeks of interviews before you are successful. Once the size of the obstacles lying in the way of each of your options is seen correctly, then the escape route is less terrifying than the inertia route.

In many cases, an obstacle to escape may be a simple skill that is lacking. Thus the cure, best taken before one quits, may be as simple as shaking off an old phobia about computers or word processors, and taking a few courses to familiarize yourself with them. In other cases, it might be appropriate to ask your spouse to stay at work while you try to make a go of that small business idea you had always toyed with. A few years later, you may well join thousands of others who have raised their glasses in a somewhat sarcastic salute to the bad boss, without whom their subsequent success would have been impossible.

On the other hand, you may, upon considering your options, elect to stay where you are and put up with an intransigent boss. This does not necessarily mean a complete surrender of all your personal pride, but rather can create a new challenge within a job. Many who have chosen this route have developed great skills in anticipating the boss's mistakes and trying to prevent them by presenting a *fait accompli*. This is seen in many executive suites, where a secretary or assistant will prepare all the documents, make sure they have been seen by all the involved decision-makers, and only then will present them to the boss for a simple signature. Although the boss may be in a fog, there will be no doubt among the others as to who is really running the show. Thus recognition from peers can supplant recognition from the boss. The net result is a compromise, allowing one to retain one's self-respect in spite of one's superior.

Depending on the situation, others find their solution in simply putting in their required hours on the job and then living for their hobbies. Many a bad boss has noted that all the staff seem to be incredibly lazy and slothful all day long. If these bosses would stand outside their offices or plants, they would witness the most amazing feats of instantaneous group resuscitation. Once free of the oppressive atmosphere of work, the employees are suddenly full of energy, which is spent on sports, gossip, friendships, hobbies or volunteer work.

People need a mission in life. If this is denied by a bad boss at work, there are other ways to fulfill this need — ways that will still allow an overall sense of accomplishment. It is obviously bad business for any company to have such a reversal of energies affecting its operation. However, concentrating most of their energies on pursuits outside of work is a common defence against the bad boss when employees elect to stay with their jobs rather than resigning.

TEN THINGS TO DO IF YOU YOURSELF ARE A BAD BOSS

To begin with, the very fact that you have come to recognize your shortcomings gives you an advantage over almost all bad bosses. Excellent turnarounds, as in the case of alcoholics, can only begin with the frank admission that one has a problem.

The next step will be reflection and introspection. Perhaps you are in the wrong job, and you don't have what it takes to be an effective boss. There is no shame in such an admission. Indeed I have seen many such bosses find great relief in quitting the office politics to go back to their old jobs in the sales force, on the shop floor, or working for themselves.

However, let's assume you are suited to being a boss, and are prepared to make the tradeoffs necessary to hold that position (such as the responsibilities of hiring and firing, the extra house of preparation for work, and the sense of loneliness in not having ready peers to confide in). Here are some action tips that will help you turn into a good boss, and a more profitable one:

1. BE A STUDENT

Even in the best business schools, not enough is taught about motivating employees to produce their best work. Read books on the subject, such as *The One-Minute Manager* by Drs. Ken Blanchard and Spencer Johnson and *Peak Performers* by Dr. Charles Garfield. Try to develop some non-monetary rewards that will encourage higher employee morale. Also read books on bad bosses, such as *Never Work for a Jerk* by Patricia King.

2. BE A TEACHER

Your superiors presumably made you a boss for more reasons than just the number of years you logged in the lower ranks. You must have a great deal of knowledge that can be shared. The good boss knows that training others benefits all concerned. It will be easier for such a good teacher to move up the company ladder when the powers that be see that his or her present department will be able to continue its good work even if he or she is moved on to higher things.

3. GIVE RECOGNITION IN FRONT OF PEERS

Feedback could be called the breakfast of champions, but it will do no good unless it is given while the sweat is still on the workers' brows. Obviously, everyone needs a certain level of salary to have the basic necessities and comforts. However, the good boss knows that, beyond this point, money alone often ceases to be such an effective motivator. I have seen companies in which a three-dollar plastic achievement plaque is given prime wall space, even by a high earner, and will motivate greater commitment to the corporate mission than a stack of ten-dollar bills.

4. ENCOURAGE RISK-TAKING AND DECISION-MAKING

Promote these even at low levels in the company, and be prepared to steer people through a few bad results. It is only by delegating stress and helping to foster a sense of entrepreneurial spirit among staff that a boss will have time to focus on issues that he or she alone can handle. As long as employees get consistent praise when they do well, and some objective tips for improvement as soon as they make mistakes, it's a good idea to encourage them to be self-starters.

5. MINGLE

The best way to instill a sense of shared commitment to a mission is to mix with the employees and be receptive to their suggestions. The bad boss sits behind locked doors with a garbage pail on his or her head, to screen out all distractions from the employees. The good boss recognizes that the experts in every phase of the business are the employees who do those jobs each day, and the customers who use the products or services sold.

6. TURN THE CORPORATE PYRAMID UPSIDE DOWN

In effect, find out who is really the boss. In a company run by a bad boss, the frontline staff are rude to the customer and save their smiles for their supervisors. A good boss inverts the pyramid so the staff can all see that the top echelon belongs to the customer, who is the rightful monarch. The next echelon will be the frontline staff who deal directly with the customer. If they realize that their real boss is the customer and not the supervisor, they will be more aware of the importance of treating the customer to the best service possible.

A good way for a supervisor to get promoted is to treat employees as his or her boss, and do whatever he or she can to help them give the best possible service to their customers. When the frontline staff see their supervisor go to bat for them in the executive office, then improved loyalty, morale, and productivity are the supervisor's rewards. All the way up the line, this inversion of responsibility can give people a most refreshing outlook and pay handsome rewards for all.

7. HOLD REGULAR MEETINGS

Preferably these should take the form of only a short "huddle" at either end of a day or week. Also communicate through the written word, in the form of *bilateral* performance evaluations. Just as the best hotel chains invite candid comments from guests, a good boss wants to find out how to be a better one. Brief *anonymous* questionnaires for employees, customers and suppliers — as well as a staff suggestion box — can help you grade your effectiveness. The very fact that you have the courage to ask such questions will earn you a lot of respect provided, of course, that you are honestly seeking input and not just using the approach as a gimmick.

8. BE ETHICAL

Conduct yourself according to the same code of ethics as you expect of your employees. If you are told something in confidence by an employee, don't betray that confidence. If you do, you'll quickly cease receiving pieces of intelligence from the staff. When promotions (or demotions) are in order, make sure you use rational criteria for the decisions. That way, even if some employees feel upset by your decision, at least they will know why someone else got the job.

9. PAY ATTENTION TO EMPLOYEE BENEFITS

To the extent that you have the power, work with your employees to establish a menu of appropriate benefits that provide flexibility. Daycare and a dental plan may cost the company a lot of money, but their value is nil to a childless widower who stores his teeth in a jar every night. Make sure some available benefits suit his needs. Assistance for educational advancement, including courses in financial planning and retirement counseling, can help round out the list of options. Medical and group insurance plans are popular but expensive options, and need to be assessed carefully by employees and management.

10. SHARE A FRACTION OF THE ACTION

Ultimately, one of the best incentives a boss can offer is a fraction of the action in the form of performance-based monetary rewards or, better yet, options to participate in company stock ownership. One of Ross Perot's greatest pleasures was to make some of his managers into multimillionaires through stock participation. They all repaid him with regenerated enthusiasm, renewed energy, and, ultimately, more corporate profits than any of them had ever imagined. Stock participation can be one of the best ways to transfer the spirit of entrepreneurship into any company. By spreading out the risk-reward net to include more of the staff, the good boss uses shared stress to encourage group excellence.

Chapter 6

THE WORKAHOLIC TRAP

MEET THE WORKAHOLIC

A workaholic, like an alcoholic, is one who lacks the ability to say "when." Workaholics are common in all walks of life, from social workers to surgeons, from stock brokers to self-employed business owners, and from ambitious junior clerks to company presidents. If the boss is an unsympathetic workaholic, then he or she may spread the habit by passively implying that emulation is the sincerest form of advancement. Some people are workaholics because they fear that, in today's climate of frequent mergers and acquisitions, only those who stay at the workplace the latest can count on job security.

The workaholic's theory is that more hours input equal more work output. "If I can do a certain amount of work in an 8-hour day," thinks the workaholic, "then I should be able to do double that amount in a 16-hour day." Taking the theory one step further, should one aim for the perfect 24-hour day at the desk, in order to really impress the boss?

Obviously, the deprivation of sleep would preclude the latter option from becoming the normal pattern. However, so too does the deprivation of relaxation time in the 16-hour workday. Efficient work requires not only a good sleep the night before. It also requires some effective time off to recharge one's energies in the other compartments of one's life — with family, friends, exercise, and hobbies. While most of us are capable of working extended hours for a few days in an emergency, the human engine cannot run at the same peak efficiency for long. The fact that the chronic 12- to 16-hour day worker appears to be more committed is only an illusion, a fact that clever managers are now noting. The workaholic is more committed, all right, but to being extremely inefficient for most of the regular workday, and then getting caught up in the evenings. Workaholics fool a lot of their onlookers since most people confuse activity with results. Thus workaholics are often revered, both by their peers and their managers. The ambitious ones keep going until divorce, bankruptcy, or a breakdown in health intervenes. Slow-learning workaholics often wait until hit by all three.

HEALTHY AND UNHEALTHY TYPE As AND TYPE Bs

Healthy Type A

Healthy Type B

Unhealthy Type A

Unhealthy Type B

Rather than direct all comments and efforts towards eliminating Type A behavior, it makes more sense to recognize the healthy versus the unhealthy varieties as well. Traditionally, all comparisons have been between the unhealthy Type A and the healthy Type B.

A healthy Type A is one who can identify true emergencies and react to these appropriately, and who can temper the hostility aspects of their responses to stress. Healthy Type As are often found in successful entrepreneurial positions. They are in good physical shape because of their attention to diet and exercise. They do not abuse alcohol, drugs, or tobacco.

For such Type As, especially if they enjoy their jobs, there seems to be no reason to expect an early heart attack, as would be the case with the hostile, unhealthy Type A.

By the same token, having the more placid, calm demeanor of the Type B does not by itself guarantee immunity from health problems. Unhealthy Type Bs may be smokers and obese. They may be out of shape and very much at risk for heart attacks the next time they are called upon to exert themselves maximally, for example, pushing their cars out of snowbanks or having to climb stairs in hot humid weather.

The problem that I see in my office is that Type As are constantly calling false alarms. For example, what happens when the red light changes to green? All of a sudden the Type A driver thinks this is an emergency, and that it's a matter of life and death whether he or she beats the adjacent hatchback full of groceries into the next block. The body responds as if a tiger is about to attack, and yet another false alarm is wasted.

Baseball pitchers or cricket bowlers are said to have only so many throws in their arms in a lifetime. The same can be said for our body's having only so many emergency responses. When we have used up our quota, something breaks down. Canada's pioneer of stress research, Dr. Hans Selye, referred to this finite adaptation energy as being like a bag of coins that we are given at birth, to be spent as fast or as slowly as we choose. The breakdown could be in any part of the body. In the case of freeway gunslingers or burnt-out workaholics, it happens to be in the brain. In the case of the alcoholic, it could be the stomach, bleeding through an ulcer. In the case of the smoker with high blood pressure, it could well be the heart that suddenly stops beating. But these unpleasant consequences can usually be sidestepped by an enlightened, active approach to stress management.

WORKAHOLIC WILLY OR WELL-BALANCED WANDA?

If you owned a company, which person would you rather promote? Would it be the workaholic who regularly sleeps overnight at his or her desk, constantly has bags under the eyes, and is distracted by constant family problems related to the inadequate time spent at home? Or would it be the well-balanced competent worker who gets the best results in the least time?

That question becomes even more pointed when you are in business for yourself, and push yourself even harder than the average workaholic. More independent businesses have failed from too much work on the part of their owners than from too little. The real cause of bankruptcy is usually undetected in the financial reports. However, it becomes clear in the doctor's office when such problems as weight loss, chest pains, burnout, and stomach disorders are traced back to the workaholic's ineffective work habits and totally incompetent management of his or her own personnel Department of One.

When big government bureaucracies perceive a problem, their reflex reaction is to lavishly throw more *money* at it. In a similar way, when modern businesses are being outsmarted, out-managed, or underpriced by global competitors, their reflex reaction is to throw more *time* at the problem. It seems to offer some solace to those whose businesses are failing that at least everyone was working long hours, if not effective ones.

In the case of machines, activity may well be equated with results, but this is not always so with people. Chronic workaholism, whether driven by the boss, one's peers, or oneself, simply corrodes the more important modern weapons so vital to the success of any business: creativity, mission, and inspiration. All three of these weapons can be best developed in a balanced environment that pays attention to the needs of our friends, our families and our bodies. The old adage that tired chickens produce stale eggs may not be precisely true in the henhouse, but it certainly is in the workplace.

In the long term, workaholics do have a head start over the rest of the workforce in many areas. The problem is, the areas they are leading in are job burnout, divorce, health crises, senility after retirement, and early death. On the other hand, greater achievement, excellence, and personal happiness are more desirable goals — goals that workaholics are doomed not to achieve in the long run. Victory does not require the exaggeratedly slow pace of the allegorical tortoise, but it does require effective compartmentalization. The great paradox with workaholism is that, for once, the treatment is more fun than the disease.

THE OVERFLOWING WORK COMPARTMENT

Workaholism causes the work compartment of one's life to overflow into the neglected and mostly vacant sparetime compartments. The result of this imbalance is detrimental to the whole person. U.S. army studies show that overworked troops generally aren't aware that their concentration and performance are falling off. The same often holds true for civilian workaholics.

DIFFERENT STROKES FROM DIFFERENT FOLKS

At work we feel in control. More importantly, our efforts are generally noticed and rewarded. Apart from the financial rewards, we get ego gratification at work in countless other ways. Coworkers compliment us on our new outfits. Customers thank us for good service. A rookie grins his appreciation when we show him how to make his first sales call. The boss turns to us for help on an important contract because no one else can handle it as well.

At home, on the other hand, our good work may be taken for granted; we may be noticed only when we do things incorrectly. Our partners leap into the breach: "Thanks for forgetting to take out the garbage."; "You're not actually wearing *that*, are you?"; or the old demoralizing praise-retraction combo: "Thanks for helping with dinner — now look at the big mess you've left." Our kids often further fan the flames: "Do we have to eat this again *tonight*?"; "How come you never take me anywhere *I* want to go."; or the all-time worst, "Don't come into the school with me; someone might see that you're my *mother*.''

With the frequent disparity between the ego-strokes received at home and at work, it's hardly a wonder that more men and women than ever before are giving in to the siren call of their work, choosing to stay late at the workplace. It is for this reason that many workaholics frankly admit they seldom need to be *forced* to work; they simply *like* to work, more than they like to spend time at home.

WORKAHOLICS AS PRIORITY ABUSERS

Workaholics are often priority abusers. They like projects that can be interpreted as earth-shattering emergencies. If the job at hand isn't shaping up to be enough of an urgent case, then workaholics have a marvellous knack of frittering away their ''in-between'' hours doing low-priority tasks. For example, workaholics love to waste minutes idly sifting through the pleasant bits of their mail, but leave all difficult matters for another day — wasting much time in the process. When deadlines are still days away, stress levels are low, and work gets done at a relatively slow pace. Often subconsciously, the workaholic wastes the early days so that the most mundane project can be elevated into a dramatic emergency. All of a sudden, the deadline closes in and work needs to be done at peak levels of speed and efficiency.

The senses — of sight, hearing, smell, touch, and taste — become more acute. The mind instantly develops an improved ability to focus, absorb, and memorize, just as it did before our school exams. The body responds with its outpourings of adrenaline, cortisol, and endorphines. The workaholic gets a feeling of power and well-being unmatched by any other experience in his or her life. This is the kind of high that memories are made of. Burning the midnight oil at the office, speeding through traffic to screech up to the door of a meeting in progress, and racing 500-yard airport hurdles like O.J. Simpson all look heroic. Unfortunately, however, they often underscore an incredible disorganization of both time and priorities.

Most people do not have jobs they would describe as exciting. Very few are stunt pilots, astronauts, or avalanche rescue workers. Most people sit all day processing information, working in a high-tech, low-touch, sterile environment. The majority would admit that looking back over their own career highlights is a little like watching Uncle Harry's 300 slides of his latest trip to the edge of town. Boring. For many, work has lots of chronic mental stress that grinds down the soul, but none of the exciting, acute, physical stress that makes the spirit soar.

It is in order to remedy this state of affairs that the workaholic invents his or her own obstacles, even if they are quite needless. The workaholic then gets a great opportunity for self-congratulation while leaping over each obstacle in its turn. There is nothing wrong with purposely injecting a little more stress into one's otherwise boring workday. Indeed, a daily dose of stress can add spice, create memories, and improve work performance.

However, I would suggest that the method of doing so should not be antisocial, dangerous to health and safety, or threatening to others. One of my colleagues, a doctor who loved to drive fast, routinely wasted time before getting into his car to drive to the hospital to attend a delivery. His need for stress was indeed antisocial, as he forced many an oncoming driver off the road. This doctor's need for extra stress in his life could have been more appropriately satisfied by attending a registered car racing school, or taking up rock climbing or hang gliding.

There are other ways of injecting stress into life. For example, one could extend oneself to one's financial limits to invest in the biggest possible house or property. This stress, too, could easily lift work habits out of the doldrums and elevate efficiency to peak levels. In other words, boredom can be beaten by stress, but please don't impose your stress and its effects on others. Remember, one person's boredom-beater can be another's panic attack.

WORKAHOLISM AND PROFESSIONAL SPORTS

A game of tennis after work may revitalize the body and brain of an office worker, but might be the last straw that pushes the over-worked tennis pro into burn-out. Famed "Grand Slam" champion Rod Laver was asked to comment on the then-teenaged Bjorn Borg's insatiable and seemingly superhuman appetite for the game. He predicted that Borg would reign at the top of his game for a lot longer if he would only learn to *not* play tennis for a part of his daily routine.

I have spoken to a number of players and coaches on the professional tennis tour, and have noted the trend towards overwork and burnout at increasingly young ages. This is a not unexpected result of taking a child out of childhood too early. Promising young stars are screened in early school years and, to the virtual exclusion of their social and even family life, saturated with one sport. To be sure, this system has developed some powerful and talented 12-year-olds, one in a million of whom will end up being good enough to stay on the pro circuit.

However, these benefits are often at the cost of developing young workaholics who are poorly equipped to cope with future life stresses. The same thing happens in other sports such as hockey, gymnastics, swimming, and figure skating.

WORKAHOLICS AS INEFFICIENT TIME MANAGERS

As we have noted, most workaholics do not schedule and compartmentalize their time well. Let's look at three areas in which they waste time in the workplace — in meetings, on the telephone, and in handling paperwork. We'll also look at ways of overcoming timewasting in these areas.

1. MEETINGS

Meetings that are unnecessarily long or, more commonly, unnecessarily held are a great roadblock to completing the eight-hour day on time. Instead of a direct conference on the phone, or in person with the two or three individuals needed to resolve a problem, there is a great bureaucratic tendency to save these problems and add them to the agenda of yet another general meeting. A workaholic manager often sees meetings as more important than anything else that might come up. Rarely will a telephone call — no matter how potentially important — be allowed to interfere with the sanctity of the all-important meeting.

For most of those present, at a workaholic manager's meeting, only a few minutes of the whole meeting relate to their area of expertise. If the agenda is not carefully planned and clustered to allow relevant parties to give their input, and then be excused, great amounts of doodling, nodding, group mumbling, and day dreaming will be going on behind the facades of interested participation. Rather than being the intensely productive heart of any business, meetings can all too easily become an end in themselves.

In most boardrooms or other meeting quarters, the chairs are far too comfortable, encouraging a slouched body language and a reclined demeanor. Some companies are catching on to the fact that these subtle nonverbal trappings, although perhaps appropriate for a past era, are actually getting in the way of doing business. Many innovative companies have come up with unique solutions, such as allowing spontaneous open-door consultations with all levels of workers involved in a project, from junior laborers to senior management, right at the outset. This is the basis of the now famous MBWA school of management, otherwise known as Management By Wandering Around. It is one reason why Japanese managers have been so effective with their desks out in the open, on the plant floor, rather than hiding in the deep pile carpets of meeting rooms all day.

Other interesting innovations abound. One company that I spoke to in Toronto had evolved a "no chair" policy for all their brief daily morning meetings. With everyone standing in an informal circle in one of the offices, they found that there were no subtle signals or incentives to waste time. People got right to the point, looked each other in the eye, and blew through the agenda in a fraction of the time of their former mid-afternoon marathon meetings. Profitability improved, the number of telephone callbacks dropped since employees weren't spending so much time in meetings, and morale soared. Interestingly enough, this company has very few people who stay late any more, but both the company and the employees are now making more money than they used to.

2. THE TELEPHONE

Like any stressor, the telephone is neutral, but in the wrong hands it can become a negative influence in any office. First of all, every phone call *is* a meeting, even though the two of you are not in the same room. And, just as we noted in the meeting scenario, if the call has no agenda, then it may become inefficient. This is often not noticed, as the total time wasted might be only a couple of minutes per call. However, when multiplied by the number of calls received each day, it can add up to several hours of time lost, which will then have to be made up after work, when the phones have finally stopped ringing. Here are two simple action tips that will help you chair your next telephone "meeting."

Act, don't react — Whenever possible (unless the caller is someone you have been playing phone tag with for days), try not to answer a call unless you are prepared. Otherwise it is the same as running any meeting without an agenda. Minutes tick away while you fluff around muttering such inanities as ". . . just a minute . . . let me see if I can find it . . . it's got to be in this pile somewhere . . . just a second while I put the phone down and check over in the filing cabinet . . ."

If it is not possible to reach people when you *are* prepared to talk to them, keep a sheet for each one in the alphabet section of your time management system. On this sheet write down all the points you want to raise the next time you speak to the person. That way, when Judy Jones calls you from overseas, you can simply flip to the J's and be instantly reminded of the agenda, which can include all the thoughts that had crossed your mind over the last few weeks concerning your business with Judy Jones.

As you talk on the phone, write notes beside each point on your agenda so that you will remember what was said. Add to the list as more points arise. Once certain points have been completely dealt with, you may want to cross them off your list.

Get to the point, and fast — If you use a non-directive greeting such as "Hi. How are you?", you will be guaranteed the equally useless reply, "Fine. How are you?" Unless you are both investigating each other's biorhythms, this opening gambit leads to a predictably unproductive interchange. Unhelpful conversation on occasion may be appropriate; for example, if you and the person on the other end of the line are personal friends as well as business associates. However, it is generally best to keep chitchat to a minimum. Get to the point or, as they say in the movies, "Cut to the chase."

The pressures of work demand that if you are to have any chance of getting your job done well and leaving work early enough to have a personal life, your telephone meetings have to be directed and structured. However, this doesn't mean you need to be rude, inconsiderate, or unfriendly. Telephone etiquette is probably a topic that should be stressed more in schools. One of the most irritating greetings is the rhetorical question, "Would you hold please?'' followed by the instantaneous supermarket music.

The caller has no idea whether he or she has reached the right number, because many offices sound like this. The person answering the phone has no idea if the call is a wrong number, which company employee is being called, or what the call might be about. Thus, with all the phone lines lit up, and demands from all sides within his or her own desk area, the person answering the phone cannot assign priorities to the waiting calls. Many times a whole conversation could be over in a few seconds with the leaving of a simple message.

By coming on the line with a friendly, "Good morning, Amalgamated Mop Handles, Robin speaking. How may I help you?" a receptionist gives a much better impression of the company. The caller, in turn, should immediately get to the point, giving his or her name if appropriate and stating the business at hand.

3. PAPERWORK

Most desks, if left unattended for reason of illness or holiday, are covered with an avalanche of paper withing a few days. It seems that your in-basket is everyone else's garbage can. Clients' letters, complaints, compliments, legal documents, junk mail, bills, invoices, magazines, newsletters, forms to be filled out, margins to be initialed, and the omnipresent memos pour in every day.

In one East Coast American computer conglomerate, the vice president in charge of administration was outraged at the slow rate at which paperwork made its way from one part of the office to another. He immediately drafted the following memo to all departments: "It has come to my attention that our employees are wasting far too much time signing their initials on every document that comes into their in-baskets. In the future, all staff are required to erase these initials. They should, however, continue to initial their erasures." There's a boss who believes in cutting red tape, but only lengthwise.

Human nature being what it is, we all like pleasant items, and dislike the unpleasant pieces of paper that await us in our in-baskets. This forms the basis for *Hanson's observation of the paper compost heap — The friendly bits are handled, and the unfriendly ones left to rot*. Letters of praise, cheques, letters with pretty stamps from exotic places, and big fat orders for company products are opened first, read, and dealt with. Complaint letters, invoices, boring quarterly reports, and complicated forms requiring filling out find their way to the bottom of the paper compost heap, either unopened or opened and then abandoned.

The longer the paper compost pile is ignored, the more it is compounded by repeat invoices, requests, and reminders. Telephone calls also increase from the parties concerned, wondering where the devil your response has ended up.

The problem can easily be solved by implementing *Hanson's antidote to paper compost: handle it only once*. If you lay your hands and eyes on a document, deal with it immediately and don't put it back on the same pile. Keep the in-basket for new entries, not for old storage. Use your desk as furniture, not as an overflow trough for your in-basket. Each item will need a finite amount of time spent on it, and that time will not be diminished by procrastinating. On the contrary, it will be increased every time you put the document aside, lose your place, and then have to pick it up again from the beginning. The positive sense of achievement gained by staying in control of paperwork, instead of being controlled by it, overcomes the initial negative responses to the *handle-it-at-once* approach. It also has the added reward of getting you home earlier, so that divorce papers will not be added to tomorrow's in-basket.

The most time consuming of all communications can be the letter. With the scarcity of office stenographers to take dictation, most office letter-writers have to dictate into a tape recorder or, increasingly, type letters on their own word processors.

Dictation presents difficulties and limitations of its own. There is a tendency to ramble, without visual guidance as to the size of each paragraph. Most people who don't have time to write a short letter end up dictating a long one instead. One of the most helpful uses of speechmaking skills (see chapter 8) is to help you formulate a good speech into your dictation machine.

If you have to type your own screed, for heaven's sake learn to type. Hammering away on the *, @, &, and # buttons because you have your fingers on the wrong row is not the way to get out of the office on time. As we discussed in chapter 4 (regarding technostress) many people fear the computer out of all proportion to its actual impact. A few simple hours spent in a basic keyboarding skills course can have even the most inflexible hunt-and-pecker typing at least somewhat faster than before. It will take only a fraction of the time that workers willingly spend to learn how to swing a club or a racquet, and can provide just as much stress relief. If you're embarrassed taking an evening typing course, take a home course instead.

Sometimes, typing isn't required at all. For many letters, all that is required is a simple answer to one question. By the time a new sheet of paper is rolled into the printer, and the address, date, and salutation are entered, the three- or four-word answer could easily have been written in pen across the bottom of the original, put into an envelope, and returned. If it is absolutely necessary for you to keep a record of it, then a simple photocopy will be a lot cheaper (and quicker) than the cost of typing a response letter. This is also a quick way to get through your daily mail pile.

COSTS OF WORKAHOLISM — FINANCIAL, MENTAL AND PHYSICAL

The price of unmanaged, long-term workaholic stress is high. The financial price is measured in the cost of errors by workers, at any level in the hierarchy, whose minds are preoccupied by negative stresses. Recently an overworked, fatigued truck driver reacted too slowly to a sudden bottleneck in the traffic and jack-knifed his tanker, releasing toxic chemical fumes into the air. No lives were lost, but a lot of people were evacuated from local houses, many of them quite ill. The resulting lawsuits almost bankrupted the driver's company. In New York a burned-out middle manager, working long after his colleagues had gone home, made a simple mental error, put in an incorrect computer entry, and lost his company several million dollars on the commodity exchange.

The mental price of workaholism is seen in terms of high rates of family breakups, job burnouts, insomnia, fatigue, depression, and anxiety. Here the spectrum ranges from minor levels of dysfunction to shocking cases of homicide and suicide.

Studies of assembly line workers have shown that repeatly-used parts of the body can easily wear out. For example, the twisting and lifting of an elbow to grasp and hoist machine parts on an assembly line can lead to inflammation, pain, and swelling in that elbow. The treatment would obviously need to include the rotation of the worker through different stations in the plant, to rest this one joint, while other parts of the body took their turn to be stressed. The analogy should be noted by all workaholics.

The modern workaholic experiences stresses revolving around the same few electrical circuits in the brain without remission. After a time, these circuits wear out. By excluding most other activities of his or her life, the person doesn't allow these circuits to rest while other interests are pursued. History has taught us that changes of scenery foster some of the most profound solutions: Newton took his break under the apple tree, and Archimedes took time out for his bath.

Most of today's successful work innovations were not discovered by workaholics logging overtime at the office, but by balanced workers, protective of their personal schedules. The everyday details are dealt with in hours at the office, but the brilliant and innovative concepts are more likely to come in a few seconds during "down time," such as during a pensive moment in the back yard, on a fishing trip, or even on vacation. (See chapter 12 on versatility.)

The physical price of workaholism can be measured in terms of impaired resistance to infections, diseases, and pains. These can run the spectrum from nuisances such as common colds that seem to last forever, to serious diseases such as (pre-existing) ulcers, arthritis, colitis, or cancers that suddenly start to flourish.

The area involved in a stress-related physical breakdown could be any organ in the body. Workaholism could produce high blood pressure in one person, colitis in another, and hives in yet another. Many times the affected organ is one that has never given any previous problems.

I saw a 31-year-old workaholic in the emergency ward with what he had initially reported to his companion as a little "heartburn." It turned out to be a full-blown heart attack. Sadly, in his case, he arrived DOA (Dead On Arrival), and all our efforts to revive him were in vain. The paradox was that this workaholic was not overweight, was not a smoker, and was fond of exercise. In fact, he was stricken by his heart attack at the squash club on one of his rare nights off; amazingly, he was not playing, just watching a game.

I saw a 40-year-old workaholic who thought she would be just the sort to have stomach problems if anything physical were to suddenly fail. To her great surprise, her health breakdown came in the form of a "curtain" falling over her vision, and a retinal detachment being diagnosed.

Workaholics usually ignore physical risks, thinking of their bodies only in the short term, attending to just the basic bodily needs. Any long-term thinking relates only from their past lives up to the present moment, but not into the future. If the workaholic doesn't feel much different now than as a youngster, then he or she will often continue along with all bad habits blazing. Although workaholics may spend a great deal of time planning for the future of their work, many feel that only wimps worry about the future of their bodies. This is a serious mistake, the correction of which is one of the major missions of this book.

A WORKAHOLIC'S LAST WORDS

For more on workaholism, see chapters 10 and 11 on low-stress and high-stress countermeasures. But for now, the best advice I can pass on to you who are workaholics is to listen to the advice of one who knows best: a workaholic at the end of a life's work. As a practicing physician, I have cared for many workaholics during their dying days, and have often been privy to their last words.

Some workaholics regret not having spent more time on their fishing boats, or on their golf courses. Many regret not having spent enough effort on making their marriages work. Many regret having not spent enough time with their children when they were young. But not once have I ever heard a workaholic take his or her last breath and whisper, "I wish I'd spent a lot more time at the office."

Chapter 7

THE IMPENDING STORMS OF BUSINESS INSECURITY

WAITING FOR THE HURRICANES

Stress is with us from our first breath until our last, so it can never be avoided. Stress is not just the turbulence of sudden hurricanes, but the chronic, gnawing anticipation of impending storms.

In the modern business world, such storms can come in a number of guises. We hear rumors of mergers, takeover bids, divestitures, strikes, job redundancies, or a possible change in office location. Long before such events occur, or even whether or not they ever do occur, our bodies and minds register that we are under stress. This stress can influence our health and our achievements. If we handle the stress of impending storms well, it can make peak performances possible. If we adopt a passive approach, then those stresses can batter us like a bird in a badminton game and leave us much the worse for wear. As I pointed out in *The Joy of Stress*, the human body is provided with a brilliant program for stress defence, but our weapons sometimes seem to be designed for the wrong war. New weapons are within every reader's grasp, and we shall look at them later in this book. However, first we should take a better look at the new enemy, job insecurity.

A NEW ERA MEANS A LESS STABLE WORKPLACE FOR MANY

Until relatively recently, a retiring employee's work record was a model of stability; it usually listed one career and only one company. That company itself was under the same ownership from one generation to the next, and often an employee's family had two or more generations working there at the same time. People became an integral part of that one company, and adopted its name almost as part of their own. Even during vacations, people would introduce themselves as, "John Smith, Dean Foods" or "Kathy White, IBM." The worker's spouse and children would also wave the company flag, buying only company brands when possible, and shunning competitors' products. Much of one's social standing, esteem, and indeed personality were seen in the context of the lifetime job.

However, in the last few decades, this orderly, sedate workplace has seen incredible changes, causing high levels of stress for companies, workers, and their families. Wild swings in international currencies, bonds, and stock markets have resulted in record levels of changing company ownerships.

A great number of these changes are now international in scope, in part because of the recent rise of most foreign currencies against the U.S. and Canadian dollars, and because North America represents a traditionally safe haven for investment, with its large pool of raw materials, markets, and well-educated workforce. This means that North American companies are currently being bought up at "bargain basement" prices, and are being run with the international management styles of their new Japanese, British, Italian, French, German, Australian, Arab, Chinese, or South American owners.

Even companies that are not being taken over are acutely aware of the need to trim any "fat" in order to avoid being taken over by another company that thinks its managers could improve things significantly. Since 1980, almost three million people have been laid off by the Fortune 500 companies. Corporate takeovers rose from 1,900 in 1980 to 3,300 in 1986. In North America, business failures have climbed steadily, and have now stabilized just over 1,000 per week.

In order to survive, two traditional competitors may merge and prune the redundant members from the corporate tree. Medium-sized independent companies with unique personalities are being acquired by faceless conglomerates. Small teams of close colleagues are being broken up, with members sent to different jobs within the parent company's world, or being let go entirely. Some entire companies or even towns can become unemployed with just the stroke of a pen on a new takeover contract.

Wild swings in world commodity prices, such as in the prices of oil and precious metals, can turn multinational corporate giants from affluent acquisitors to cash-poor divestors. The effect can be to turn booming cities into ghost towns. Captains of commerce may be the subject for "Who's Who" one year, and "Where Are They Now?" the next year.

Strapped for cash after a stock takeover or leveraged buyout, most companies sell off major portions of their assets to raise money to pay down their bank loans. This allows them to focus on a smaller number of "core" businesses that are more in keeping with their expertise, long-term corporate goals, and missions. However, it can be most unsettling to all employees involved.

As a result of all these high-powered financial manipulations, the bottom line is that job insecurity has now become the number one stress for many employees. For centuries before the end of World War II, the changing political map of the world made it possible for people to find themselves living in a new country and speaking a new language, even though they had never left their hometown. Today, when one looks at the globe, the political map has largely stabilized. However, it is the corporate boundaries that are doing the shifting.

Stress levels are easy to understand when workers have to uproot their families and move to a new city, a new country, and a new culture or language. However, significant changes and stresses are also imposed on those who stay on when their com-

pany changes its flag of ownership. I have met many people who
have worked for at least three different companies in the last
decade, each with its own distinct management team, culture,
and style. Yet they are still behind the same desk.

EFFECTS OF JOB INSECURITY ON EMPLOYEES' PERSONAL LIVES

With companies changing hands more often than a hot potato in
a buffet line, the effect on all employees is dramatic. Usually,
a period of rumors lasting months or even years precedes the
event. This prolongs the stress. For many, the impending storms
may be much worse than the real thing when and if it eventually
hits.

During the "impending storms" phase, anxieties abound.
"What if my job is declared redundant?" "What if the new boss
is a fiendish tyrant?" "My family would never follow me if I have
to move to another city." Such negative thoughts, given free
reign, frequently consume more than half the worker's time.
Coffee room talk is of nothing else. On the job, daydreaming —
or worse, *nightmaring* — about these negative possibilities makes
it difficult to concentrate on the immediate job at hand.

Decreased morale and efficiency at work produce frustrations
that are taken home, and a vicious circle is created. At home
the number of arguments increases, as does the number of times
the kids get scolded or the garbage can gets kicked. The urge
among habitual self abusers rises: latent alcoholics drink more,
smokers smoke more, and drug abusers abuse more. Tragically,
incidences of child abuse, wife-battering, and suicides also increase
dramatically.

When Baxter Travenol Laboratories Inc. merged with American Hospital Supply Corp. in 1985, 4,000 jobs were eliminated.

Managers from both companies had to reapply for jobs in the new enlarged corporation, and stress levels were high. Levels of alcohol, drug, and child abuse went up significantly.

The layoff of 6,800 employees since 1984 at Phillips Petroleum Co. has had far-reaching effects in Bartlesville, Oklahoma, the company headquarters. Statistics from Women and Children in Crisis tell a grim tale: women attending support groups for battered wives leapt 41%; the number of children in counseling groups rose 74%. These problems do not affect only those who are laid off, but all those in the companies involved.

Job transfers, whether initiated by employee or company, have consequences that can be stressful indeed. The changes that are to be faced are enormous in all respects. They include new work responsibilities, new colleagues, new home, new friends, new schools for the kids, and even problems with breaking up the family unit, such as leaving older teenagers behind.

Two trends are at work here. One is the change from the old "Father Knows Best" model of one income supporting the whole family. Transfers are now more stressful because the costs of housing and educating a family now often necessitate the two career household as the norm. Unless both spouses work for the same company, it is most unlikely that both will be able to satisfactorily relocate their careers.

The second trend is that the ubiquitous Information Age has meant there is now a greater need to think in terms of global markets. Virtually all major financial institutions have had to establish some sort of representation in Japan, London, and other investment centers. Manufacturers are finding that by setting up a foothold on a new continent, as Apple, Raychem, and Amdahl have done in Ireland, new sales are generated that would have been missed if they had stayed back in California. This means that the impending storm of being told to move hovers over more workers' horizons than ever before.

BUSINESS DOWNTURNS — WISE AND UNWISE CORPORATE RESPONSES

Most businesses are cyclical, or are affected by outside cycles such as interest rates, oil prices, or housing starts. In our rapidly changing markets, even the best-run companies experience downturns, and these can have a severe impact on their workers. Employees of blue chip companies such as IBM, Caterpillar, and John Deere, for example, thought their traditional policies of lifetime employment would insulate them from severe changes in the marketplace. They thought that all their retirement, insurance, and financial needs would be looked after by the company.

However, in the 1980s, these companies experienced a radical change in their markets, and tens of thousands of loyal employees were laid off. The stress levels on these workers were felt right through their industries, around the world. People thought, if employees of these outstanding companies could be on the unemployment rolls, then the same could happen to anybody.

Some of the downturns were handled better than others. Some corporations made the best possible effort to reassign employees to other jobs (even at much lower pay rates; for example, Delta's pilots who worked as clerks, baggage handlers, and sales agents during a recent recession). If they couldn't reassign employees, some companies tried to help them find other employment through retaining assistance, in addition to giving them severance pay. Companies that showed this kind of consideration saw the best results in terms of productivity among the rest of their employees and in the long term, the best profits. When markets rebounded and more staff was needed, these considerate companies were rewarded by a ready pool of loyal, experienced, and committed people to fill the positions.

On the other hand, companies that undervalued their people, didn't communicate with them in the period leading up to the layoffs, and didn't treat them fairly afterwards fared far worse.

They were often left with an unmotivated, complacent workforce, high levels of absenteeism, deterioration of product quality and profits, and in many cases, financial ruin.

In the corporate sense, then, the same stress of a market reversal can bring out one of two quite different results. Corporations that choose to manage their stress and their employees' stress competently and ethically will do well in the long term. In the short term it may seem that this means the expenditure of considerable and seemingly unnecessary sums for stress defence. However, those corporations that choose to ignore the effects of stress on their people will pay a much higher price in the long term.

BUSINESS DOWNTURNS — WISE AND UNWISE PERSONAL RESPONSES

From the personal point of view, crises among the most solid blue chip companies underline the importance of taking more personal control of one's future. All workers and their spouses could benefit greatly if they assumed they were in business for themselves, and therefore learned more about means to save and invest their money and to protect themselves against sudden cuts in income.

Judging by the unbridled consumer spending spree in the United States, which has depleted individual savings to an unprecedented extent, thrift went out of style along with the manual typewriter. By having too much month left over at the end of their money, workers at any salary level can leave themselves unduly vulnerable for stress-related health breakdown, possibly even a fatal one. I have seen this repeatedly in my practice, and not just among the lower-paid employees.

One of my patients, whom I'll call Steve, was a 36-year-old

investment broker who had been with a prestigious firm for five years. During this time the market kept rising to new highs, right across the board. In the trade, a period like this is known as a "no brainer" because, even if one threw darts at the list of stocks, one would come out making money. And make money Steve did. By the end of the second year, he was making over a million dollars a year.

But, like most employees in a big firm, he didn't take much active interest in his own investments and securities, and in fact was spending money even faster than it came in. Steve and his wife acquired three houses, and were lavishly renovating them all. Holidays were exotic, and the kids went to the most expensive private schools. Even though he was an investment counsellor to his customers, Steve, like a doctor who tries to be his own patient, gave himself the worst possible advice.

He did not own one stock outright, but was instead levered up to the hilt, borrowing against each of his houses, and even against his wife's jewelry. On October 19, 1987, the world stock markets crashed, and Steve lost everything. His levered loans were called in, his income fell to one-tenth of its former level, and 150 of his colleagues were laid off. He was beginning to regret his poorly worded pre-crash wish that his income would break out of the million-dollar plateau. The "head hunters" had been trying to find him another job, but with the streets bulging with young ex-millionaire investment dealers looking for work, chances were slim that he could earn even a fraction of his former salary (and meet current expenses).

Steve was having a terrible time sleeping, and for that matter he wasn't having a very good time when he was awake either. Headaches pounded at him incessantly, and his heartburn was threatening to turn into bleeding ulcers. About eight weeks after the stock crash, he suddenly felt a "heavy weight" upon his chest. After tests done in my office and in the hospital emergency room, it was determined that Steve was in the middle of a heart attack. Actually, it was only because he had promised his wife that he would come in to see me that he survived.

I visited Steve daily in the cardiac intensive care unit, and listened to him curse the market, curse the banks, and curse the stress that he thought had brought him there. It took a good deal of talking on my part, but finally I was able to get him to see the light. If he had not been so greedy and shortsighted in his own preparations, and had followed the example of some of his more conservative colleagues, he could easily have entered the crash with one house paid for, a couple of modest cars, and a portion of his money left in an easily redeemable form so that he could cash some of it in when stress struck.

People who had made stress defence plans similar to those thought October 19 was like a giant Boxing Day Sale: some stocks they had been eyeing could suddenly be bought at a 50% reduction! More importantly, their personal health did not decline with the market. The object in the workplace is not to hope that stress will go away, but to count on stress always being there, even though it may change its intensity from one year to the next. Both individuals and corporations who invest a little time and money on stress defence will outperform those who passively wait, unprepared.

QUALITY AS INSULATION AGAINST BUSINESS STORMS

In a global economy, it's open season on inefficient companies. No longer can corporations grow fat behind protectionist trade barriers and produce inferior goods and services. Two American researchers, W. Edwards Deming and J.M. Juran, helped win World War II by developing new methods for improving manufacturing quality. Unfortunately, U.S. companies paid scant attention to them, perhaps because their corporate focus was on quarterly reports to their shareholders, and most quality improvements take a few years to bear fruit. But the researchers' advice was not totally ignored; one need not stretch one's imagination to figure out which Asian nation invited them across the Pacific to train their engineers. Today experts credit Deming and Juran for Japan's dramatic improvement from "junk merchants" to purveyors of prized quality goods.

Many companies are facing storms because they still have not learned the lesson. For these slow learners, including some of the major American giants, quality is regarded as something they can add to a badly designed, poorly made product to help hold it together until the buyer gets it home. However, the key to survival in today's competitive climate is real quality through every step of production and service. It is as essential to the work done by the lowest paid individual on the payroll as to the chairman of the board. Without quality, things don't get sent out properly or on time, and huge service departments are working flat out to repair flaws that should never have been allowed into the products in the first place.

In service industries lack of quality means having to send out corrected invoices to replace the previous ones, which had mistakes and omissions. Lack of quality means having to take a lot of heat and bad publicity from irate customers who demand value for money. For both companies and individual workers, quality is one of the best weapons to fight back against stress at work. Quality work is one commodity that will always be in demand. Thus, when one faces the impending storm of an upcoming merger or possible layoff, one should make quality work an even more important priority. Even if your whole division is terminated, it will be easier for you to retain your pride and self worth — and find another good job — if genuine quality is your goal.

FOR POSITIVE THINKERS, JOB LOSS COULD HAVE SILVER LINING

Positive-thinking people treat the impending storm of layoffs or job loss as an opportunity, not just as a crisis. They assess their skills and aptitudes, supplement existing skills with additional training in favorite areas, and keep their eyes on the job markets. Instead of dwelling on the huge numbers of people fired by big companies, they note that the overall levels of unemployment are lower than they have been for years. Obviously the unemployed do not stay unemployed long. Indeed the remarkable upturn in small entrepreneurial businesses has provided more options for career choices than ever before.

In their personal lives, positive people avoid thinking about themselves excessively. Instead they try to help others with their problems. They keep varied interests, hobbies, and friendships alive, and eat, sleep, and exercise effectively. Thus, when they begin the next day at work, they do a much better job of concentrating on work and performing well. They afford themselves the luxury of a little peace of mind in the face of impending storms of job insecurity.

When one studies case histories, the fact emerges that, when negative thinking employees are laid off, the event can ruin the rest of their lives. When interviewed five years or more after they lost a job, negative thinkers are found to be even more embittered and inflexible than before. They now have a past event to justify their lifelong pessimism. Most say they find their new jobs boring but, for the moment, secure.

They often have less enthusiasm at the start of each day, make less money than they used to, and have not made any real efforts to learn new skills. Some, unwilling to move to a more suitable area to find a new career, stay behind in an economically depressed town and survive on welfare or pensions. These pessimists blame their failure on the same stress event (the layoff five years ago) that their positive thinking colleagues credit for their new successes.

On the other hand, when positive thinkers are interviewed five years later, they will usually say that this same "crisis" (of being laid off) was a blessing in disguise. When they were forced to take new career paths or move locations, hidden talents and potentials come to light. Such happy discoveries can carry a person's career in new directions and result in achievements beyond all former expectations. Some of the greatest success stories would never have happened if individuals involved had continued with their safe, secure jobs and not been forced through an involuntary job change or an early retirement.

So common is this finding that, if one asks self-made people what they did before becoming wealthy or famous, almost all have a story of facing seemingly insurmountable hardships. A failed unorthodox get-rich-quick scheme may sound hilarious in retrospect, but at the time it flopped, taking the person's life savings with it, it seemed the end of the world. Thus can the school of hard knocks be a fine preparation for future successes. It is somewhat reassuring to note that, in countries that have virtually taken stress out of the workplace, as was done in Russia and China until recently, everyone had a secure job but the countries virtually went broke.

The very lifeblood of our modern economy depends on having stress in the workplace, and our success depends on how well we cope with the challenges. Sometimes the blessings each challenge presents can be very well disguised, as Sir Winston Churchill noted after being thrown out of office after winning World War II. However, it behooves all of us to seek out the potential for good that can come out of any crisis. To do otherwise is to ignore life's lessons. If one views each of the lows in one's career as a postgraduate course in business, philosophy, and human resilience, then it is easier to retain a positive attitude. Lessons learned in difficult times come back to pay extra dividends when times improve.

WHAT TO DO WHEN UNEMPLOYED — SOME PRACTICAL EXAMPLES

Often the key to dealing with temporary unemployment, whether resulting from a layoff, strike, or firing, is better management of one's newly-found spare time. I have seen many cases in which temporarily unemployed workers have successfully "moonlighted'' doing home repairs, landscaping, or gardening. Or they have changed directions entirely.

I have seen some who recognize the difficulty in continuing with a career that is destined for continued shrinking of its workforce, possibly leading to a complete bankruptcy of the company itself. These industrious few have taken their unemployment as an opportunity to make a course correction before they hit the rocks. If they are living in a one-company town, then the course correction will probably include moving to where the jobs are. In addition to holding their household's finances together with odd jobs, they use their time to engage in learning a saleable skill that suits their current aptitudes and future goals.

One of my patients, aged 24, learned how to run computers, worked her way into a responsible "white collar" job, and never regretted leaving her old job on the assembly line. Another, age 35, was fascinated by numbers, and took courses in accountancy. He pursued this hitherto suppressed ambition by doing part-time bookkeeping as well as attending accounting school. Five years later he graduated, and is now happy in a job he loves far more than the one he left.

Another one of my patients, a gentleman aged 57, came to me in despair. As a result of the strike in his plant, he was given early retirement with insufficient funds to continue living in his house. As a part of my questioning, it came out that activities that had given his satisfaction during his life included gardening. Indeed, I had noted on a previous housecall that his garden was beautifully manicured. I suggested that, instead of undervaluing this very saleable skill (which he often did by helping neighbors with their gardens and never charging them a cent), he should recognize that he could earn a living doing what he had been doing for pure enjoyment. This gentleman started by putting an ad in the local newspaper and distributing notices of his new business in mailboxes around his neighborhood.

He sold his car and bought a used truck and a few new tools. Almost from the first week, he was in great demand. Soon he needed help. He went back to the newspaper ad department, this time to find an assistant. Two years later, I saw him again and asked about his new life. He now had a fleet of four new trucks, each with two workers. During the busy summer season, he supplemented his staff with student workers. During the winter he kept busy with snowplowing and repairing lawnmowers for customers. His crisis of being terminated because of a long strike turned out to be the opportunity of his lifetime. Not only was he making more money, which allowed him to pay off his mortgage, he also felt a sense of job satisfaction that he had never known before.

We can rarely influence the impending storms that threaten our work. However, we can at least adopt the flexibility and positive attitude so necessary to being able to protect our future.

Chapter 8

STRESS AND PUBLIC SPEAKING

SPEECHMAKING — A STRESSFUL NECESSITY

Over the past seven years, I have traveled all over the world giving speeches to audiences from 10 people to 5,000 people at a time. The audiences have included representatives of virtually every job category imaginable: traders on commodity and stock exchanges, newspaper editors, reporters, clerks, professionals, schoolteachers, government and military staff, union members, and jetsetting chairpersons of international corporations.

In almost every case, pre-speech surveys of audiences list one of the greatest stresses at work as having to get up on one's feet to make a speech. This fear can exist even if the audience consists of only a few close colleagues.

Medical research has now shown the dangerous self-fulfilling nature of the fear of public performance. Researchers headed by Dr. Alan Rozanski at the Cedars-Sinai Medical Center in Los Angeles have found that during mentally stressful tasks, of which public speaking is one of the most severe, 60% of heart disease patients experienced silent myocardial ischaemia. Dr. Andrew P. Selwyn, an associate professor of medicine at Harvard Medical School, notes that these mental precursors of heart attacks are, like many physical risk factors, amenable to preventative therapy. It is to help defuse potentially dangerous as well as embarrassing situations that we shall now see how to use the stress of public performances to bring out excellence instead of discomfort or even disaster.

Speechmaking skills are vital in making a sales presentation, or making your own pitch in a job interview with an audience of just one or two. If you are cursed with a bad boss (see chapter 5), then your speechmaking skills may even help save your career. It is vital to be able to think on your feet in a one-on-one situation with a boss, client, or customer.

Self-employed workers, from doctors and lawyers to consultants and crafts experts, are recognizing that the best advertising is by word of mouth. Particularly effective are the words of their own mouths, in the form of interviews in the media, or free instructional talks or seminars to groups of potential customers. With the omnipresence of roving reporters, it is also not unlikely that most who hold positions of responsibility will be called upon to say a few words into the microphone or camera on short notice. Again the skills of public speaking are put to the test.

MANAGING PHYSICAL RESPONSES TO SPEECHMAKING STRESS

Speaking in public is rarely a natural skill, but it can always be learned. Not everybody can learn to be scintillating or charismatic as a public speaker. But everybody can at least learn to use the high levels of stress generated by speechmaking in a positive way. We can all learn to present ourselves in our own best light. Before learning how to make a better speech, we should first take a look at dealing with the internal stress responses taking place in the speaker.

HOW TO COMBAT MOUTH DRYNESS

For dryness of the mouth, drink water before your presentation, and even quietly retain some in your mouth during the last seconds before you are on. Never drink milk or have ice cream before you speak (although they are good foods at other times). We are all familiar with the increased mucus in our throats after we drink a big glass of milk, and that is one reason why only water is served on the speaker's lectern.

However, many speakers forget this during dinner, and have their ice cream or coffee with milk just before stepping up to the microphone. As a result, they suddenly find they have the handicap of a throat full of rubbery secretions at the same time as the stress response is drying up the throat.

If sufficient water is not available, a good trick is to emulate the desert soldiers of the North Africa campaign in World War II. When water rations were running low, each man would place a pebble under his tongue to stimulate saliva flow. Pebbles aren't recommended for public speakers, but it's a good idea to carry a small piece of hard candy for just such dry-mouthed emergencies. Use it *before* you start speaking, but don't keep it in your mouth during the actual speech. That way you avoid the unsettling distraction of choking. Whatever you do, don't chew gum during a speech, as it inevitably looks as if you have peanut butter stuck to the roof of your mouth.

HOW TO EAT BEFORE A SPEECH

If you are nervous about your speech, don't eat anything just before it. Plan ahead by eating a light snack that is high in fiber, such as wholewheat bread and an apple, several hours before you are due to go on. If you should be an after-dinner speaker it is best to only eat sparingly. Do not eat anything fatty, or heavy with protein, or too great in quantity. If you do, your stomach may be competing with the audience for your attention. A prespeech meal that is too high in sugar or salt can also make your tongue feel swollen and dry. If your speech is first thing in the morning, you could even plan on eating after the speech instead of before.

OVERCOMING SHAKINESS

Avoid all caffeine, as it will exaggerate all the stress responses by causing enormous surges of adrenaline and other hormones.

I have seen a lot of speakers give themselves an unnecessary handicap, just for the sake of a couple of absent-minded cups of coffee or tea. The time spent making the jitters worse with caffeine could just as easily be spent in calming those jitters with some relaxation techniques.

If you already have the skills to call up the Relaxation Response — such as with yoga, or meditation, or the *Stress for Success* Power Nap — try them before you speak. If you don't yet have such an ability, then focus on a spot, perhaps the back of the room or the back of your hand, breathe in through your stomach, and feel the waves of relaxation that suffuse your body, counteracting the natural jitters that attend stage fright.

If you are reading from a prepared text, make sure it is written in the largest possible type and triple spaced, to allow you to let it rest on the lectern. That way your shakes won't be noticed by the audience, as they would if your notes were flapping helplessly in your grip.

KEEPING YOUR VOICE CLEAR

If you are a smoker, don't smoke just before you speak. (For that matter, once you have made it that many minutes without poisoning yourself, keep on quitting!) A speaker should not drink any alcohol before the address. If you wish to have a drink, wait until you have concluded your remarks.

I know many celebrities who drink prodigiously before a speech (much to the alarm of the meeting planner) and still get away with it, but don't count on being able to pull off this stunt. Even 14 hours after the ingestion of a few drinks — when blood levels of alcohol are back down to zero and the mind registers no sense of inebriation — significant impairment is noted in both concentration and fine motor skills (see chapter 14). For the same reasons as you would rather fly with a sober pilot than an inebriated one, present your audience with the kind of speaker they deserve — a sober one.

AVOIDING BOWEL AND BLADDER URGENCY

For heaven's sake go to the bathroom a few minutes before your

time, even if you are the featured guest at the head table. This
is another reason to avoid putting much food in your stomach,
as the stretching of the stomach wall increases the urgency of
the normal stress response of emptying one's bladder and bowels.

MINIMIZING PERSPIRATION PROBLEMS
If you are prone to profuse perspiration, dress in lightweight clothing and check the room temperature an hour before people start
filing in. It is not just your stress making you feel warm. Often
it is also the presence of all those other people in the room. If
the room will be full, it is best to set the temperature a few
degrees below the normal level. If the room is hot to start with,
open the doors and ventilate it as much as possible.

DEALING WITH CHEST TIGHTNESS
For a tightness in the chest, take some slow deep breaths, as
this complaint is usually related to bronchial spasms similar to
those experienced by an asthmatic. Chest tightness is not a
problem for all speakers, but can be alarming if it does occur.
Obviously more severe heaviness that gets worse when you walk,
and goes away when you are standing, brings up the subject of
what to do in the case of a heart attack. However, we are supposing for the purposes of this discussion that, like most speakers,
you only *feel* as if you are going to die.

COPING WITH A RACING HEART
If you have done all the above and still feel your heart bounding
under the ribcage, then the most important tip I can give you
is to ignore it. There is no harm in having your heart race. As
long as you aren't thinking more about it than you are about your
speech, it will settle down on its own once you get going.

If you are prone to heart disease, your doctor may suggest
that a simple beta-blocker taken before the stress would be helpful. However, I have found that, for healthy people, taking a
placebo under the same circumstances will do the same amount
of good.

The object of the foregoing advice is not to remove all the

body's reactions to stress, but to control them so that they can help you give a better performance. The audience can't see your blood pressure or your pulse rate, or your internal stomach and hormonal changes. All they will remember is whether or not you did a good job.

It may be easier if you keep in mind that almost all professional entertainers experience the same symptoms, and that they consider the beforehand stress necessary to a good performance! Studies have shown that even pros like Bob Hope, Johnny Carson and Bob Newhart all have incredibly fast heart rates just before they start a monologue, but those rates quickly return to normal once they are into their deliveries.

STAGE FRIGHT — FIGHTING BACK WITH ENDORPHINE

Endorphine, the body's own molecule of morphine, has great powers to calm jangled nerves. It can be released in many situations, such as during labor or in the heat of battle, but neither of these cases is of much help to the trembling speaker trying to get those first few words out. Slow abdominal breathing, exercise earlier in the day, or even massaging one of the acupuncture pressure points (such as in the V between the base of the thumb and index fingers or the shouldertips) can all prove effective and yet socially acceptable ways to get the endorphine going. Except for vigorous exercise, all these techniques can be used right up until the last moments before you are introduced to the audience.

SEVEN ACTION TIPS FOR SPEECHMAKING

In my own case, I learned the skills of speechmaking in a rather unusual way. At the age of 14, when our family was living in the city of Moose Jaw, Saskatchewan, I worked parttime in the local television station as a studio "director." I organized the lighting and microphones for the local news, weather, and sports reports. Sometimes the preceding movie finished early. Having to bridge the gap, I would do a live comedy monologue, it having been determined that government film clips of loons or frostbite were not readily appreciated by the audience. Because there was no video tape, stress became a great teacher for me in doing these instant speeches. Each monologue had to be spontaneous, and timed exactly to fit the space available.

Most speakers don't have such a unique opportunity to hone their craft in front of live cameras, and most audiences are not as patient as the good people of Moose Jaw. Thus, for most readers who are serious about learning to be better speechmakers, I would suggest seeking professional training. From my discussions with many professional speechmaking instructors and with many of their graduate trainees, as well as from my personal experiences as a speaker, I have distilled the following techniques, which I heartily recommend.

1. KNOW YOUR AUDIENCE

Know what they already know about your topic, so you won't be talking down to them. Know what they don't know so you won't be blathering over their heads. Many people are under the illusion that a lot of questions at the end of a speech means that the speaker was thought provoking, but it could also mean the speaker had no idea whom he or she was addressing.

The presence or absence of questions after a speech is influenced by a lot of factors, such as the size of the audience and the time allotted before the next scheduled part of the program. Although the presence of a lot of questions could mean the speech was a good one, it could also mean the opposite. I have seen expensive and world famous speakers pull out a few well-worn pages of notes, and proceed to read the same canned speech to an audience of executives as they would to an audience of union workers. When the speaker concluded with a call for questions, each member of the audience had one. In this case it was not because of a witty, controversial, or thought provoking speech, but because of a poorly researched analysis of the audience's realities.

2. PREPARE AND REHEARSE YOUR SPEECH

Audiences don't want to waste their time listening to a musician who is a little rusty, or watching an unprepared dancer flub around trying to get the steps right, so don't expect your audience to be happy listening to your first draft of a speech. Practice at home or even "off Broadway" with some of your peers at work. You can even rehearse mentally on your way to and from work as you commute.

The point of rehearsal is to familiarize yourself with your material and, where possible, to familarize yourself with the setting and audience. By repeating the material many times, you will be better prepared when your mind switches on to "automatic pilot" for those first few moments as you start. Your store of positive images and expectations will be the first thing your blank mind will reach for.

Once you have had experience in giving a prepared speech, then it will become much easier to think on your feet and give a spontaneous one. However, as the golfing great Sam Snead advised when asked about using a tee under the ball for even the shortest of par three holes, always take an advantage if it is offered. If you are given advance warning of your speech, use this advantage well, to make for the best possible results.

3. CHECK OUT THE SETTING IF POSSIBLE

Often familiarization with the setting is possible only on the day of the speech, but I always suggest a preliminary scouting to rule out any last-minute mistakes that could sabotage your speech. If time permits, a "dress rehearsal" will also help the novice.

If the microphone is fixed for a person only half your height, if its cord is too short, if the sight lines for the back half of the room are interfered with by the crowd in the front half, or if the loudspeaker shrieks whenever you stand right where the stage is lit, the time to find out about the problem is before the speech, not during it. If you allow at least one hour for any needed changes, most convention and hotel staff can remedy the situation with risers, different sound arrangements, adjustment of the seating, and so on.

4. VISUALIZE THE PEOPLE IN THE AUDIENCE

When most novice speakers are being introduced, they stare at the floor or the wall above the last row in the audience. The audience thus seems to be like a faceless monster, ready to devour them as soon as it can. By remembering that those people wouldn't be there if they didn't want to hear what you have to say, you can take a lot of the threat out of the encounter.

If you pass some members of the audience as you walk to the microphone, don't ignore them. Pick out a couple and shake hands, or exchange a few words. When you get up to the mike, shut up. Resist the temptation to race right into your speech. Instead take a couple of slow breaths as you focus on a few individual faces in the crowd. It's a good idea to personalize your opening comments with a few words directed at some of the well-known people in the audience or at the head table. Notice the expressions on their faces — they don't hate you, they wish you well.

5. GREET THE AUDIENCE AS A WHOLE

To begin, the audience usually claps for you, so common courtesy dictates that you should return the favor by greeting them. This is best done in a way that makes clear that you appreciate their being present and, if you are not in your own home territory, that you have enjoyed coming to their part of the world. Most politicians have mastered this practice, but only a few are believable enough to pull it off. The technique can fail miserably if it is not sincere.

I heard one professional speaker at a lakeside resort hotel start out by telling his audience he appreciated them so much that he felt as if he were one of them (he was lying; the audience was a group of nuns). He felt so glad to see them that he wanted them to join him in giving themselves a big round of applause. Next, a somewhat less enthusiastic bit of clapping was elicited as a show of appreciation for the resort staff who had served dinner. However, the speaker lost all forward momentum with his third fatuous exhortation: ". . . so let's really hear it for the *lake*."

6. USE NON-VERBAL CUES

The use of non-verbal cues such as loudness, intonation, phrasing, well timed pauses, and body language can make an enormous difference to the meaning of any sentence.

SOME UNSPOKEN METHODS OF CONVEYING MEANING

If you are going to make them listen to the whole speech, let them see the whole speaker.

For example, the sentence, "Glenn did a terrific job" could be interpreted in one of two ways. If said in a sincere tone of voice, it means Glenn did well. If said with a mocking emphasis on the word *terrific* accompanied by a rolling of the speaker's eyes and a holding of the nose, then it is clear that Glenn did

SOME UNSPOKEN METHODS OF CONVEYING MEANING

Poor (shifty)

Good (credible)

Philip Rostron/Instil Productions

In both sets of photos, the speaker is saying the words, "You can believe me when I tell you. . . ." Note how the poor body language on the left undermines the message, whereas the good body language on the right supports the message.

poorly. However, the reader of this sentence cannot guess which version was intended from just the words themselves, nor could he or she guess if the words were delivered by a speaker with a flat, monotone voice, hiding behind a lectern.

Knowing that your body language conveys about half of your meaning (making it even more important than your words), it makes eminent sense to rehearse your body's messages as well as your verbal message. If you have access to a videotape or even a mirror, you may find it useful in checking how you look as you speak.

You may also want to seek professional guidance. Consulting organizations such as Toronto's Fraser Kelly CorpWorld teach communication skills and crisis management by putting clients on the "hot seat" and then critiquing the results on videotape. Clients, who come from all levels of the corporate and governmental hierarchies, are not humiliated. Rather, they are taught in the most vivid terms how to best present their points of view. The skills gained are useful not only for public speeches and media interviews. Attendees also note that their confidence levels improve during direct interactions with customers and clients.

7. LOOK AT THE AUDIENCE AND BE AS NATURAL AS POSSIBLE

If a speech must be read, make sure it is well rehearsed and written in large letters with colored cues for emphasis and phrasing. Then you can look up at the audience most of the time instead of down at the script. If at all possible, just use headings, written on small index cards, as a map to guide you through the areas you wish to cover. If you step away from the lectern, the audience can see all of you, which means that, in addition to reading the expressions on your face, they can catch the messages of your body language.

Expect to stumble over the occasional word; don't apologize and don't let yourself get rattled. The object is not to deliver each word in staged dulcet tones, but to be human, to communicate, and to make your impression. No one thinks twice about stumbling over a word in a personal conversation among friends or for that matter, with any individual member of the audience. However, most novice speakers feel that they will be held in scorn by the audience if they stumble on a word.

It would be impossible to be effective on long-distance phone calls if you concentrated on speaking only perfectly structured phrases, as if each conversation were an English exam. The same is true in a speech. Although Oscar Wilde's arrogant opinion was that the worst advice you can give most people is, "Be yourself," that turns out to be the best advice I can give a speaker.

THREE RULES FOR STRUCTURING SPEECHES

The oldest three rules for making a speech are still the best: Tell the audience what you are going to tell 'em. Tell 'em. Then tell 'em what you just told 'em.

1. TELL PEOPLE WHAT YOU ARE GOING TO TELL THEM

A brief statement of your intentions reassures the audience that you have organized your thoughts and gives them a preview of what to expect. It reestablishes your structure to yourself, so that minimal reference need be made to your cue cards or slides. If part or all of the speech is a precisely worded legal statement or careful pronouncement to the media, it is best to show everyone the document and let people know you are about to read the exact words so that the meaning will not be misinterpreted.

Be considerate of the audience's realities and attention span. If you are going to stand there and bury your nose in the text for the entire speech, then your audience would far rather read the text themselves, because they can read faster than you can speak. The goal is to communicate by reading your audience, not your speech. That way you can tell if it is appropriate to cut one section short, or elaborate more on another.

2. GIVE PEOPLE YOUR MESSAGE

Use the medium of speechmaking for its own unique features. A speech can convey your opinions, missions, and passions in a way that can never be communicated in print or over the telephone. (This is of course why the skies are filled with business travelers.) If you have a long list of statistics to read, make up handout sheets and then simply refer to them by holding up your copy. After drawing the audience's attention to it, give them a brief summary of your conclusions, but don't read each line out loud. They can read the document for themselves.

3. TELL PEOPLE WHAT YOU JUST TOLD THEM

Wrap up your comments with a brief summary of what you would like people to remember about your speech and then sit down. Always know what time you are supposed to conclude, and never overstay your welcome. There hardly ever seems to be a timepiece that the speaker can see; thus the prepared speaker should bring one along. Some use a small travel clock, which they secrete behind the water glass. Others lay their watch on top of the lectern. I have found that wearing a wristwatch with black hands on a white face allows me to get a subtle peripheral glance at the time without having to rudely hold the watch up to the light. Another good technique is to ask someone to give you a signal when you have five minutes left.

FACING THE MEDIA

Although it may not happen often, there could come a time when you will be asked to speak to the media. It may be only a few seconds of response to a breaking news story, or it might be an extended interview for closer scrutiny. However, if you have never been told how to handle yourself, then the exposure could be nervewracking or even disastrous. Armed with a few simple tips, however, the experience can be both exhilarating and rewarding.

REMEMBER THE REALITIES

In any interview with the media, remember that the parties involved each have their own realities. For example, *your reality* is that you want to represent yourself or your business in an honest and clear light. The reason most people, even the highest paid movie stars, give interviews is to sell their products or reflect their knowledge. The same is true for the accountant who consents to a show around taxtime, the yoga instructor who is seeking new clientele, or even the private citizen who wants to "sell" his or her political or religious opinions.

The audience's reality is that they want to be entertained, told something they never knew before, or given something of value. If at least one of these elements is not immediately forthcoming, the audience will turn the page or change the channel. If some or, ideally, all of the elements can be combined in one interview, the audience will be most appreciative and attentive.

The media's reality is that they are judged by their ratings, whether they sell advertising space or whether they are government funded. If an interview is bland and uninformative, audiences will switch off, ratings will dive, and somebody will be called onto the carpet.

All of the realities — yours, the audience's, and the media's — can be easily satisfied if you bear them in mind and conduct yourself accordingly. If you have a product to plug, don't hesitate to mention it; the interviewer is mindful of your reality. For the audience's sake, put yourself in their shoes and keep your comments concise and interesting.

PRINT, RADIO, AND TV MEDIA

There are three main kinds of media to consider, but all require extensions of your speechmaking skills.

The print media's reality is they have only a limited amount of space for printing a given story and a limited time in which to print it. You can help a lot by choosing your words thoughtfully. In many cases it is appropriate to hand out a brief statement of facts to supplement what you say in your interview. It doesn't mean the press is obliged to print your interpretations, but at least it does minimize the chances for misunderstanding your position.

Evasive, rambling diatribes must be rewritten or reinterpreted by the reporters. In the end they may not even be used (unless they are issued from high government offices, in which case they are repeated verbatim; the reason, one supposes, is so they can be entered straight into the history books).

Radio media exposure can come in a number of different formats, from a quick question to a two-hour "phone-in" show. Brief interviews can be some of the most difficult, whether conducted over the phone or into a microphone. This is especially true when they are live or taped only once. Speaking on radio can be difficult the first time you try it, especially when you realize how many thousands of people will be listening. As soon as you are given your cue, there is a great tendency to chatter on and be cut off long before you have made your point. For brief interviews, be prepared to condense your material. A 30-second interview will probably allow only 80 words.

If the interview takes a hostile turn for some reason, don't panic and don't get mad on the air. If you keep your voice level down when an irate caller raises his or her voice, it is the caller who will sound out of line.

Don't feel compelled to fill every silence once you have finished your point. Many an unsuspecting guest has proceeded to dig his or her way into a hole by facing a suddenly silent host and a red "on-air" light after finishing a response. The old adage, "He who speaks next loses," is very appropriate at moments like these. Rather than being a negative feature, a bit of silence on the air can actually add impact to your comments. When you are stumped for a moment, take a pause, even in mid-sentence if necessary, to collect your thoughts (as you would in normal conversation). And above all, keep your sense of humor. As has often been said, if you end up in a shouting match with a fool, the audience may not be able to tell the two of you apart.

The television media is the one with the most power to persuade, and very little time to do it. The first sight of all the bright studio lights, with the cameras and crew hovering around, is usually imposing to a novice. With training, one can be taught to ignore all the fascinating details of the studio and to conduct a face-to-face interview as if the interviewer were the entire audience and there was nobody else in the room.

The crew is paid to correctly position the lights, microphones, and cameras, so just ignore them and focus on your conversation. Talk naturally to the interviewer, understanding that he or she may have to look at the producer instead of at you during your responses. Give concise answers, but generally not one- or two-word answers that convey little information.

Remember to assume you are always on camera. Don't pick your teeth, fiddle with your tie, or scratch your ear when you think the coast is clear, because you could well embarrass yourself.

DANGERS OF THE "SNEAK ATTACK" TV INTERVIEWS

Be careful about nodding your head too vigorously, even if you think you are off camera. I have seen inexperienced interviewees being led through a classic car salesperson's "yes set," in which a series of quick "yes" answers is followed by a sudden "no" question.

Once your head starts rocking back and forth to answer in the affirmative, it will probably still do so when you are saying "no!" and the verbal message will be erased by the visual one. The same obviously applies for a series of short negative questions followed by a quick "yes" answer. When responding to a lengthy question, especially one that has frequent pauses, do not try to coax the interviewer along by nodding or shaking your head. Just be patient.

By being aware of the physiological changes that will be taking place in your body as you rise to the microphone, you can take simple preparatory steps such as breathing through your abdomen (see chapter 10 on "belly" breathing), modifying your diet, and using positive mental imagery to defuse the potential dangers. Once you have rehearsed to the point of being able to read your audience instead of your speech, and are flexible enough to edit your words into easily assimilated "clumps" of information, then you will see the best results of all. The stress of facing the audience will not only be neutralized, but will become your ally for excellence. It will bring out your best possible performance.

Chapter 9

TRAVEL STRESS

STRESS AND THE SINGLE (OR MARRIED) MOTORIST

Any discussion of stress in the workplace would be incomplete if the subject of travel were not included. We travel to get to work, we travel during our work, and we travel to get to distant meetings. Admittedly, for some workers, the distances are minuscule; for example, for the consultant who works out of her basement or the shopkeeper who lives above the store. Such people have other stresses on the job. However, in this chapter, we will deal with people for whom working at home is not an option, making travel a fact of their working lives.

Travel comes in all forms: short and long time frames, and short and long distances. For most people, the commonest hurdle is the daily grind to and from work. This is most acute in large cities. The problems are truly international, but some of the ugliest and best-studied traffic jams are in the United States. The five-county area around Los Angeles has some of the most extensive acreage of paved roads and the world's highest concentration of fast cars, such as high-speed Porsches, Mercedes, and Jaguars.

However, most of them never get out of first gear, because of the highway traffic that moves at a 24-hour average speed of a mere 30 mph (50 kph). During peak periods on weekdays, the situation degenerates to a standstill.

There have been many efforts to encourage car pooling, such as by having fast lanes for cars containing more than one passenger. This has spawned several consumer innovations such as the inflatable passenger dummy, and the net result is still a horrendous snarl of traffic, which worsens every year.

The picture is not much rosier elsewhere. The air shuttle from New York to Boston, a distance of 200 miles, takes 55 minutes, but the drive from the airport into the city's core, a distance of half a mile, could easily take as long. The same problem plagues big cities from Canada to Europe, and from Rio to Tokyo, with no letup in sight. With the post-World War II baby boomers raising families, demand has risen for homes. The affordable ones are usually located in the distant suburbs around cities. Thus more cars are commuting longer distances to work, and funneling into the crowded central roads.

The levels of stress that this brings are extremely significant. For those who handle it poorly, it can be damaging to their health, and may even endanger the lives of others. Medically, we know that stress mechanisms all fire at once when the body identifies a crisis. Adrenaline pours out, the stomach shuts down, the pulse races, and the hair stands up on end. The blood pressure soars, muscles clench in spasms around the shouldertips and jaw, and primal aggressions rise, ready for fight or flight.

With immediate flight being out of the question, more and more frustrated drivers are turning to the fight option — either inside their cars as they nip at the heels of slower drivers, or outside their cars, where they may stomp up and beat a dent into the roof of an offending vehicle. Even the mild and polite become aggressive when they strap themselves into their bumper-cars to drive to work. This means they usually arrive late, enraged and spent before they even start to face the day's stresses on the job. Although stress can be joyful, these commuters would never believe it.

However, stress is not the real enemy here; it is what these commuters are doing in response to the stress that brings on disasters. Their response is typical of what we now call the Type A personality, which includes hostility, aggression, impatience, and chronic "hurry sickness." Of all these traits, hostility seems to be the most accurate predictor of impending heart attacks, though the whole complex of behavior usually comes as a package.

Some experts have suggested that we should be trying to eradicate all Type A behavior, but indeed this is not always desirable. Apart from the hostility, which of course is never appropriate (except perhaps in the middle of a raging battle in wartime) the other traits are potentially good ones. Many psychiatrists and psychologists insist that we should strive to be mellow and relaxed all the time, but sometimes this may be greatly detrimental to handling our stresses. For example, if your office building were on fire, I would not recommend that you have everybody break off into small study groups to come up with a consensus on escape. There is a time to panic and a time to use our Stone Age emergency reflexes, but the routine travel to and from work is not a situation that will even be improved by these reactions.

SEVEN COMPETENT COMMUTER TIPS

The competent commuter recognizes that traffic stress can be either a crisis or an opportunity. Choosing the latter means he or she can face exactly the same stress and have few ill effects — only beneficial ones. Rather than waste life wishing other drivers would speed up, the competent commuter chooses from a number of options to make this traffic time an opportunity. The following commuter tips are designed with the automobile commuter in mind. With a few minor modifications, such as a portable taperecorder and earphones, they could easily be adopted by commuters on public transport.

1. BE REALISTIC

Never tell anyone you live only 17 minutes from work, door to door. Just because you did it that fast once, at 3:00 a.m. with a passenger in advanced labor and a police escort, does not mean this will ever happen again during your lifetime. However, if you keep telling people how quickly you can get to the office, it becomes an ego game like bragging about how much money you made betting. Eventually you start to believe your own exaggerations.

By relaxing over the paper in the morning and finally leaving for the office at 17 minutes before your first appointment, you can count on being enraged at all the idiots on the road, even if they are traveling at the speed limit. When a student driver in the car ahead lurches to an unscheduled stop, making you miss two green light cycles, your tight schedule could make this essentially nonthreatening event into a life or death emergency. The trouble is, it will usually be your life, not the other driver's, that will be at the greatest risk.

On the other hand, if you had recognized that the trip to work usually takes 40 minutes, then you could easily allow an hour and arrive relaxed. If circumstances permit, perhaps you could plan to read the morning paper after you arrive. The same incident with the stalled truck would then not be such a big deal after all.

Commuters who use public transport can make the same modifications in their schedules to avoid having to make a last-minute race down the length of the platform to catch their train or bus. During rush hour, there is usually another one coming in a few minutes anyway. A year from now, people would never remember whether they arrived at 8:45 or 8:50. However, in the heat of the chase, they are so focused on the artificial ''emergency'' that some have died during a frantic gallop for a bus or train.

2. HAVE AN AGENDA FOR GRIDLOCK

None of us would like to interrupt our busy work schedules to attend a meeting where the chairperson has no agenda, and is in no apparent hurry to get to the point. And yet that is exactly what happens in a traffic jam. When you are alone in your car and the traffic seems to have lost the concept of forward motion, there is no need for you to be without an agenda. You cannot control what others do, but you can control what you are doing in traffic; you are, in effect, chairing your own meeting. If you find that nothing is getting accomplished, then blame the chairperson.

If you have an agenda, you can accomplish a lot in traffic. When the car is moving every few seconds, but only a few feet at a time, there are many other tasks that can be safely accomplished without taking your attention off the road. An upcoming sales pitch can be rehearsed out loud. A big speech can be timed with a stopwatch. A strategy for a new account can be plotted, or problems and/or ideas can be worked out mentally.

In situations where you might anticipate being stuck in your car for an extended period, i.e., several hours during a major snow storm or holiday traffic where the roads have been known to become "clogged up" for several hours, you may wish to keep a book you've always been meaning to read in the car, or perhaps a portable cassette recorder just in case you happen to come up with a sure-fire get-rich-quick scheme.

3. STUDY WHILE YOU'RE STALLED

Your car may be idling, but that doesn't mean your brain should be. In the number of hours most workers spend on the road, a lot of learning can be done. Audiotapes of experts in any field can be inspirational, and can make a real difference in your own performance. Almost every conceivable subject is now available on tape, from learning a foreign language, to home repair tips, to religious study, to literary interpretation of Shakespeare. Some tapes will help you hone the perfect golf or tennis swing, or ski the perfect turn. When one hears how American POWs in Vietname were able to maintain sports and music skills through imagery while in solitary confinement, one realizes that, with modern teaching techniques, the potential for learning during "wasted" time on the road is prodigious. You could even earn a correspondence diploma or degree in a few years if you plan to study while you're stalled.

4. PRACTICE RELAXATION SKILLS

When stuck in traffic, take a mental trip to your favorite relaxation destination. By practicing some of the skills mentioned in chapter 10, you can be relaxed in spite of the external tension of traffic.

Ideally, until your skill levels are good, it is best to try slow breathing and self-hypnotic techniques only when you are not moving. Even if the traffic is moving in a steady crawl, there will be occasions at stop lights when you can fix on a spot, loosen your belt for comfort, take a couple of slow deep breaths into your stomach, and enjoy the relaxation response. Please remember to do your belt up before you leave the car; otherwise the results could prove embarrassing in the parking lot.

5. TAKE A DOSE OF LAUGHTER

Laughter is the best medicine of all. There is nothing wrong with hearing the morning's bad news once. However most traffic jamees hear it repeated at least five times a day if they keep their car radios on. Though bad news can appeal to the same base animal instincts that make all drivers slow down to see an accident, there is no personal advantage is listening to reruns of the airplanes that did not land safely, terrorist bombs that exploded, and more government bungling with your hard-earned tax dollars.

Instead, laughter can be stocked in portable form, on tape cassettes in your car. A good belly laugh with an old radio show or a modern comedy concert can reverse all the nasty changes of blood pressure, adrenaline, and stomach acid that attend negative responses to a traffic jam.

6. CONSIDER GETTING A CAR PHONE

Since car phones are expensive, make sure that yours will give you some kind of payback. Obviously, if you make 100 calls a day from the office, some of these could easily be taken care of in the car, giving you more time for business or pleasure in a day. If your being stuck in traffic means a customer will take his or her business elsewhere, then the car phone makes sense. However, if all your calls could easily be made from the office, and the only person who ever needs to call you in the car is your spouse, reminding you to pick up a bag of milk, then the expense may not be worth it.

If you do decide that a car phone is a necessity, the Traffic Safety Division of the Canada Safety Council has recently published a set of guidelines for the safe operation of cellular phones.

- Buy a hands-free phone that allows you to memory-dial with the touch of a button.
- Install the phone on the dashboard rather than in the console beside the driver's seat so you don't have to take your eyes off the road to make or respond to a call.
- Dial only when stopped. If necessary, pull off to the side before you make a call.
- Don't answer the phone in heavy traffic conditions. This will only add to your stress and make a bad situation unbearable.

7. UTILIZE TECHNOLOGY IF NEEDED

Many sales representatives spend considerable time in their cars traveling from customer to customer, and stress levels may rapidly rise if they do not have the most current information when arriving to sell an account. Telephones may not always be available and, even if they are, the people at head office who supply your data may be tied up with other calls, attending meetings, or may themselves be out of the office. With the rapid developments in business technology you and your employer may wish to discuss whether or not you and the company would benefit from even more communication equipment. Consider the various laptop computers with modems to communicate over the phone. You could also invest in a portable facsimile machine, to send and receive whole documents and pictures. Again, however, make sure the presence of these tools in the car really benefits you, and does not get in the way of safe driving.

JET LAG — A MAJOR STRESS OF FLYING

Airline travel has become more frustrating, delaying and nerve-wracking over the last few years. A combination of deregulation, cheaper fuel, and the expansion of markets from the local to the global scale means the skies have never been more crowded. A few years ago, if a management executive wanted to see how things were going on the production side, he or she would only have to walk down the hall to enter the shop floor. Now the shop floor is likely to be across an ocean, or in a small rural center where labor costs are cheaper than in a big city. If the same executive next wants to visit the advertising and promotion advisers, they will probably be located in the heart of New York, Toronto, Chicago, London, Sydney, Los Angeles, or another big city.

In the not-so-old days of local or regional horizons, the company representative could visit all his or her accounts by car and usually be home every night. Because of today's ease of transmitting information by satellites and phone hookups, the business territory is now unbounded. But because words, even spoken ones, make up less than half the message (see chapter 8), travel is needed to add body language to satisfactorily conclude most business arrangements.

A personal sales or promotional call to a customer might require travel to the far corners of the globe. Many middle managers and even many junior workers on the staff are traveling great distances on the job. With the internationalization of company ownership, it is not unusual for assembly-line workers in a new car plant in Tennessee or Ontario to be flown in to visit their peers at plants in Japan or Europe.

With the ascendancy of women in the business world, there are even more complications to the flying family relationship. For example, if one spouse has a promotion to a different part of the country, the other partner may choose to stay in the original location. This means that a lot of people are using airlines to commute (daily or weekly) back and forth to see their own spouses. Even career couples who don't fly on the job find they cannot easily get two consecutive weeks of vacation together, and are thus flooding the travel market with brief three or four day excursions. All this adds up to a lot of jet lag.

In the animal kingdom, all creatures are guided by an internal clock. In humans, it runs on a 25-hour day. This means that bodily functions are not constant all day, but have peaks and valleys at specific times of the day. For example, body temperature drops at night when we sleep, and is at its lowest first thing in the morning. Urine output is much less at night, as is heart rate and blood pressure. Our eyes produce fewer tears at night than during the day; this makes our eyes feel more comfortable when they are closed. The body's internal clock programs the rates of secretion of hormones such as insulin (which affects blood sugar levels and the sense of hunger), cortisol, and thyroid. The internal clock cues our stomach to start secreting acidic digestive juices when mealtimes are due.

When we suddenly move into a new time zone, the body's internal clock will still keep ticking to its old rhythms, making us feel wide awake when everyone else is sleeping, and sleepy in the middle of daytime meetings. Fortunately these problems are self-correcting, given enough time (about one day for each time zone change). However, given the realities of business travel, or even the abbreviated vacation times many working families take, few people can wait for their bodies to adjust naturally. Besides, when they come home, they will be out of step again for several days.

The challenge of jet lag is not as much a question of fitness or inherited abilities, but a question of competent management of our bodies. Since human beings have had the intelligence to invent the stress of jet travel, one would think they should be able to invent the cure to jet lag. That cure is indeed now at hand, but it must be learned.

In my capacity as a speaker flying to over 100 cities a year, all over the world, I have had ample opportunity to put all the academic jet lag theories to the ultimate personal test. Although there are a few people who withstand jet travel naturally, with few side effects, I am not among them, as I discovered to my chagrin in my earlier trips. My current ease with jet lag is purely learned, not congenital. I have also had the chance to meet large numbers of senior executives, entertainers, and sales representatives who spend more time in the air than pilots. I have spoken to the airline professionals themselves, including flight crews.

The conclusion that emerges is that people who have conquered the time changes all have a system, which can be adapted and used by any traveler. What follows is based on their experiences, the results of two decades of medical research, and books such as *Overcoming Jet Lag* by Dr. Charles F. Ehret and Lynne Waller Scanlon. I recommend the above book as a further resource for specific diet programming for longer trips.

SOME JET LAG STATISTICS

In a study of 800 experienced travellers flying across multiple time zones, 94% were found to suffer from jet lag. For 45%, the problems were severe. Fully 90% were sleepy and fatigued on arrival and remained so for up to several days. Most were wide awake at night, but ready to doze off at mid-day. The effects were less when traveling west since the body is trying to lengthen the day into a 25-hour cycle. The major complaints were poor concentration (69%), slow physical reflexes (66%), irritability (50%), and upset digestion (47%).

It is important to note that the shift worker who does not travel faces the same changes (except a change of place). He or she can thus take almost as many days to recover when starting a new shift as the transoceanic traveler, and can thus benefit from the information in this chapter. For all those who must, for reasons of business, make quick trips across many time zones, there are some valuable tips that will help prevent many of typical jet lag problems. The following seven involve tricking the body clock.

1. USE LIGHT-DARK CYCLES

As light strikes the retina of the eye, the pineal gland at the base of the brain is stimulated to secrete melatonin, a hormone that plays a role in fatigue, the immune system, sleep disorders, and memory. Night shift workers and east-west air travelers are forced to disorient themselves from their natural cycles, but the strong role of light in telling our bodies the time can help them adapt.

The most important consideration when traveling for a brief visit is to get onto the destination time as soon as you board the plane (unless you are returning home the same day and wish to stay on your own time). If this means that you are supposed to make your body believe that it is daytime when the plane is dark, then turn your light on.

When I arrived in Australia for a full day of meetings recently, I was asked where I wished to have lunch. I chose an outdoor restaurant, and when I arrived, was offered a chair that faced the scenic Sydney Harbor and Opera House. I immediately asked to trade seats. Unfortunately, that meant my back was to the scenery. But it was more important to me that the sun be straight in my eyes. Since I didn't wear my sunglasses, this bolt of stimulation helped convince my doubting internal clock that it was day, even though it was night back in Canada. If I had instead traveled from Vancouver to Toronto, and was trying to convince my body to go to sleep right after the meal in order to get onto local time, then I would choose to eat in a dark restaurant.

To control your sleep-awake cycles before arrival, I suggest requesting a window seat on the plane. That way you will be able to pull down the window shade. Another method is to take along an effective eye mask to give your body the illusion of night. Some travelers even pick the side of the plane that will serve them best. If they want to be awake, they will sit by a south facing window during the day (at least in the northern hemisphere). If they wish to rest, they will chose the opposite side of the plane.

2. USE PROTEIN AND CARBOHYDRATE

We humans have two main pathways of electrical and neurological activity: one to wake us up, and one to begin the sleep-inducing process. The adrenaline pathway, which keeps us active, is stimulated by high protein foods such as fish, fowl, meat, eggs, dairy products, and beans. A meal of such foods can thus give us up to five hours of long-lasting energy.

The indolamine pathway, which induces the shutdown process for sleep, is stimulated by high carbohydrate foods such as pasta, salad, fruit, and rich desserts. A meal of such foods typically gives you energy for an hour or so and then leaves you drowsy, all set to sleep. Thus, even at home, if you start off the morning with a sweet bun, orange juice, and a donut, you may well have the mid-morning "blahs." On the other hand, if you don't have much time to eat during the day and then have a huge portion of steak before going to bed, you will probably sleep fitfully, dream furiously, and wake up exhausted.

These well-known facts about food can help the traveler plan a counterattack against jet lag. If you are boarding an evening plane to Europe from the east coast of North America, it would thus be best to have eaten a light carbohydrate meal a couple of hours earlier. You should then decline the in-flight meal so you can sleep right away, because sleeping is what the Europeans will be doing at that time.

When you are awakened in the morning, six hours later — with a honey bun, croissant, jam, and orange juice — it would be best to decline the whole meal and instead try to have some high protein food. If you request them in advance, most airlines will now offer high protein meals, in the same way as they provide other special meals such as kosher and vegetarian plates. If you cannot arrange to be served a high protein breakfast, then take along a high protein snack such as cheese, nuts, or even a disposable container of beans or chick peas.

For an evening meal, when you are trying to make your body believe it is time to retire, try to pre-order a vegetarian meal, or just avoid the meat portion of the meal you are served and eat the rest including dessert. What most travelers do, of course, is exactly the opposite. They eat the high protein meat course for dinner, followed by a considerable amount of alcohol (especially when it is cheap or free), and thus sabotage any chance of having an effective few hours of sleep. Once you arrive at your destination, the same principles hold true, although it is best if you do not eat great quantities of anything for the first day.

3. USE FLUIDS

Alcohol is a disaster when you are suffering from jet lag, but water is a great help. By drinking great quantities of water on the plane during your destination's daytime, and cutting it off a few hours before your destination's nighttime, you can help reset your kidneys into the new routine. If you do not stop drinking water a few hours before you sleep, then you will probably be awakened by your full bladder, as the kidneys will be producing more urine (in effect, at the normal rate for daytime) than during your normal sleep at home. Once you get up to relieve yourself, it can be very difficult to go back to sleep.

As drinkable water can be difficult to obtain on airlines, I suggest taking along at least a quart in your carry-on bag for a six-hour trip. Bottled waters come in a great variety, and are all suitable. However, in general, the noncarbonated types make a little more sense during flight, as the gas released by carbonated waters in the stomach can cause uncomfortable bloating or even pains on the rare occasions when the cabin pressure drops.

On the other hand, carbonated beverages have a distinct advantage on ground level when visiting tropical countries. This is because their higher acidity makes it more difficult for infections to survive the voyage through the stomach.

4. EAT HEAVILY AND THEN LIGHTLY

Laboratory experiments with rats can be useful for jet lag studies, because the budget for their "air fares" is so low. Rats can be given jet lag by simply changing the artificial lights in their indoor environments. For that matter, so can humans when they change shifts at work.

Experiments have been conducted by artificially switching the lighting regimen to correspond to a sudden eight-hour time change, such as would be experienced in traveling from Tokyo to Denver, or from Vancouver to London. It has been shown that the rats who were eating whenever they felt hungry took four to six days to resynchronize naturally, not unlike the expected human recovery. On the other hand, rats that were allowed to eat very little for the day before the time change and were then fed a high protein meal at what would correspond with breakfast time in their new "destination" had a remarkably rapid resynchronization.

It has also been found that preceding the day of light eating with a day of heavy eating can increase and then decrease the body's stores of glycogen in the muscles. This further sets the stage for a resetting of the metabolic clock upon arrival. Although this may sound complicated, and can vary with the length of trip and the direction of travel, the moral of the story seems to be: If you're leaving on Thursday, eat generous servings on Wednesday. On Thursday, the day you leave, eat very little. Do not break the final "fast" until breakfast, destination time. At this time a high protein breakfast would be best.

5. USE TEA OR COFFEE

Although I do not favor drinking regular tea or coffee under normal circumstances, at least not in excess of two cups per day, the methylated xanthines in them have been shown to help the body fight jet lag. Caffeine (found in coffee, tea, cola and chocolate), theobromine (found in coffee), and theophylline (found in tea) are all members of this chemical family. In people who can tolerate these substances, they can provide a useful method to trick the body's clock.

You can make a considerable improvement in your adjustment to time change by avoiding coffee or tea for a few days before the flight. Then have two or three cups of coffee or tea on the morning of your flight if you are traveling west, or on the evening of the flight if you are traveling east.

6. USE ACTIVITY-REST CYCLES

One's level of fitness alone offers little protection from jet lag, as is witnessed by the number of world class athletes who suffer from it. However, physical activity in flight and after arrival can help reset the body's time clock. Exercise basically wakes one up. The stimulation of the blood pressure, heart rate, and lungs — added to the general muscular flush of fitness — help signal the body to stay alert for at least the next few hours.

EXERCISES TO DO ON THE AIRCRAFT

If the morning sun is shining in your new destination but your body thinks it is the middle of the night, 20 minutes of exercise can be a great help in tricking your inner clock. On the plane, some brief isometric exercises are about all one can manage in a crowded seat. However, a few shoulder and head rolls, and then a bit of a stroll along the aisles can improve the circulation (reducing the risks of deep vein thrombosis, or blood clots in the legs) and waken the senses if you are trying to stay synchronized with your destination time.

If there is room and you are not too self-conscious, good exercise can be obtained by standing in the aisle, slowly raising yourself up on your toes, and then lowering your heels to the ground. Sets of multiples of 10, alternating your weight to first one leg and then the other, can give the most powerful muscles in your body, the calf muscles, a good workout. Modified dips with your hands on the armrests of your seat will give your chest, shoulder, and arm muscles a bit of work.

Upon arrival, more normal sorts of exercise are again possible, but make sure you do them at a time conducive to waking yourself up in your new time zone. You may feel like a brisk jog at 3:00 a.m., but resist the temptation until daytime, or you risk delaying your adaptation process. An important caveat here is never to underestimate the effects of jet lag. Do not do any vigorous exercise on the first day. For example, if you can usually run for 20 minutes, just walk briskly instead. Your body has enough to contend with on that first day without being pushing to its pre-travel limits. (See Appendix A.)

EXERCISES TO DO IN A HOTEL ROOM

Activity also refers to mental stimulation, such as social contacts, loud music (turn that headset up), or reading a thrilling page-turner of a novel. The fact that your companions on the plane may all have fallen asleep on their old time will probably make it hard for you to find that social interaction, but disciplined alternative stimulations such as reading or doing crossword puzzles can be effective. (See Appendix A.)

JOHN W. MORRISON

The rest cycle is just as important and just as difficult to satisfy as the activity cycle. However, great success here depends on some disciplined relaxation skills, such as the *Stress for Success* Power Nap audiocassettes. By learning a self-hypnotic technique (see chapter 10), virtually anyone can go to sleep on command. Relaxing music casettes will help as well.

Though one might think tranquilizers would promote relaxation, it is really best not to take them at all during the week of your flight, as they linger in the blood stream and increase the adaptation time. Many experts note that triazolam (Halcion) works well to help some people avoid jet lag, but I prefer to approach jet lag without drugs unless problems persist in spite of conservative measures. I have found many tranquilizer users will complain of mild amnesia for the first day, which could be disastrous in a business meeting. If airsickness is a problem, a nausea pill such as dimenhydrinate can help, and may also increase drowsiness. However, the dry mouth and residual drowsiness it can cause make it unwise to take just for sleep.

One new adjunct to the dietary tricks mentioned in this chapter, however, has been developed, and, although not supported by any large body or research, seems to be promising. The Anti-Jet-Lag Formula* is a simple package of six pills, starting with two taken one hour before bedtime after arriving at your destination, and the remaining four tablets taken the following day with breakfast and lunch. They are comprised of vitamin and amino acid supplements, and contain no drugs, caffeine, or other additives. Taken at the same time as the recommended foods, these pills are said to assist the body's response to changing cues.

These tablets are not prescriptive, and have been used safely for decades, so there would appear to be no potential for side effects. Remember, though, that the pills do not mean that other dietary recommendations for jet lag, such as abstinence from alcohol, and avoiding late high protein dinners can be ignored.

If you plan to sleep on board, try to grab a blanket, no matter how hot the plane might be at ground level. Your body temperature will drop naturally in sleep, and feeling cold can keep you awake. If you have a coat with you, you can use it instead of or in addition to a blanket.

* The Anti-Jet-Lag Formula is produced by American Biosearch, Inc., 5820 Oberlin Drive, Suite 202, San Diego, California 92121, U.S.A.

7. USE TIME TO YOUR ADVANTAGE

Set your watch on destination time as soon as you get on our plane. Don't do it earlier, as it may confuse you as to departure time, and you might miss your flight. Your watch provides yet another external cue to trick your internal clock. This cue works most effectively if you use your imagination to visualize your normal energy level at this new time, and let it dictate your corresponding activities in flight.

LEG LAG — IT COULD BE FATAL

Medical scientists have recently uncovered a rare but significant health risk for those who travel long distances in cramped airline seats. Drs. Cruikshank, Gorlin and Jennett have recently published an article documenting six passengers who ended up in hospital due to prolonged periods in a confined space. Two of the patients were Drs. Cruikshank and Jennett.

In 1986, at Heathrow Airport, a three-year study of over 60 cases of sudden death following long-distance flights reported that in 18% of the autopsies deaths were due to blood clots in the lungs. The diagnosed cause of these clots was from restricted circulation in the lower extremities. Gravity pulls the blood to our feet and lower legs, with the result that the blood in the veins of our feet has the same pressure as a column of water as tall as we are, when standing. Apart from a few thin valves in the leg veins, the only thing propelling this blood back to the heart is the pumping action of the leg muscles. This job is made more difficult by anything that thickens the bloods, and by anything that impedes the natural channels of venous return.

In an airplane, then, a number of factors conspire to make these problems more likely to occur. The lack of humidity, salty foods and snacks, and alcoholic beverages all dehydrate the body, making the blood thicker, while the shape and space provided by an airline seat restrict the return venous flow. This latter problem is easily noted by any passenger who takes his or her shoes off inflight, and later can't get them back on due to swelling of the ankles.

The simple fact of life is that the majority of the traveling public cannot afford the stiff premium charges for the extra space and comfort of the first-class section. Therefore, it is important for economy travelers to identify the potential for problems, and to actively defend against them. The following action tips will provide good help.

- Exercise before travel. Obviously the condition of venous pooling will be worse in people whose leg muscles are never worked, so this is just another reason to keep in reasonable condition. A good walk around the airport complex before flight time will be much more beneficial than spending the time sitting in the bar or cafeteria. If you are sequestered in a lounge at the gate, then choose to stand rather than sit, and slowly exercise your calf muscles by rising up and down on your toes.
- Don't smoke. Smoking is known to impair the circulation of the blood, and increase the risk of venous clotting. If you are a confirmed addict, at least try not to smoke while in-flight.
- Wear loose clothing. Girdles, elasticised knee-high socks, tight jeans, and tight belts all make venous pooling worse. Support hose, either with calf-high socks, or ladies' pantyhose will help.
- Drink lots of water, even if you have to bring a bottle of your own.
- Avoid salt where possible when in-flight. This means avoiding the snacks offered, and not adding any salt to the actual meals served. (Plenty is already added.)

- Exercise during travel. Fellow passengers don't mind disturbing themselves to let you up for a visit to the washroom, so don't feel shy about getting up for a stroll and stretch. Standing in the aisle, you can repeat your slow calf exercises to help "reactivate" the venous "pump." Walk around the aircraft when possible, or stand out of the way and slowly rise up on to your tiptoes, one leg at a time. When unable to move from your seat, isometric exercises and slow ankle circles will help. Make sure that some exercise is forthcoming upon arrival, such as a brisk walk, to return the blood circulation to normal. If your flight is making a stop to take on more passengers, take advantage of the opportunity for a brief stretch and walk in the airport lounge.

CULTURE LAG — WHAT TO DO ABOUT IT

The stress of doing business in a foreign environment can be greatly reduced by doing a little research into the local history, customs, and — if appropriate — local health threats to outsiders. Language tapes can not only help pass the time in traffic jams and on the flight to your destination. They can also give you the distinct advantage of at least a little fluency when you arrive.

Because of the global nature of modern work and travel, it is critical to study the local cultural features of the countries with whom you do business. For example, much body language that we take for granted is at odds with the body language of other cultures. For example, North Americans consider the Japanese penchant for looking away when one is being stared at to be "shifty." The Japanese consider the direct "look-'em-in-the-eye" style of North Americans to be insensitive and rude. In the West the motto is, "The squeaky wheel gets the grease." In Japan, by contrast, the motto is, "The pheasant would not be shot but for its cry."

In many European homes, an American business guest might bring along a gift of flowers to the hostess and get his face slapped, because such gifts are considered highly personal, like lingerie. Unlike the Americans, the Brazilians are forever patting, touching, and poking you (and each other) during a meeting — behavior that to some puritanical types can seem downright fresh.

Confusing? Yes, but such cultural differences are all a part of life's rich pageant, whether we like them or not. It's best to be aware of them and try to adapt as well as we can.

POWER PACKING VERSUS PANIC PACKING

One key to easy traveling is the packing. Mark McCormick, in his excellent book *What they don't teach you at Harvard Business School*, notes that, when he flies to Paris or London, he takes only his briefcase. This is because he has fully stocked closets and drawers in his European homes, so who needs suitcases?

Well, for the rest of us, who have not yet fully stocked our foreign closets, packing is the only way out. After talking to hundreds of experienced business travelers and traveling several hundred thousand miles a year myself, I have developed a system that I call *power packing*, which I highly recommend.

POWER PACKING — THE RIGHT CHOICE
- Plan your wardrobe no later than one week ahead, so all dirty items can be washed or sent to the cleaners, and all supplemental shopping can be done for the trip.
- Never store an empty suitcase. Use it to store duplicates of toiletry kits, swimsuits, exercise outfits, running shoes, hairdryers, and any other routine items. The first thing you will do for your next trip is repack them anyway, so you might as well save yourself a step.

- Prepack for the different lengths of journey that you are likely to take, leaving the easier parts until just before the trip itself. It is false economy to try to save on duplicate items, so you may as well invest in a complete set for every kind of travel requirement. For example, many frequent flyers pre-pack one carry-on bag with its routine inventory for quick trips and a checkable suitcase for longer trips. In the suitcase might be some different items, such as a travel iron that is too heavy to carry in the hand luggage. Both can be stocked with a supply of packing tissue for the next trip.

- The night before you leave, lay everything out around your open suitcase on the bed. Pick colors that allow you to wear the same shoes to work as you will be wearing on the plane. Thus you avoid packing extras (except for your exercise shoes, if needed).

- Use your prepacked sheets of tissue paper between the layers of clothes. Roll pants and shirts, or skirts and blouses, and fold jackets around them to avoid wrinkles. Ties can be kept in a handy travel pack or even coiled around a pair of socks.

- Pack things in the appropriate sequence, so the heavy items don't shift onto the delicate ones. Even the rookie grocery clerk knows better than to bag jugs of milk on top of the ripe tomatoes.

- Secure the zippers and latches, and lock your luggage. Affix some identifying mark on it, such as a bright sticker or a colored ribbon or tag. This will facilitate identification on the carousel or in the hotel lobby.

- Take along some of your desk work or reading material in your carryon bag. One can count on traffic delays on the runways (an activity now known as *tarmacking*) and in airport terminals. Travelers who get out their laptop computers and dictation machines when they are stalled in transit may not be workaholics, despite appearances to the contrary. Probably they are just well organized workers who would rather sit around doing something than nothing.

- Get a small amount of the local currency before you leave, so you don't have to rush around the airport looking for the exchange counter.
- If possible, have a map of where you are going, to cut down on initial disorientation. Often, your local library will be able to provide you with a xerox copy if there is no tourist bureau in your area.

PANIC PACKING — THE WRONG CHOICE

- Postpone all packing until the taxi arrives to take you to the airport.
- Race like a maniac, half dressed, soapsuds still in your hair, from one end of the house to the other, and from attic to basement, screaming, "Who's the idiot that hid my other shoe?"
- Don't waste precious seconds by turning on the closet light. This way you won't be offended by those soup stains all over your lapels, or the subtle differences in color (such as between your blue suit jacket and your brown pinstripe pants).
- When in doubt, stuff everything you can lay hands on into your empty suitcase. Can't decide which of five outfits to take to your two day conference? Take them all; might get a little cool in the evenings.
- Leave all bottles of fluids ajar, and don't bother to put them in zip-lock bags. You brought extra suits, so who cares if one gets a little wet?
- Just get the zippers of your cases three-quarters closed; that'll do.
- Leave the house at least eight times, and each time bring out another forgotten item. Taxi drivers just love to watch a show.
- Help the passenger service agent at the airport by running alongside the conveyor belt, picking up bits of laundry that have exploded out of the side pockets of your suitcase.
- Panic packing comes with a guarantee: Once your plane is airborne, you will suddenly realize that you forgot something crucial. If you remembered your fancy new imported razor blades,

you forgot the handle. If you remembered your lap-top computer, you forgot the power cord. Panic packers should always take along lots of coins, so they can rush to the nearest pay phone to find local stores carrying replacements. The problem is, panic packers usually forget to pack any coins, and waste even more time trying to find change.

- If you are traveling to multiple destinations, this will require multiple panic packing episodes. The corollary is that, no matter how much time you wasted on the first leg of the journey, the full damage cannot be assessed until you return home, with a considerably lighter load than you started out with. At least one item of your inventory will be left somewhere in each hotel room, and no matter how quickly you call the hotel when you get to the next city, the cleaning staff will have found nothing. The supplemental corollary is that all lost and found departments carry only what you found and what somebody else lost, never the other way around.

FEAR OF FLYING

The fear of flying, which affects many people, is of course reinforced by the live pictures of every plane crash in the world, replayed dozens of times a day on TV. "White knuckle" flyers fear being out of control of their own destiny. Even if they would make incompetent pilots, they would rather fly the plane than be passengers, since then they would be the first to know they are going down. The reality is, of course, that if you need to travel from New York to Edmonton, or from London to Rome, there are far more chances of a fatal accident if you drive your own car than if you travel with a quality commercial carrier.

One of the best ways to offset fear is to travel with a friend or spouse but, by making a point of not reading the bloody details of any plane crash (just as you should not watch a *Jaws* movie before going on a skindiving holiday), and instead reminding your-self how many millions of air passengers arrive safely each day, you will be better able to get on a plane in comfort. It is, of course, advisable to pay attention to the demonstrations of safety fea-tures and exit routes on board.

One paradoxical aspect of all this fear of flying is that most of my patients who have such a phobia do not bother to buckle up their seatbelts in their cars. Many even allow their young chil-dren to stand up on the seat or to sit in their laps, thus allowing their child to be used as an air-bag during a crash.

Realistic fear can be a healthy, even lifesaving, characteristic, but an unrealistic one can be self-damaging. If the pessimistic comments of relatives or friends start to reactivate your worst fears, tell them to change the subject, especially if you have an impending flight. If all else fails, then try hypnosis. I have seen large numbers of patients with phobias, including flying. Virtu-ally all improved with post-hypnotic suggestion.

In any event, travel is and always will be a fact of working life. By following some of the above tips, you can at least make the experience useful and not just exasperating.

Chapter 10

DE-STRESS OPTIONS

BECOMING AWARE OF YOUR TOTAL STRESS LEVELS

As I explained in *The Joy of Stress*, it is important to be aware of the total stress levels in your life. The Holmes-Rahe values listed below apply to events you have gone through in the last 24 months. Below that I have included several more work stress selections that may apply to you. Assign a score to each of your stresses, based on the values given in the charts.

The Holmes-Rahe scale of stress ratings

LIFE EVENT	VALUE	YOUR SCORE
Death of a spouse	100	
Divorce	73	
Marital separation	65	
Jail term	63	
Death of a close family member	63	
Personal injury or illness	53	

LIFE EVENT	VALUE	YOUR SCORE
Marriage	50	
Fired at work	47	
Retirement	45	
Marital reconciliation	45	
Change in health of family member	44	
Pregnancy	40	
Sex difficulties	39	
Gain of new family member	39	
Business adjustment	39	
Change in financial state	38	
Death of a close friend	37	
Change to a different line of work	36	
Change in number of arguments with spouse	35	
Mortgage over one year's net salary	31	
Foreclosure of mortgage or loan	30	
Change in responsibilities at work	29	
Son or daughter leaving home	29	
Trouble with in-laws	29	
Outstanding personal achievement	28	
Spouse begins or stops work	26	
Begin or end school	26	
Change in living conditions	25	
Revision in personal habits	24	
Trouble with boss	23	
Change in work hours or conditions	20	
Change in residence	20	

LIFE EVENT	VALUE	YOUR SCORE
Change in schools	20	
Change in recreation	19	
Change in church activites	19	
Change in social activities	18	
Mortgage or loan less than one year's net salary	17	
Change in sleeping habits	16	
Change in number of family get-togethers	15	
Change in eating habits	15	
Vacation	13	
Christmas	12	
Minor violations of the law	11	
Miscellaneous		
Enter your total here		

Under "miscellaneous," assign values for your own additional work stresses. Here are some examples from "the Hanson scale of work stress ratings."

WORK EVENT	VALUE	YOUR SCORE
Withdrawal from smoking or other addiction	60	
Public speaking before a major work audience	55	
Daycare problems	55	
Corporate merger/acquisition	47	
New technology in the office	40	

WORK EVENT	VALUE	YOUR SCORE
Workaholic hours (more than 12 hours per day)	35	
Travel stress (away from home more than 4 days per month)	30	
Commuting stress (more than 5 hours commuting per week)	25	
New Boss	20	

Once you have rated all stresses that apply to you, add the numbers to arrive at your total. You now have some objective idea of the amount of stress that faces you. If your score is less than 150 units, you have a 30% chance of a change in your health within the next year. Up to 300 units gives you a 50% chance. More than 300 units gives you an 80% chance. By having regular checkups from your doctor, at least annually if you have a high stress score, you will gain insight into your own target areas and be better able to prevent crises.

Now that we have established your level of stress, we should find out whether you need to worry. As my own score on the Holmes-Rahe scale is 510 points, I should be in great danger — 80% risk. However, my +550 points of resistance serve to negate that risk. Let's see if your choices in response to stress decrease or increase your risk.

The Hanson scale of stress resistance

WEAK CHOICES	VALUE	YOUR SCORE
1. Bad Genetics: You have a family history of deaths before age 65 from natural causes.	-10	
2. Insomnia: You are insufficiently rested to have enough energy during the day, yet cannot sleep effectively at night.	-20	

WEAK CHOICES	VALUE	YOUR SCORE
3. Bad diet: Your diet is unbalanced because you eat too many junk foods. You also qualify if you go on fad diets that allow some but not all the recommended food categories (see Appendix B).	-30	
4. Obesity, bulimia or anorexia: You are 10% or more over or under the weight at which you look your best in a bathing suit.	-40	
5. Unrealistic goals: You continually fail to meet goals you've set for yourself.	-50	
6. Poisons: You take drugs including: prescriptions such as tranquilizers or anti-depressants; street drugs; too much caffeine or too much alcohol in order to get through your day.	-60	
7. Smoking: You smoke cigarettes, cigars, or a pipe	-70	
8. Wrong Job: You find your career boring or downright unpleasant. You love weekends and holidays, but dread going back to work.	-80	
9. Financial distress: You can't support your current lifestyle and pay your debts, as well as maintain some savings for future needs.	-90	
10. Unstable Home and Personal Life: You do not get along with family members and/or close friends. Also assign yourself this score if you see yourself as ''lonely'' or as having many superficial friends and bouncing from one meaningless relationship to another.	-100	
Your Total	-550	

STRONG CHOICES	VALUE	YOUR SCORE
1. Good Genetics: You have "chosen" your ancestors well; most of them have lived well past 65.	+10	
2. Sense of Humor: You can laugh *with* others, and *at* yourself.	+20	
3. The Right Diet: You eat a balanced diet (see Appendix B) including the right number of calories to maintain your ideal body weight.	+30	
4. Alternate Activity: You have a balance of physical and intellectual activities in your life. You exercise at least 3 times a week and strive to maintain tone and flexibility in your body.	+40	
5. Realistic Goals: You try to set clear, attainable goals regarding your work and your personal life.	+50	
6. Stress Skills: You know how to identify stress in your life and are aware of what is happening inside your body during times of stress.	+60	
7. Relaxation Skills: You sleep sufficiently well at night to have full energy levels during the day. If you become fatigued, you have the ability to take a refreshing nap.	+70	
8. Thorough Job Preparation: You are fully rehearsed and mentally prepared to handle the routine stresses at work. When unexpected job stresses hit, you have some contingency plans, and skills in crisis management.	+80	

STRONG CHOICES	VALUE	YOUR SCORE
9. Financial Stability: You have the savings, insurance policies, and/or marketable job skills to protect yourself and your dependants should you lose your job because of changes in the economy or your health.	+90	
10. Stable Home and Personal Life: You have an understanding confidant, a best friend, and a loving partner (even better if your spouse qualifies for all three). Your family is supportive, and your friends make you feel good about yourself, through good times and bad.	+100	
Your Total	+550	

Enter total of **Weak Choices** _____
Add Strong and **Weak** choice points
for **Stress Resistance Total** _____
Subtract your Holmes-Rahe stress
score to get your **Net Stress Score** _____

If you obtain a score of more than -300 that indicates an 80% chance of serious change in your health. Consult your doctor soon. Remember, even if you score well today, stress is dynamic. Review your position on the scale often.

DE-STRESS WITHOUT DISTRESS

Stress is a significant problem in the workplace, and many people are searching for effective antidotes. Unfortunately, most look in the wrong places. The answer is not to follow the crowds who take sedatives or tranquilizers (see chapters 14 and 15), but to take control. It is for this reason that the following *de-stress* options to control your symptoms are critical to learn. All the *de-stress* options are easy to master and free from side effects. They will improve your health today, and may even save your life tomorrow.

TEN DE-STRESS OPTIONS

1. THE RELAXATION RESPONSE

Boston cardiologist Dr. Herbert Benson of the New England Deaconess Hospital first coined the term *relaxation response*, by which he meant the physiological change in our bodies that occurs when we alter the state of our consciousness through non-drug means. Benson's original quest, which turned out to be successful, was to find a way to help victims of heart disease without risking side effects. The physical changes that he found during patients' relaxed states included such easily measurable parameters as a lowering of heart and breathing rates, a lowering of arterial blood lactate concentration (a measure of the end products of metabolism in the muscles), and even a lowering of blood pressure. Relaxation can help the body's immune mechanisms improve, with measurably increased levels of killer "T" white blood cells in the bloodstream.

The relaxation response is quite distinct from actual sleep, and is best described as a wakeful hypometabolic state. The relaxation response produces low-end alpha and high theta waves. (See the biofeedback section of this chapter.)

The relaxation response helps elevate circulating levels of endorphine, making pain tolerance much greater. This explains why headaches can often be aborted in their early stages by relaxation techniques.

Best used daily for 15 to 20 minutes, the relaxation response demonstrates our physiological power to counteract our bodies' negative, inappropriate responses to stress. This power is so profound that it can offer lifesaving benefits to post-heart-attack victims and, even more importantly, to pre-heart-attack victims.

The relaxation response can be reached through a wide variety of simple means, such as through prayer, meditation, yoga, or hypnosis. However, it is not obtained by simple relaxing. To obtain full effectiveness, the best thing to do is to follow an example such as Dr. Benson's protocol.

The relaxation response in practice

1. Sit quietly in a comfortable position, and loosen any tight clothing around your waist.
2. Close your eyes.
3. Deeply relax all your muscles, beginning at your feet and progressing up to your face. Keep muscles relaxed.
4. Breathe through your nose. Become aware of your breathing. As you breathe out, say the word "one" silently to yourself. In effect, breathe in . . . out, and say "one." Breathe in . . . out, and say "one." Breathe easily and naturally, into your stomach.
5. Continue for 15 to 20 minutes. You may open your eyes to check the time, but do not use an alarm or you will be subconsciously cringing as your time comes up. When you finish, sit quietly for several minutes, at first with your eyes closed and later with your eyes opened. Do not stand up for several minutes.

Do not worry if you are bothered by extraneous thoughts. Just acknowledge them and then get back to your breathing routine. Soothing background music, or the *Stress for Success* Power Nap tape, may also help your relaxation process at first. However, when you have fully mastered the skills, you will be able to practice them even in the heat of the most stressful days at work. If time does not permit a 15 to 20 minute break at work, then I have found that even a few deep breaths while on "hold" on a phone call can replenish some of your energy.

If you are having difficulty mastering this on your own, consult your doctor or local hospital to find the name of a skilled practitioner in your area. Courses are available that take anywhere from a few minutes up to years to master. I have found excellent benefits from programs lasting one evening a week for a month, such as those run by Toronto's Eli Bay, of the Relaxation Response Institute.[1]

[1] The Relaxation Response Institute's address is 858 Eglinton Ave. W., Toronto, Ontario, Canada, M6C 2B6. Telephone number is (416) 789-7261.

2. BIOFEEDBACK

Biofeedback, a "pop psychology" rage back in the 1970s, is now an accepted medical option to help teach patients how to control their state of mental alertness. When we are under acute stress, electrical activity in our brains sends the EEG patterns into wild, random activities, making it hard to concentrate, relax, or sleep. However, by concentration and learned relaxation techniques, one can control this electrical output and begin to emit regular coherent wave patterns. These can easily be measured on any EEG or biofeedback machine.

The following brainwaves are not in any alphabetical order, not even in the Greek alphabet, from whose ranks the letters have been chosen. The brainwaves were named more or less in the order they were discovered.

- Beta: 13-25 cycles per second (c.p.s.) — a super–conscious state permitting enhanced concentration. Seen in the prepared student during an examination.
- Alpha: 8-13 c.p.s. — A state of relaxed vigilance.
- Theta: 4-8 c.p.s. — yoga trances, relaxation response.
- Delta: 1-3 c.p.s. — deep sleep.

Biofeedback, by showing us which kinds of waves we are emitting, can help reveal to us the power that we have to adjust our brainwave activity along the continuum between 1 and 25 c.p.s. By training and practicing, we are able to relax or focus on command. As in many new areas of stress relief, there are a number of charlatans in this field. However, your family doctor, local hospital, or university center should be able to refer you to a skilled biofeedback expert who could give you some initial training. Once you have mastered the skills of shifting your levels of consciousness, then the hardware becomes unnecessary unless you wish refresher courses.

3. MUSIC

Music has a special ability to tranquilize or agitate, distract or help us concentrate, make us get up to dance, or thump on the neighbors' door demanding silence. Music can color our moods. It can help improve our concentration at work or it can make us fall asleep at work.

Music actually has healing powers. Pablo Casals, the late musical genius, spent his latter years racked with pains and stiffness in his joints. He was unable to mobilize his limbs each day until he played a vigorous Bach selection on his cello. After that, the levels of endorphine and cortisol were raised in his bloodstream, and he was able to carry on with the zeal of a younger man. Because tastes in music vary so much, I suggest you make a tape of the music that most relaxes you and play it when you need to calm down. With a portable tape recorder, this can easily be done in your car in traffic or during a break at work. If you find you are always tired on the job and agitated at home,[*2] try playing rousing music in the office and the soothing varieties at home.

One of the reasons for the popularity of music as an escape from work stresses (unless one works all day in the music business) is that music completely fills up one compartment of our lives and effectively seals out work distractions for a time. This is why many people find that attending a live concert is so valuable to them, and why attendance at such events is now outstripping attendance at professional sporting events for the first time in the United States. Almost all the people in the audiences have jobs (ticket prices virtually dictate this), but few are giving their jobs even a moment's thought as Michael Jackson, Anne Murray, Bruce Springsteen, Nana Mouskouri, or a Philharmonic Orchestra mesmerize them for a few hours.

[*2] If you have trouble deciding on musical selections to help you unwind, write to New Music Distribution service at 500 Broadway, New York, 10012, or send for the Sound Health Catalogue, c/o The Relaxation Response Institute, 858 Eglinton Ave. W., Toronto, Ontario, Canada, M6C 2B6.

4. ART

The role of art in molding attitudes in the workplace has been well established from the beginnings of civilization, as we have seen from archeological finds. More recently, in Germany during the depression of the 1930s, Adolf Hitler demonstrated his understanding of the power of art when he removed many classic masterpieces from public view, and commissioned massive new sculptures, murals, and paintings to glorify the spirit of the Aryan worker. While this was done for highly political motives, to manipulate public opinion in favor of his party and himself, the undeniable fact is that it worked.

Given the unavoidable fact that we are all influenced by visual imagery, it makes sense that this power be used to achieve good purposes, such as improving morale, attitude, and productivity in the workplace. In many businesses, from jean giant Levi Strauss to T. Eaton department stores, old artifacts and photographs can link the values of company founders with those of even the most junior employees and customers. If you have some control over your work station, you may be able to inspire yourself in a similar way by placing favorite photographs, paintings, or other *objets d'art* on your walls, shelves, or desk.

Recently I met some of the top executives at Paine Webber's Head office building in Manhattan. Their chairman, Don Marron, has been an avid collector of contemporary art for 20 years, and has amassed one of the most daring and spectacular corporate collections in the world. Some of the largest canvases I have seen grace the tall walls of the main lobby, and brilliant expressions of color and line hang on virtually every bit of wallspace in the office tower. Marron knows that, by surrounding his employees with the most daring modern art, he is nurturing an atmosphere conducive to innovative and aggressive thinking.

5. ACUPUNCTURE

One of the oldest forms of medical treatment is acupuncture, which has its roots in Asia more than 4,000 years ago. Small combustible deposits, not unlike the material that makes up the "punk" that we used to light firecrackers as children, were placed in various places on the skin, and would cause certain pains to go away. Over the centuries, acupuncture needles replaced the hot embers, and a "map" of points on the surface of the body was charted, with specific points identified with different kinds of medical pains.

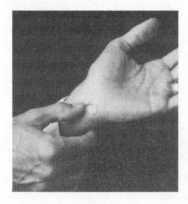
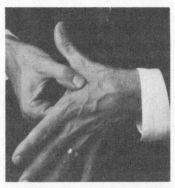

JOHN W. MORRISON

Although not taken seriously by the Western medical establishment until relatively recently, acupuncture is now widely accepted by our own doctors. It is a useful weapon to fight pain — a weapon that is virtually without side effects. The only caveat here is that the practitioner must be properly trained. In lay hands, one could experience some harm. I saw a case in which an unqualified practitioner inserted a too-long needle into the shoulder tip area and punctured the patient's lung. There is also the ever-present worry of spreading diseases such as hepatitis and AIDS through improperly sterlized needles.

While these problems can be avoided by disposing of the needles or sterilizing them under strict conditions, my own preference is to use the benefits of acupuncture without breaking the surface of the skin. New technology has given us electrical devices such as the laser, and Codetron and TENS machines, which can all be used instead of needles. (However, there are still a number of resistant conditions, such as severe migraines, that may continue to require needles if noninvasive substitutes are not strong enough.)

Acupuncture has been used in the field of sports for years. As long ago as the early 1970s, when I was speaking to the team doctors of American NFL clubs about players traded to our team in Toronto, I was fascinated to hear their stories about the benefits of Trans-Cutaneous Nerve Stimulation. When a player came off the field with a painful "jammed" knee, the joint was first examined (and sometimes X-rayed). Then one or two pairs of electrodes would be pasted to the skin just above and below the sore knee. These were connected to a small portable transformer, which emitted a low-frequency current. The player would be able to pace around in front of the bench for about 20 minutes, and then the pain would be reduced enough so that he could get back into the game.

One interesting thing is that Trans-Cutaneous Nerve Stimulation, or the more modern equivalents — laster and Codetron therapies — work best when the electrodes are placed over the same points found by Asian acupuncturists centuries before. A skilled massage therapist is also aware of these points. The therapist uses direct finger pressure, which may be painful at the time, to make tense muscles go a little numb. Such finger-pressure techniques are otherwise known as Shiatzu or accu-pressure, and again use exactly the same points on the body.

Particularily when one is under a lot of chronic stress at work, and when one's shouldertips become tense and stiff, it can be of great benefit to fight back with a simple dose of one of the acupuncture-based therapies. If you have access to a whirlpool, then try to have one of the jets point directly at one of your accupoints. If possible, have your spouse or a friend learn how to massage these points as well, since a daily treatment is better than having one just once or twice a month.

6. FASHION

To maintain our maximum energy levels on the job, it is helpful to dress for each compartment in our lives. The costumes we wear can play an integral part in defining these boundaries. It can be helpful to have a working wardrobe that is quite distinct from our evening and weekend clothes. Styles that are up-to-date (but within our budget) help improve our self-image. Off-duty clothes can put us in a relaxed mood, while on-duty clothes can help put us in a working mood.

A football player loses his normal, calm behavioral patterns when he changes out of his civilian clothes and into his pads and uniform before a game. I have been in many a pre-game locker room, and have always been amazed by the consistent increase in players' aggression levels as they don each new article of equipment. The same phenomenon can be seen in reverse. After a long day of shooting in front of hot camera lights, the first reaction of the professional model is to shuck off the fancy clothes and shuffle around in loose, well-worn jeans and a sweatshirt.

One problem with wearing business attire when we're trying to relax is a matter of our bodies' functions. As we can see from watching babies, it is natural for us to breathe by moving our stomachs in and out. Modern styles make it virtually impossible to continue this method of breathing. Narrow waists, narrow hips, and tight belts have thwarted natural "belly breathing," and combined to force men and women to breathe by just moving their chests in and out.

The problem with this is that we do not breathe as deeply or exchange oxygen for carbon dioxide as efficiently as we could. This means that, when we are under considerable stress, there is a buildup of the products of metabolism, including carbon dioxide, and we are not able to blow them off properly. This can, paradoxically, make us yawn even in the heat of the most stimulating crisis. (It's interesting to note that it is virtually impossible to yawn without letting your stomach do the breathing — go on, try it!)

Thus an integral part of learning to master our relaxation powers is to at least modify our clothing a little. This may mean closing your office door to unbutton your waistline or unbuckle your belt, or loosen your collar and tie. If you do not have the luxury of privacy, then make sure the clothing you choose fits loosely enough to let you breathe properly.

Pierre Elliott Trudeau, former prime minister of Canada, displayed an understanding of this principle by frequently wearing comfortable turtlenecks, even to high-level meetings where the other men wore tightly collared shirts and ties. Once your clothing is no longer fighting you, then you can relearn all those years of bad breathing habits to be able to take charge of your relaxation. (See The Relaxation Response, earlier in this chapter.)

7. POSITIVE IMAGERY

Positive approaches to stress at work can make an incredible difference to outcomes, as long as these approaches are realistic and backed up by discrete, goal-oriented steps.

For example, the imagery of language can determine the outcome before the battle is joined. For example, in response to the common greeting of, "How's it going?", a response of, "Great!" sets up a positive attitude. It can put one on the lookout for the opportunities instead of the crises inherent in the day's stresses. The habit of responding with a negative response such as, "Not bad," "So, so," or the brutally blunt, "Lousy!" encourages a negative outcome from the same stresses.

Remember the power of speech in shaping your images, and

make sure to try to shape positive ones. If you don't, your negative words may well become self-fulfilling prophecies.

8. PLACEBOS

Placebos (from the Latin meaning "I shall please") are imitation medicines. Their effect on our health can be strong. I recently had a harried, over-stressed executive in my office complaining about the pills the specialist had given him for his rumbling ulcer. His old pills — which were shiny and yellow — worked instantly, every time he felt his stomach flare up. The new pills — green, less expensive, and with a different name — did not work in the least. He then produced the prescriptions to show me. Both pills were actually the same chemically. One listed its well-known brand name, the other its generic Latin name. The yellow capsule was taken with the expectation of improved health, and it produced exactly that result. The green tablet, taken with heavy reservations, did just as poorly as was expected of it.

The reality, then, is that a good part of what makes us feel better is nothing more than marketing. Virtually all medicines could be made the same color; for example, white. However, after all the scientific research has determined the exact combination of molecules to comprise the medication, the drug companies then spend additional large sums to find out which cosmetic appearance will be the most effective for each group of patients. This is how colors, shapes, flavors, sizes, prices, and dosages of each new medicine are test marketed. In other words, if it is found that a bold red pill is the best format for fighting arthritis, while a soothing blue pill makes a better anti-depressant, then these colors will contribute to the overall effect of the healing process.

In the modern workplace, a similar placebo power can be harnessed in a number of nonmedical ways, without risk of side effects. For example, if you always feel serene and peaceful at the cottage in the summer time, then a photograph of your favorite fishing hole can bring back those feelings in the midst of the hustle of a city job. So too can the sounds of rain on the cottage roof, birds on the water, or wind in the trees. These tapes can be store-bought, recorded yourself, or — if you are particularly good at self-suggestion — simply imagined.

9. HOBBIES

Hobbies can do a lot to divert our attention from the stresses of work, especially when they force us to concentrate on something quite different. For example, if your work is high tech, a hobby such as building an old model sailing ship or train set could be highly therapeutic. If your job involves physical danger, then reading might be an excellent hobby. If your job is impersonal, your hobby might involve socializing in a club atmosphere.

Winston Churchill was able to cope with the awesome pressures of wartime leadership by painting in oils. (Churchill also tried his hand at bricklaying, but his skills were apparently better applied to canvas than to clay.) The list of hobbies is happily endless, but the most important aspect is that you choose one that fits into your lifestyle, aptitudes, and time schedule. Your hobby should be one that distracts you from your work stresses, and that motivates a sense of mission in this compartment of your life.

10. HUMOR

Laughs can save lives. Humor has the power to release high levels of endorphines and cortisols to make us feel better and heal better. Laughter can provide an essential escape from stress, and can literally prevent heart attacks, nervous breakdowns, and suicidal tendencies. As Norman Cousins illustrated in his books and articles on the subject, laughter can release the powerful "doctor within" us that Albert Schweitzer first noticed among his African patients. In terms of the modern workplace, the levels of laughter seem to fill the levels of need, as seen in what I term the other D.J.I.

I refer not to the Dow Jones Index, but that other powerful indicator of the stress levels in the marketplace, the Daily Joke Index. When times are good, stable, and prosperous, nobody at work seems to have heard any good jokes lately. The value of a good laugh is deemed to be minimal, and thus the D.J.I. is low. However, tough times seem to provide the ideal medium for jokes to flourish and abound. An atmosphere of economic depression means that a premium is placed on the value of a good, relieving laugh, and the D.J.I. is high. The consistency of this index is remarkable, in all kinds of industries, in all kinds of cultures, all over the world.

As opposed to negative, sick humor at the expense of others (such as the terrible "gallows humor" that circulated after the African famine, the assassination attempt on the Pope, and the AIDS death of Rock Hudson), the full benefits of humor can only be applied by laughing *with* others, or *at* ourselves.

Humor, hobbies, placebos, positive imagery, fashion, acupuncture, art, music, biofeedback, the relaxation response — all these options are open to you. They can be powerful de-stressing tools not only in the workplace, but in all compartments of your life.

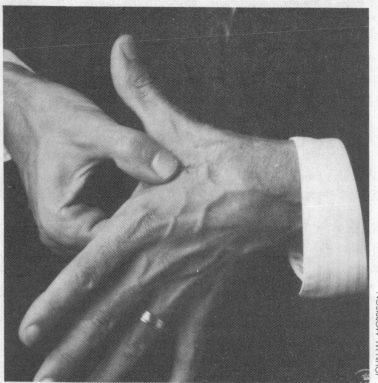

Chapter 11

USING STRESS TO FIGHT STRESS

STRESS CURES AND HOW THEY WORK

When a grass fire is raging out of control, we can douse it or burn off key areas ahead of its progress so that the fire will run out of fuel. In other words, we can fight fire with water or we can fight it with fire. In a similar way, we can fight stress with the seemingly contradictory weapons of relaxation (see chapter 10) or with more stress. Depending on the situation, one or both of these may be appropriate to help close the doors to other compartments of our lives (other than the work compartment), and thus prevent the stress of work from overwhelming the rest of our lives. A stress cure, which often involves high stress, works only if it applies a different stress from the one that is bothering you at work.

Many of us have paid to buy stress on a rollercoaster, and the memories do not soon fade. As soon as our car has reached the top and begun its sudden descent, our stomachs are suspended midway up our chest cavities, our heads are thrust back, our hearts race, and every muscle tenses.

Mentally, there is great stress, requiring the most intense concentration and the focusing of the mind on a new task; namely hanging on for dear life. Not one person in any rollercoaster car is talking about the office as the car hurtles down the rails. Thus, the stresses of one's work can be effectively displaced by stresses of quite another kind. This allows the brain to regenerate its circuits back in the work compartment.

Stress cures need not be as exciting as that. They can be as mild as the commitment to keeping score during a round of golf, or paying tuition and facing examinations in adult education courses. The discipline and study required generate more stress than would be the case in hitting a plastic golf ball on your lawn or studying at your own speed.

The more modest levels of stress, such as studying for an exam or playing a few holes of golf, may be helpful as a part of one's daily routine. However, the most dramatic levels of stress, such as rappelling down a cliff face, need not be used as often. These more dramatic stresses will occupy one's mind during the months of preparation before the event, as well as provide strong memories afterwards. People have dined out on such stories for years!

The type of alternate activity that we choose for our stress cure depends on the types of stresses we face in our work. It would thus make sense that, with our high-tech work environments, many of us should consider cures that offer more primitive, high-touch stresses, such as those found in natural outdoor settings. With time being so overprogrammed in our lives, it would be desirable for our chosen stress cures not to require bringing along a stopwatch. Since most of our jobs are sedentary, we should also seek some exercise. No one stress cure method is best for all. The following Outward Bound method is cited as an excellent example from among the many stress-cure possibilities that exist.

THE OUTWARD BOUND STRESS-CURE METHOD

Founded by Kurt Hahn, a distinguished educator who founded the Gordonstown school in Scotland, the organization known as

Outward Bound has become one of the best vehicles for injecting high stress cures into the lives of sedentary workers. As well,
it offers a sort of civilian "boot camp" for youth over the age of 14.

In 1940 Hahn noted, with considerable concern, that younger
members of the crews of sunken convoy ships did not survive
as well as their older mates in the icy waters of the North Atlan-
tic. It was found that the teenaged boys were more likely to see
their ship as a symbol of stability. Once it was gone, they were
more likely to soon give up hope of survival. The older salts
seemed to have a much greater fount of mental strength to draw
upon, and thus had a better chance to save their lives in the face
of the same fearful stresses.

Motivated by such observations, Hahn founded the first Outward Bound school in Wales in 1941. The same principles of using
stress to improve survival skills were found to be just as relevant after World War II ended in 1945. They have continued to
prove their worth in over 30 schools around the world today.

In addition to teaching the young, Outward Bound, a non-profit
organization, has become a popular outlet for deskbound office
workers, from executives to the rank and file, and from the ath-
letic to the elderly and even cancer victims.

LAURIE SKRESLET

The various Outward Bound options include the Mountain School, the Sea School, and the Wilderness School. The stresses involved in each can change with the seasons. In all disciplines, new stresses completely distracted the participant from the ones left behind. Some of these new stresses include rock climbing, digging snow caves for a night's shelter, surviving in wilderness and ocean settings, and kayaking down whitewater rapids.

Apart from the simple act of replacing one stress with another, to allow one to recover from the original stress, these courses teach powerful lessons about the hidden strengths that lie in the individual, and about the even greater strengths that lie in comradeship and teamwork. These lessons can be applied back at work to just as great an effect as in the field.

For example, if you've learned you can kayak down whitewater rapids and survive, dealing with the boss's pettiness back on the job becomes a much smaller problem than you once thought. If you've learned interdependence and mutual respect while climbing a steep rock slope with a team, it suddenly becomes a relatively simple matter to cooperate with your colleagues in solving that seemingly insurmountable problem in the warehouse. These benefits can be amplified by having "antagonists" on the same rope, such as representatives from labor and management. For each person who has chosen the Outward Bound method of stress cure, the organization's motto rings forever true: "To serve, to strive, and not to yield."

DR. JOE MacINNIS AND PRESSURE PROOFING

One of the foremost marine explorers, Canadian Joe MacInnis is a medical doctor and world authority on human performance in high-risk environments. Dr. MacInnis was the first person to scuba dive under the ice pack at the North Pole. He was the discoverer of the world's most northerly shipwreck, the *Breadalbane*, and has also been down to the deck of the *Titanic*.

Dr. MacInnis has taken citified workers, from union representatives, to executives, to prime ministers, to Prince Charles, to parts of the planet they would otherwise never have seen.

I have had the pleasure of working with Dr. MacInnis in seaside resorts in front of audiences from all over the world. His approach to stress cures is unique. After a morning of his slide presentations and my talk on the positive value of well-managed stress, seminar participants are taken out for a "Discovery Day." Landlubbers are given professional training by qualified scuba instructors, and then taken under the ocean for their first look at the wonders it contains.

Sometimes Dr. MacInnis takes participants to see coral formations, and to marvel at the brilliantly-colored fish that inhabit the shallow reefs in places such as Bermuda and Florida. Other times he takes them deeper. He has even taken some down to explore sunken Spanish galleons from a bygone time. For each of the participants, such gripping adventures will form the basis for stories they will tell their grandchildren. The memories will far outlast those of just another routine holiday at the beach.

By using real "hands-on" experiences to reinforce the verbal and slide presentations, Dr. MacInnis aims to prove to people that they have great reserves of strength to "pressure-proof" themselves. These reserves can be applied back on dry land just as well as in the ocean depths.

CHOOSE YOUR OWN ADVENTURE

In many other cases, people have chosen to use their own imaginations and aptitudes to seek their own stress cures. For Paul Newman, the best way to offset the stresses of the movie industry is to buckle up and drive his racing cars around the most demanding tracks in the world. Robert Redford skis the high powder snows. Other people buy high-risk shares in oil wells, gamble in casinos, or spend their vacations living in primitive jungle conditions, using their unique skills to help improve the basic quality of life among underprivileged local people.

There is real danger in all such endeavors, which could result in loss of health, loss of life, or loss of fortune. It therefore behooves the participants to play it smart. There is no benefit in being a showoff and tackling a winter mountain with no skills or guide. There is no sense in trekking off into the jungle as a heroic health care worker without proper immunization against local diseases. There is no wisdom in kayaking down rapids with a group of drunken amateurs. There is no glory in betting the farm at a casino and coming home wearing a barrel. Whatever stress cure you choose, never place yourself in unnecessary jeopardy.

It is best if your stress cure offers you a *perceived* risk rather than an ill-prepared-for *real* one. Thus it is best that you seek expert advice and guidance so that you will not recklessly expose yourself to unnecessary danger.

The human capacity to withstand stress is formidable. The positive imagery and depth of resourcefulness that stress cures bring out in us can be a kind of "rehearsal" for work stresses. They can give even the most pessimistic worker cause for inspiration, confidence, optimism, and renewed vigor.

Chapter 12

MENTAL FITNESS AND VERSATILITY IN THE WORKPLACE

THE IMPORTANCE OF MENTAL FITNESS

Victory against work stresses requires a lot more than money. It requires a new spirit of cooperation between all levels in an organization. No longer can a company improve its profitability by sending out insensitive notices such as "firings will continue until morale improves." The following is becoming an axiom of today's enlightened managers: "People are not a cost; they are a resource." Just as it takes time and money to extract rich metals buried in the ground, it takes time and money to bring people's mental resources to the surface. However, it is only by making commitments to do so that long-term profits can be maximized.

In terms of today's workplace, the tools needed are not in the form of "hardware" such as picks and shovels, but in the form of "software" such as practical seminars and study sessions, with books, tapes, and lectures from selected experts. For the first time in the history of modern work, the interests of business owners and employees have converged into the same humanitarian path.

The late American golf great Bobby Jones was once asked what the most difficult distance on the golf course was for him. He replied that it was not the 200-yard approach shot or the 20-foot putt, but the distance of six inches that mattered most: the space between his ears. The same is true for all of us, whether our business is professional sport, word processing, or people management.

Investments in one's mental fitness for work will pay handsome dividends, whether the resources of time, money, and energy are underwritten by one's organization, or one has to go it alone at a necessarily slower pace. By learning the latest development in one's field, adopting a positive approach, and keeping the versatile side of the brain alert to new solutions, one can actively reduce the number of "bad days" each week, increase personal morale, and improve the overall efficiency and viability of one's business.

Let's take a closer look at two particularly important aspects of mental fitness — positive thinking and versatility.

POSITIVE THINKING AND REALITY

Millions of people have read the book *The Power of Positive Thinking*. However, even its author, Dr. Norman Vincent Peale, would agree that, without realistic goals and positive behavior, positive thinking alone is not enough.

We have all seen positive-thinking political candidates on the eve of a landslide defeat still insisting they can sense victory in spite of the polls. Positive thinking alone will not guarantee top marks for a student on her upcoming final exam, if she has never studied or attended classes. Positive thinking that is unsupported by any cooperative actions can become simply wishful thinking. This was demonstrated by the great positive thinker, Mohammed Ali, near the end of his fabulous boxing career. Appearing for his later fights out of shape, overweight, and showing signs of having been hit by too many punches, Ali's positive boast of "I'm the greatest" fell sadly short. He retained his positive attitude, but lost his realistic goals and appropriate behavior leading to those goals.

On the other hand, even the best-trained people will never win if they lack positive mental images, because the resulting lack of confidence will always distract concentration and diminish ability.

I have spoken to a number of Apollo astronauts, and asked them if it ever occurred to them that their spacecraft might not get back to earth. Without exception, they hadn't really given that option much thought. Through simulator trials, the astronauts had been programmed to face almost any eventuality, but had never even considered being left to die on the moon. Fear was simply not to be taken along on the journey. There was no room for it as the trained brains were filled to capacity with scientific data, along with positive images.

Athletes use similar mental techniques to achieve heights of excellence in their work. Baseball's great Babe Ruth used to step up to the plate and point to the spot in the outfield bleachers where he proposed to hit the ball. Although he didn't succeed with every pitch, or even in every game, he did enact his prediction enough times to set baseball history.

In a more recent example from the world of sports, hockey great Wayne Gretzky was interviewed before the second game of a playoff series. His team then, the Edmonton Oilers, had not looked good in losing the first game, and the interviewers asked whether Coach Glen Sather had shown the players their mistakes on video.

Gretzky's response was illuminating. Rather than showing only errors on the video, which would have mentally reinforced the wrong images, Sather showed highlights of the players performing well. His strategy has certainly proven effective, and in this particular case the Oilers stormed back to win that second game and subsequently take the Stanley Cup.

The same powerful principles of imagery apply to enhancing performances in the working world. Rather than taking untrained young graduates and plunging them into stressful work situations, enlightened companies are first investing in the building of positive images to enhance performance and confidence. Imagined experiences can be as good as real ones in building up a store of confidence.

For example, videotapes and role-playing seminars can prepare inexperienced sales trainees for the kinds of objections they will encounter in the field. Demonstrations by talented professionals on how to overcome these objections will leave trainees justifiably enthused instead of pessimistically terrified when they make their first real calls. The learned premonition becomes the earned outcome.

In any job, a style of language can set the tone for a positive or negative approach. The power of words in establishing an image has long been recognized by public relations and promotion experts. For example, the careful turn of a copywriter's phrase can make or break an advertising and marketing campaign. A major promotion for a new hot dog weiner could be a success if the featured ingredients included "beef by-products," but could fail miserably if the more graphic "animal lips" were mentioned.

However, even more influential than the choice of words to sell products or concepts to large audiences is the impact of the

wording of our internal communications, otherwise known as
"self-talk." For example, Sharon, the boss, tells two of her office
managers that they will be giving a presentation to a company
sales meeting with over 100 people in the audience. Josh sets
a negative tone to the project and undermines his mental fitness
by saying to himself, "Oh no, I've *got* to give a speech." Les,
on the other hand, gives his mental fitness a positive boost by
saying to himself, "Now I *get* to give a speech." It should come
as no great surprise that Les makes the better speech.

With so much of our economy now based on service industries, the positive attitude behind every employee's smile
becomes an essential ingredient for success in the workplace.
An individual who thinks positively and gravitates towards positive-
thinking friends and colleagues, or a corporation that consciously
nurtures a positive culture, will always outperform those who
wallow in doom and gloom.

MENTAL VERSATILITY AND THE ANATOMY OF THE BRAIN

In Treviso, a little walled town north of Venice, Italy, a promising young boy of 10 quit school to support his sister and two
younger brothers when the father of the family died. Luciano
worked in a clothing store, and his eight-year-old sister Guiliana
stayed home sewing sweaters for a local manufacturer. Guiliana's
design skills soon became better than those of the people she
worked for.

Young Luciano, using the versatile side of his brain to dream
the unconventional dream, encouraged his sister to do more knit-
ting. He began "repping" her sweaters to store buyers, often
using his bicycle to get around. Luciano's first break came when
he did a roaring trade with a load of his sister's sweaters that
he took to the Rome Olympics in 1960.

Five years later, Luciano and Guiliana Benetton, along with their younger brothers Carlo and Gilberto, opened their first production facility. Today they oversee an empire spanning all continents, with sales of over a billion dollars per year. Building an empire in a field where none had grown before, the Benettons, who all still live in their little home town of Treviso, forged their way to success with style.

Mental versatility such as that shown by the Benettons is a key ingredient of success and of managing modern stress. Although outstanding individual examples abound, in most people versatility does not just flourish on its own, but must be nurtured carefully. That nurturing begins with an anatomical understanding of where versatility lies in the brain.

THREE MAJOR PARTS OF THE BRAIN

The lower brain stem is home to all the primitive reflexes that are triggered by our "fight or flight" stress response. These reflexes include the racing of the heart, the outpouring of adrenaline and cortisone, the increase of TSH (the precursor of thyroid hormone), and the dilating of our pupils.

The left hemisphere of the brain is the side that absorbs all our memorized data. In this hemisphere we store phone numbers, addresses, facts, and past details. With the left hemisphere, an actor can memorize whole scripts, and a mathematician whole theorems. Linear, logical thinking is done here, and instructions are memorized that will help an assembly line worker know exactly what steps to follow the next time there is a breakdown in part of the plant machinery. Through this side of the brain, people can be made much alike, reciting the same poems, playing the same songs on their musical instruments, and having memorized the same cultural and political history.

The right hemisphere of the brain is the seat of imagination, of versatility, and of creativity. It is this side of the brain that gives a child whimsy, or an adult a playful sense of humor. It is this side of the brain that the composer uses to write a new song, or the artist to paint a new image.

The right hemisphere creates new inventions, new strategies, and bold designs. It is this side of the brain that can come up with a new end-run when the traditional linear lines of attack have failed. In other words, this is the source of our best weapon to fight modern stresses in the workplace. (References here to the functions of the left and right sides of the brain are for right-handed persons. These functions are in the opposite hemispheres of left-handed people.)

In today's tough markets, a product line that stays on top of the heap for a year is doing well, and even a great product may be eclipsed in 18 months. Thus versatility is critical to survive and thrive in business. It is the right brain hemisphere that we need to fight the new stresses of the Information Age, in which the rote regurgitation of what has been tried before will often not be relevant.

The division of labor among the three brain areas means that versatility is discrete, and has nothing to do with intelligence (although it can't hurt to have a well-stocked databank in the left brain). Thus the way to harness it at work is often simply to utilize the suggestion box. The best solution to a problem that has been stumping the high-priced help may come from a summer high school student on the plant floor, or from the suggestion of a customer. Similarly, at home, the solution to your next problem may come "out of the mouths of babes."

WHY NOT TRY AN IDEA INCUBATOR?

Mental fitness can be maintained and honed by physically defining a separate compartment, such as the Japanese "idea incubator" room to sit and use the other side of your brain. Simple tricks of decor and sound effects can provide a completely different environment for counterpoint to the routine kinds of stimulation that pervade your work.

VERSATILITY AND INTELLIGENCE

The world-famous pioneer of stress research, Montreal's Dr. Hans Selye, once told me of an experience that happened to him in Harvard in 1940. Selye, along with a number of eminent experts in medical research, were having lunch in the staff cafeteria when they were joined by a Harvard bacteriology professor. He was having a terrible day, and needed the group's help urgently.

It transpired that the professor had been out of town over the weekend, and had returned to find a disaster. Some "idiot" had left a cheese sandwich on the lab bench on Friday, and it had grown moldy. When the professor returned on Monday, he found that the mold had killed all his beautiful bacteria cultures, which he had been planning to photograph for textbooks.

The brain trust around the table sprang into action. They all canceled the rest of their schedules for the day and stayed at the table with pads of paper and sharp pencils, trying to work out the best solution. After midnight, the experts adjourned for sleep, and then reconvened at dawn in the bacteriology lab, ready to put their plan into action.

They donned special masks and fumigated the whole lab. They boiled all the petri dishes, and sterilized all the instruments.

Pleased with their concerted efforts, the medical researchers then helped the bacteriologist set up new plates so he could start his cultures all over again. They all agreed that it was a good thing this had happened at Harvard, because this was a place where it was possible to assemble some of the most intelligent medical brains in the world to solve the problem.

Unfortunately, each expert was using only his left brain, attacking the problem from the traditional point of view. What they missed, even though it was growing right under their noses, was penicillin.

Penicillin, though discovered years before, had not yet come into general use. If, instead of concentrating on how to kill the mold, the researchers had instead concentrated on how to use it, many lives would have been saved. Alas, they missed their opportunity.

However, supposing one of the brilliant experts had asked the opinion of the woman who was clearing their trays off the cafeteria table. She might well have said, "So you fellows have this fuzz that's killing all your germs. I thought germs caused people to get sick. Isn't there some way to use your fuzz to make people healthy?"

Now, a member of the cafeteria cleanup staff might not seem worthy of a consultation at this level of academia, because she would probably have none of their lofty left-brain academic degrees. She might not even possess a grade school diploma, never mind postgraduate letters after her name.

However, because creative solutions come from a different side of the brain than memorized intelligence, the cafeteria staff member's versatile hemisphere had just as much chance of developing a solution as the learned professors' versatile hemispheres.

Similarly a staff suggestion box, or feedback cards from customers and suppliers, can yield a motherlode of brilliant suggestions that can solve the next problem you are stumped with. Many modifications to computerized parts that put human beings on the moon, and simple household inventions such as the paperclip and adhesive tape, which we now take for granted, have had humble beginnings. In this age of change, victories against stress will be made by those who can harness creativity by drawing on their own right hemispheres, as well as the right hemispheres of those around them.

It is also the creative side of the brain that sees the humor and the ridiculousness of our actions, and offers us the benefits of laughter. (It is the left hemisphere that memorizes other people's jokes.) Whenever you find yourself baffled by a problem that seems to defy all traditional solutions, which will happen more and more often in the future, try switching over to the versatile side of your brain for the solution. Even if you don't immediately come up with the answer, you may well have a good therapeutic laugh.

MAKING BETTER USE OF THE BRAIN'S VERSATILE SIDE

As a medical doctor, I have worked with many patients who have suffered strokes on one side or other of the brain. In watching them recover the lost facets of each side through the attentive care of nurses and occupational and physiotherapists, I've discovered some lessons that can help all of us learn to make better use of the creative sides of our own brains:

• Do not trace; do not copy. Start with a fresh blank page and try your own drawings. Make your own images.
• If you can play a musical instrument, spend some of your time trying new chord progressions, or even arrangements of existing melodies. Although one still needs to fill up the mental data-bank with examples of other people's songs, remember to balance these exercises with a few for the creative side. Don't be afraid to meet the challenge of putting together a whole new arrangement or song, even if you are the only one who ever hears it.

• Listen to the great humorists, or read some of their thoughts, because they can provide excellent examples of how to view things through the versatile side. Steve Allen, in his book *How to Be Funny*, points out that the best way to stimulate humorous thinking is to keep the company of people who are funny. The next best thing, if all your friends are dour, is to read and listen to the best.

A waiter working in a restaurant next to a theater complex told me that he could tell which "tables" had just come out of the Robin Williams movie, because those groups were wisecracking, taking the waiter's comments out of context, keying in on alternate meanings of words or phrases, and generally having fun. It is obvious that versatility can be learned, and without any pain.

• Be a student of history, with a view to extracting past examples of versatility that might have relevance to your own stresses. Some excellent examples are found in military history; for instance, in a case where a general or admiral rejected the traditional strategies of the day. Before Horatio Nelson fought the combined French and Spanish fleets off the coast of Trafalgar, lines of opposing battleships almost always converged in parallel lines to fire at each other. However, Nelson was outnumbered and outgunned; thus this tactic would probably have led to defeat.

Instead, Nelson's right brain came up with a new idea; namely, attacking in two parallel columns at right angles to the enemy. As a result, he broke the enemy line into thirds, and effectively removed the enemy's front ships from the battle. Nelson called his plan the "Nelson Touch," and it helped earn him his place in history.

The same quality of versatility from highly active right brains has created legends in all walks of life. From explorers who dared to defy past wisdom (the world was flat) and sail out in search of new lands to business legends such as Lee Iacocca and Howard Hughes, an active right side of the brain has always been a stepping stone to success in the face of stress.

• Be a student of the fine arts, as well as of your own chosen field. A few hours spent in an art gallery or museum can rest the electrical circuits of the left brain. Looking at works of art allows you to imagine the vision that brought light to a picture, or that released the beautiful statues once buried in blocks of marble.

An overworked clerical employee or executive can get a lot more out of a 10-minute noontime stroll in the park if he or she notices the details of light and shadow in the trees, or the juxtaposition of colors between natural and humanly created structures, or simply watches the people pass by, imagining how great artists might interpret the scenes.

Liberal arts courses offered in universities are seeing renewed interest, because more people are recognizing the need to improve interpersonal skills and understanding of the humanities. This is what separates an education from a purely technical training. The arts are a healthy part of the curriculum of job-oriented courses such as business and the professions.

• Reach for the possible, not just the expected. Walt Disney had a famous motto that summed up his life's accomplishments: "If you can dream it, you can do it." When people are discounting your ideas because, "It's never been done that way before," then you know you are probably on the right track. Treat past experiences as a set of building blocks. Tear them down and rearrange them to see what the possible solutions could be.

Adults at work can learn a lot from children at play. When a child is presented with a pile of odd blocks and asked to build something, he or she will reverse, rearrange, substitute, and otherwise modify the pieces to make them fit the problem. When others were asking, "How can we get the customers to come to us?" Mary Kay substituted elements of the problem to ask, "Why not have us take the products to the customers?" Her enormous cosmetics empire was thus born.

Estée Lauder, using her versatility and vision to come up with a totally different approach to the same industry, created her international dynasty. Thus it is clear that there are many pathways to a particular goal.

You can use similar techniques just as easily, and the results can be just as rewarding. When others ask you how to improve profits by cutting more costs, rearrange the elements of the problem. Perhaps spending a little money on employee training would result in improved customer service, which might generate a lot more profits, especially if all your competition is cutting down on their personnel.

During the famous silver rush brought on by the Hunt brothers' speculations, investors were rushing to sell stocks in film manufacturers such as Kodak, fearing that the high price of the silver ingredients would hurt the industry. However, versatile investors discovered that the incremental rises in the price of silver would have very little effect on the price of the finished film, so they reversed their thinking and bought stocks. What happened, of course, is that film prices increased dramatically. Silver then crashed from about $50 to $5, but the price of film stayed right where the high silver markets had taken it. Stock prices soared, and the versatile thinkers were smiling.

• Even though English is acknowledged as the "universal" language, the act of learning a new language is an excellent way to develop one's versatility. Assuming the language is not an esoteric or dead one, there will be added benefits in terms of relating to people from different cultures and markets. These benefits will be seen readily when one travels to another country, hosts visitors from another country, or conducts business abroad.

In North America there has not been a historical tendency for English-speaking people to learn another language. However, with the tremendous advantage of having immigrants from almost every country in the world living in close proximity, there is the unique potential for greater use to be made of this untapped resource. Fluent teachers and tutors can readily be found. Radio and television transmissions in foreign languages can be tuned in. Magazines and publications in foreign languages can be readily obtained. Most importantly, daily practice with neighbors and your customers can reinforce greater levels of fluency than all the lessons in the world.

Countries without this rich cultural mix, such as Japan, cannot find such a ready source of exposure to these added stimuli in their lives. Even so, the Japanese have been able to teach second and third languages in schools, language labs, and with the ever popular tapeplayers in evidence on every bus and train. For a good deal of their listening time, the teenagers are learning their English lessons instead of just tuning in the local disc jockey. The result of these techniques in developing new patterns of thought are beneficial to both the individuals and to their businesses, as foreign languages broaden their ability to expand into new markets.

Chapter 13

PHYSICAL, NUTRITIONAL, AND ENVIRONMENTAL FITNESS

WORKPLACE FITNESS — NOW MORE IMPORTANT THAN EVER

The profitability and productivity of any business depend on the fitness of its individual components. Throughout the Industrial Age, poorly maintained mechanical components were clearly seen as poor management, because the results would be the breakdown of the assembly line or even the whole factory. Now that the Information Age has replaced the simplicities of machines with the complexities of people, the consequences of poor maintenance at work are less obvious, but just as serious.

However, it seems that there has been as little attention paid to prevention in the workplace as there has in the rest of our health care, and it shows. Incompetent management of human resources, by both employers and the employees themselves, is the single greatest waste in the cost of doing business in the world today. For people who own any business, large or small, this is the equivalent of handing every worker a $100 bill every Monday morning, making sure the workers set fire to their bills, and then telling them their jobs are in jeopardy because they can't seem to control costs.

When companies are in financial troubles, the "soft" costs of maintaining employees' physical fitness are usually the first to be axed, when top management starts playing more "by the book." The company aerobics classes are deemed unnecessary, and budgets for training seminars to improve mental fitness and facilities for exercise to improve physical fitness are slashed. Morale and motivation among employees suffer.

At a time when competition allows only the strong to survive, there is a real long-term danger to cutting down prevention budgets. It is relatively easy to cut down spending from "fat and slothful" to "lean and mean." But continued enthusiasm for spending cuts can easily cross the fine line into "thin and frail." Individuals and their companies both share a stake in trying to achieve the best possible physical health and fitness at work.

The traditional North American business school approach worked well for over a century, until the 1970s, when technology revolutionized the workplace. Since then, a new style of management has emerged, first popularized by the Japanese (borrowing heavily from unappreciated American innovations such as Westinghouse's "quality circles"). The results have taken the traditional business world by storm, pushing the United States out of sole possession of world economic leadership and beating the traditional experts at their own games.

The principal exports out of New York harbor to Japan are now scrap steel and waste paper. These materials are processed and shipped back to the States in the form of automobiles and cardboard boxes containing electronic equipment. Japanese shipbuilders have so outperformed the world champion Scots that the once bustling shipyards on the banks of the Clyde now sit relatively deserted. The Germans once had a monopoly on high quality cameras and optics, but today sell only a small fraction of the world's lenses, having lost a good share of the market to their Far Eastern competitors. The Swiss used to be the watchmakers for the world, and now find they are being heavily outsold by Asian brands. American banks, which used to fill the list of most important financial institutions in the world, now occupy only one spot out of the top 10, being surpassed by Japanese and European banks.

It has thus become painfully obvious to all levels of the workplace that old approaches to new realities are doomed to failure. The traditional disregard for individual fitness, both by management and by the workers themselves, has been shown to be economic suicide.

The Japanese miracle since 1945 cannot be attributed to simple good luck; it has been due in no small measure to an enlightened approach to the fitness of people in the workplace. This tactic has also proved to be a key to success when used in other countries.

To maximize personal and corporate potentials, the ideal preventative medical plan should address the following areas of fitness for work: mental, physical, nutritional, and environmental. The area of mental fitness is so important and extensive that it warranted a chapter of its own (see chapter 12, Mental Fitness and Versatility in the Workplace). In this chapter we will consider the other three areas of workplace fitness.

PHYSICAL FITNESS AND THE WORKPLACE

Until relatively recently, the work that most people did gave them plenty of exercise on the job. Our bodies are built for motion, but in the modern era of sedentary information processing, we receive little. For all the attention given to complicated fad diets, it still remains that the most effective way to reduce the risk of a heart attack is simply to exercise at least three hours per week.

If you are out of shape, then have a preliminary examination by your doctor. A consultation with a fitness professional can help customize exercises to fit your needs. If you have not had an exercise ECG, the old rule of keeping your exercising pulse rate at or below 180 minus your age is a good guideline.

Remember also to check your pulse in the sauna, steambath, or whirlpool, as overheating the body will cause the same skyrocketing of the pulse rate as seen with too much exercise. A sudden heart attack can be the result. (I do not recommend prolonged heating of the body immediately after a vigorous workout, as the body temperature will already be elevated enough.)

Although the body should have at least three hours of exercise per week, even greater benefits can be achieved by exercising daily. To do so on one's own time requires a modicum of discipline, which is usually missing in the population at large. (If one is ever in doubt of this phenomenon, one needs only to sit on a park bench in a crowded amusement park and observe the body shapes of the vast majority of the general public.)

Exercise not only benefits physical fitness, but also helps our mental outlook and our approach to work. By releasing the body's own stores of endorphine, exercise can give a sense of well-being, relief of minor aches and pains, and a mild euphoria: all elements that people become addicted to.

Indeed, many people do get withdrawal symptoms when they stop exercising. They develop all the reactions of exercise deprivation: loss of energy, increased aches and pains, and depression. Fortunately, addiction to exercise is perfectly benign, and treatable by returning to more exercise.

WORKING WORKOUTS INTO YOUR LIFE

When you just can't find time to fit fitness into your work, try to fit it into the other compartments of your life. Following are some suggested workout routines for the home, fitness club, and even for the hotel room when you're away on a business or personal trip.

Companies are increasingly instituting fitness programs at work, and these are proving to be popular beyond initial expectations. These programs are best if they address the needs of the whole staff. White collar workers, in general, are somewhat more aware of fitness issues, and tend to do more exercises than blue collar workers. However, the physical strain of manual labor places blue collar workers at greater risk of physical injury, which means that this group will benefit even more from physical fitness and warm-up exercises before each shift.

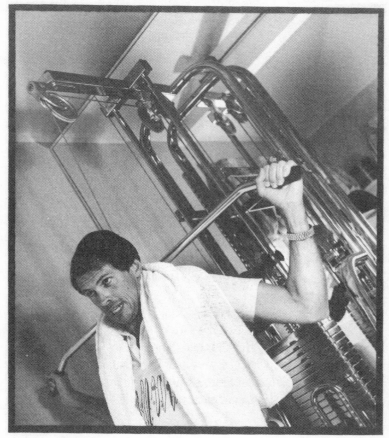

JOHN W. MORRISON

Most company fitness programs are voluntary, taking place during the lunch hour or at either end of the workday. Even with only 40% of the workforce participating, companies have noted an increase in morale, loyalty, and productivity, and a marked decrease in absenteeism. Participating employees have a consistently better attitude towards their jobs, and are more able to cope with stresses when they occur.

The per capita cost of physical fitness classes and facilities decreases tremendously when attendance is compulsory. In today's free societies, compulsory attendance might seem difficult to enforce, but not when the activities are scheduled on company time and when the nature of these exercises is compatible with the interests of the staff. The time could be as brief as 20 minutes, which is less time than most employees spend on coffee-and-donut breaks. The Japanese have learned this lesson well, and encourage aerobic and stretching exercises on company time to start each workday. Many European and North American competitors are following this lead, with similar good results (though disguising the exercises in different sports, dances, or martial arts, depending on the culture). The costs to the company are more than repaid by the increased productivity, attendance, and attention to quality displayed by workers who are physically fit.

One practical point to note is that, unlike soldiers, not all workers will be of the same age, or share the general good health of their coworkers. Some may have particular health problems that would preclude their joining their peers in exercise sessions, but they could still participate in modified levels of stretching and toning. In larger organizations, workers with similar levels of fitness can form their own groups and exercise at a pace appropriate to each group.

Obviously, it would be advisable for all employees to have a full medical examination before they start an exercise program, and any special recommendations should be followed. (In addition to suggesting particular levels of exercises to some of my patients, I have also sometimes recommended particular modifications in clothing such as appropriate footware or support hose to help reduce leg and back pains.) Some health problems, such as tension headaches and chronic repetitive strain injuries, such as backaches and stiff shoulders, may indeed be improved by a daily fitness break at work. If obesity is a problem for some, then special incentives should be given to help these employees resume their ideal weight (no, I don't mean narrowing the doorways to the pay office).

Many companies, such as IBM, Sony, and Ross Perot's EDS, have a paternalistic approach to encouraging employees' physical fitness. Others, such as the Harris Corporation, find success in leaving it up to their employees, especially when they are scattered over decentralized locations. Due to the vast differences in size, complexity, and employee needs, it is impossible to impose one style of fitness training that will be the most cost and time effective for all companies.

Actually the most successful plans have not been the ones imposed by consultants, from the top down, but those that have been developed by the employees themselves. Drawing from the good and bad experiences of competitors and using a suggestion box to keep the lines of creativity open from all levels in an organization, uniquely effective ways to encourage corporate fitness have been developed.

Workers in one plant or branch office may prefer to start an in-house baseball league, or set up contests such as tug-of-wars or regular team relay races. One energetic group in a large insurance company devised a contest to swim around the world. Each employee would try to swim a few miles a week in the company pool and record the results on a master sheet in the office. At the end of a few years, the cumulative total of miles swum was calculated, and sponsors were tapped for a donation to charity.

Companies that lack their own fitness area can often take advantage of neighboring facilities. The Harte-Hanks corporation, in San Antonio, Texas, built its new head offices in the same building complex as an independent fitness club. Bob Marbut, the chief executive officer, listened to the suggestions of his staff and began a program whereby all office staff could have 50% of their club fees paid. By having his employees pay some portion of the dues themselves, much greater participation was ensured, than if the memberships were made free.

NUTRITIONAL FITNESS AND THE WORKPLACE

Early industrialists, although not noted for any excessive concern for their employees, achieved great wealth by pampering their inanimate printing presses, blast furnaces, and steam engines. Even when times were a little tight, they would economize anywhere but in the care, nurturing, and maintenance of these iron servants.

Today's sophisticated horse breeders have no difficulty recognizing the source of their incomes, and the animals are pampered accordingly. Nobody would ever think of feeding a prize quarter-horse a bag of junk food before a race. Sensible marathon swimmers also recognize the importance of their bodies in their work, and pay careful attention to the nutrients they feed them. Obviously nobody would consume three helpings of prunes before diving in to swim the Channel.

In today's competitive workplace, where people are the engines of profit, it is surprising to note the pervasiveness of poor nutritional maintenance, which can only diminish performance. For those who have an expense account, this form of self-sabotage can be seen in the traditional business lunch, with its huge portions of meat and alcohol, followed by huge portions of dessert and alcohol.

Top executives, in some cases making huge salaries, become passive seductees for an hour-long sales pitch if they are being treated to a $70 meal. If they were not being taken to a posh restaurant, they would never have given the pitch more than a few minutes of their precious time.

It is the constant excuse of pudgy, middleaged, pre-cardiac desk workers that they can't drop the required 20 pounds because they have expense account lunches. In just the same way that there are pastry chefs who remain thin, and movie stars who remain faithfully married, anyone who is eating "on the company" can also learn to resist the temptations of free fare.

Until recently, the etiquette for taking someone to a business lunch required that the host order the same size of meal as the guest, to avoid making the guest feel awkward. "Power lunch" specialists insisted that, even if your guest ordered a slab of brontosaurus, four double cocktails, and three desserts, it was essential for you to follow suit, even if you simply consumed your desired eating quantity and left the rest. The present attitude, fortunately, indicates that such large lunches are unnecessarily expensive and are, generally speaking, unhealthy for a person with a sedentary job. What is more commonly seen in North America today, are business lunches conducted over salads and Perrier.

The safest option is to avoid the old protocols and order whatever you feel your day's calorie burnoff would justify. A plausible excuse, (if one should even be needed) for choosing a more appropriate meal for yourself could be "doctor's orders," even if I am the only doctor who has ever mentioned it to you.

In the case of self-employed individuals, it is up to them to see the absurdity of temptations to eat or drink too much, and to instead take the kind of control over their food and drink intake that their bodies, minds, and careers require. In larger organizations, it helps if expense accounts are monitored, and if strict policies of alcohol avoidance during work hours are adhered to. A fuller discussion on alcoholism will be seen in chapters 14 and 15 but, in terms of nutritional fitness for work, even a moderate use of alcohol during business hours is detrimental and costly.

Companies that have their own cafeterias in house are in an ideal position to positively influence the nutritional fitness of employees. In addition to providing some basic form of labeling, such as listing calorie and nutritional contents of foods along with their prices, companies with their own eating facilities can see that the foods offered are skewed towards greater nutritional fitness. For example, substitute high fiber natural foods for artificial ones; one way is to offer wholewheat bread instead of the flannelette white variety. Enough good-quality protein should be provided to help stimulate the adrenaline pathways. (See chapter 9, jet lag diet.)

However, the passive presentation of good foods does not ensure such foods will be chosen. Even in a hospital setting, where good foods are readily available (if one knows which foods and, more importantly, which hospitals to look for), I have seen staff, including elite surgeons, cruise past the fresh vegetables and fruits. Instead, they will unthinkingly choose to fill their lunch trays with colas, chips and gravy, and ersatz desserts.

It may help you to think of your body as a finely tuned racing car. You should pay the appropriate attention to using the best blend of fuels to feed it. This is especially true in mid-race, at lunchtime. No matter how well the employees in any company are doing their job during the morning, if they fill their lunch tray with the wrong fuels, they will waddle out of the cafeteria all set for a nap, an antacid tablet, and a low-performance afternoon.

To encourage high performance instead, simple nutritional education can be included in the company newsletter, on the employee bulletin board, or right in the cafeteria. If applicable, the help of a dietician can be enlisted. For those workers who do not eat at a company cafeteria, the nutritional information provided can still be used as a guideline for the right foods off a menu or off a supermarket shelf.

ENVIRONMENTAL FITNESS AND THE WORKPLACE

Some simple and inexpensive adjustments to the workplace environment can make a big difference to performance, and to the reduction of stress. The most frequent complaint noted by occupational health and safety experts is poor air quality. It can cause acute illnesses such as nausea, or chronic problems such as headaches, lethargy, dizziness, and irritated eyes, nasal passages, and throat.

These conditions are often called the "sick building" syndrome, and are the result of hermetically sealed office buildings with insufficient fusion of fresh clean air. Computers and other machines generate heat, and can contribute to an overall sense of dryness in the air. Particularly if there are any smokers using the same air supply, even on a different floor, everyone will be breathing poisonous fumes in mild concentrations.

Secondhand smoke can be very damaging to non-smokers. I have seen many cases of lung cancers, emphysema, and heart diseases caused by cigarettes that the patient's spouse or coworkers smoked. Some people with heart disease are so sensitive to smoke that they develop angina when anyone smokes near them. Some have even died from entering a smoke-filled room. Thus, it is medically clear that a smoker's rights are only to harm themselves, and that the current moves to eliminate smoking from public places is fully justified, and will continue to grow.

Because of the widespread use of air conditioning in the modern office buildings, none of the windows open. This means that all the air supply to the occupants is shared, passed through a useless dust filter (carbon monoxide and other gaseous poisons in tobacco smoke pass right on through), and then recycled back to every corner and every floor of the building. In other words, the real question when a co-worker pulls out a cigarette in the coffee room is not, "Do you mind if I smoke?" but rather, "Do you mind if I force everyone in this building to smoke?"

The ultimate answer is not to try to reinvent a better air filtration system, or designate a particular room or floor as the smoking area. Tobacco smoke should be confined where it belongs: in the lungs, hair, and clothes of those consenting adults who have chosen to suck poison gas into their body as a way of "defending" themselves from stress. Because this ludicrous habit is a very personal choice, it should be condoned only on personal time and in a personal environment. In the workplace, the infliction of these clouds of toxins on innocent bystanders should not be tolerated. In North America, great strides are being made in this area, and for once are being put into practice more quickly than in Japan. Over half of all businesses in North America now have some form of smoking restriction in the workplace.

To keep workers and customers awake and alert in late evening hours, casino owners know that a fresh supply of clean air and, in some cases, the infusion of extra oxygen is immediately effective. What seems to be largely ignored, however, is that stale air has the opposite effect, making people drowsy and less efficient. In many buildings, landlords may actually cut down on ventilation to reduce heating and air conditioning costs.

If you are building a new office or renovating an old one, see what arrangements you can make for proper ventilation. Should you be currently renting or leasing, speak to the landlord if you find ventilation is poor, and strive to have improvements made. Many offices report that using an air ionizer or charcoal filter seems to help, but chemical ''fresheners'' usually just make everyone sneeze.

The following are other action tips on how to better design the work environment.

WORKPLACE STRESS: DEFEAT OR VICTORY BY DESIGN

Some characteristics of a poor work station:
- Chair too short.
- Desk too tall.
- Cigarette butts in ashtray.
- Permanent crook in neck from telephone.
- Squint due to glare and poor lighting.
- No reading stand—just an avalanche of papers.

Some characteristics of a good work station:
- Chair just right—adjustable for arm, seat, and back support, with the all important wheels for quick escapes for exercise breaks.
- Adjustable keyboard.
- Stand for reading at same height as screen.
- Top of screen at eye level, at a comfortable distance from the viewer.
- Optional shade to reduce glare from room lights.
- Incandescent lamp over reading stand, to counter fluorescents.
- Telephone headset if needed (or, if preferred, a headset attachment for the phone, to keep one's hands free to use the keyboard).
- Footrest if needed.
- Well organized desktop.
- Window or distant object to provide periodic long focus to rest eye muscles.

Chapter 14

SUBSTANCE ABUSE — THE LOSER'S OPTION

A DANGEROUS AND COSTLY PROBLEM

Substance abuse is the inappropriate ingestion of legal and/or illegal chemicals, drugs, and alcohol. Virtually all participants cite stress as one of the main reasons for starting their habit. The list of substances abused is broad. It includes cocaine, which currently produces the most headlines, alcohol, which causes the most damage, and nicotine, which causes the most deaths.

Substances have been abused in all parts of the world since the beginnings of civilization. Indeed, some tales of inebriation in ancient Egypt and Persia sound much like todays' headline stories.

Although the abuse of alcohol, chemicals, and drugs is truly an international problem, the most dramatic and well-studied abuses are in the United States. When addressing a group of 100 American workers, it is statistically safe to assume that 25 of them are abusing something; the figure rises to over 50 if we include those who use tobacco.

In terms of hard drugs, there are an estimated 25 million drug users in the United States alone, and over one million of them are medically addicted. They spend more money on drugs in a year than a company like General Motors earns. The great publicity this has been getting — with high profile "role models" such as movie and sports celebrities checking themselves in for detoxification or burial — has been substantial.

In counterpoint, there is a whole subculture of unheralded poor children being raised on "crack" and other street drugs. The ongoing costs of these habits propel users into a low life of high crime that has the added impact of threatening the safety and security of citizens and workers everywhere. The U.S. Justice Department notes that, in some cities, an astounding 8 out of 10 criminal defendants test positive for drug use. An alarming rise in youth gang wars is terrorizing shopkeepers and customers alike in areas of Los Angeles, San Francisco, Miami, and other cities.

However, between the headline stories of stars and street gangs, lies an even bigger story — that of substance abuse among average workers, from blue collar to executive suite. The hidden costs of poor concentration and higher error rates lead to dramatic losses of productivity, which can directly cause the demise of not only the individual, but affect the bottom line of an entire company.

To a self-employed worker, mistakes made while on drugs or alcohol can quickly mean bankruptcy. In larger companies, there is a greater reserve of capital, and an individual's mistakes might be compensated for by the nonabusing members of the staff. But such compensation is not without impact. When overall quality declines, or costs increase because some employees are not pulling their weight, then the entire organization can suffer.

The effects of substance abuse are considered to be a significant factor when comparing Japanese workers' efficient performance with the often less efficient performance of their Russian, North American, and other Western counterparts. In addition to the cold monetary arguments against substance abuse and the concern for the health of abusers, an even more compelling reason to deal with the problem lies in the area of public safety. Obviously this is true in such sensitive areas as transportation jobs, where an impaired driver or pilot can kill a lot of people. However, it is also true in many other jobs. Consider, for example, the workers who produce brakes for our cars, smoke alarms for our homes, and foods for our families. Furthermore, even if a substance-abusing worker is not likely to cause any direct damage to others while on the job, he or she might well become a killer once in the driver's seat of a car while returning home.

In a recent study of Navy P3-Orion pilots using simulators, the effects of as little as three ounces of spirits, or three glasses of beer or wine, dangerously impaired performance *even 14 hours later*, after blood levels had fallen to zero. This contradicts the prevalent opinion of private pilots who, according to a survey, believe it is safe to fly four hours after drinking. It is interesting to note that over 400 private pilots who augered their planes into the ground between 1968 and 1985 had postmortem blood-alcohol levels of over .04. One now wonders how many of the other 5,000 private pilots who died during that interval had been impaired by recent alcohol ingestion even though blood levels might have fallen to zero. Similar results have been shown in simulators when pilots are tested 24 hours after the ingestion of a single "joint" of marijuana.

It is certainly relevant that 80% of all air accidents in the world, whether commercial or private, are due to human error. The fact that pilots who have previously taken marijuana or alcohol often feel they are performing brilliantly causes considerable concern. The implications are significant for all weekend imbibers who return to jobs of potential danger, such as operators of heavy equipment, public transport, or even their own cars. It is no wonder that most work accidents take place on Mondays.

THE WHY, WHO, AND WHAT OF SUBSTANCE ABUSE

In the workplace, what initially gets people into substance abuse is complex, but what keeps them there is simple: the drugs make them feel good. A vicious cycle is thus built up, whereby the addiction enters the culture of the family, peers, or even the society. This encourages more people to experiment, and thus become addicted.

In most cases, the precipitating cause of substance abuse is related to stress: either too much or too little. Workers suffering from chronic boredom in an assembly line, or those who are laid off, might turn to substance abuse to add a little excitement to their weekly routine. On the other hand, those suffering from too much excitement, such as in middle management or the executive office, may seek drugs to help them relax. Soldiers suffering the incredible horrors of war may turn to drugs or alcohol as a quick escape from reality. Whatever the initial reason for abusing substances, they are highly habit forming. Initially it is the individual who abuses the drug, but soon it is the substance that abuses the individual.

Once thought to be the problem of lower social classes, substance abuse is now present in virtually all walks of life. The sight of millionaire stockbrokers being escorted off in handcuffs for trading in psychoactive commodities has put an end to the stereotype that drug abusers were simply indigents lounging in smoky opium dens, or street gangs in tough neighborhoods.

The list of substances abused is long, and varies considerably from one culture or region to another. It includes a broad range from the easily available (such as alcohol, cigarettes, hair tonics, and prescription drugs) to the illicit (such as narcotics and street chemicals). Self medication with drugs such as cough, cold, insomnia, and headache remedies has become so common that people consider these tablets and elixirs as harmless as condiments on the kitchen shelf. The emergency wards (and indeed morgues) have been kept busy by the tragic consequences of people overdosing on these "benign" drugs.

Some cases of abuse of common household remedies are the result of deliberate suicide attempts, and others are the result of accidental overdoses, such as by children, or adults who unknowingly take incompatible medications. Specific details about the substances most relevant to you can be obtained through your doctor, hospital, or a local public health office. A great many support groups are available to back up professional treatment programs.

CIGARETTES — A HAZARD TO HEALTH AND CAREER

As if the litany of medical reasons to quit using tobacco weren't enough, smoking has now been proven to be hazardous to your career. With a groundswell speed that has amazed even the most jaded observer, limitations on smoking in the workplace have recently affected nearly all U.S. and Canadian workers, with similar patterns following in the rest of the Western nations. Even in countries with strong smoking traditions, such as Japan and France, nonsmokers are starting to fight back. Increasingly nonsmokers (who are in the majority) aren't afraid to tell the truth when someone asks, "Mind if I smoke?"

However, despite all the health awareness and the ineffective warnings on cigarette packages (which serve mainly to protect cigarette manufacturers from future legal battles), many ardent nicotine addicts still insist on their freedom to smoke at work.

What is now giving smokers cause for second thoughts about igniting a rolled vegetable leaf is a simple bottom line fact: cigarettes are hazardous to your career. In the boardroom, it is now considered suicidal to a career to light up a cigarette while the nonsmoking chairperson glares down the table. For that matter, it is equally foolhardy to smoke in front of a nonsmoking client or prospective customer. Smoking can even make it difficult for job applicants to start a career. In the personnel offices of many companies, a cup of coffee is proferred to help the applicant feel at home during the interview, and an ashtray is placed in front of him or her as bait. If the applicant accepts the bait and lights up a cigarette, then the job will probably go to a nonsmoking candidate of equal qualifications.

The problem extends beyond the obvious costs to a company of having smokers on staff, and the costs to the health of the smoker and those sharing the same air. The image presented by a smoker lighting up is also a factor. It is an image of poor self control, lack of self discipline, and disregard for others. This negative image is why one rarely sees a corporate spokesperson (even from a cigarette company) or a politician risk lighting up in front of an audience.

As for smokers already on staff, many companies have taken a sympathetic approach initially, offering prospective quitters a carrot such as a monetary reward, instead of a stick such as, "You're fired." For example, Houston's BMC Software sends its employees to anti-smoking hypnosis sessions. Texas Instruments designs and builds special rooms for smokers, and keeps the rest of the workplace air clear.

Allstate has recently announced a ban on smoking in all its offices. Other companies, such as USG Interiors (because of the added risks of lung diseases in smokers who work with their insulation products) have gradually instituted a policy of non-smoking even in a worker's sparetime. In the case of USG, this drastic step was cushioned by educational discussions of the risks, as well as extensive "smoke-enders" classes on company time for all workers and their spouses. Over the course of a year, smokers were convinced (a few left the company), and today there is full compliance.

A LESSON FROM VIETNAM

Statistics can be boring, and most of us are immune to their impact after being bombarded with the latest ones in each day's newscasts. However, statistics, if visualized, can be powerful tools for motivation.

The Vietnam War Memorial in Washington, D.C., is a massive wedge-shaped wall of granite containing the names of every American soldier known to have died in that conflict. Crowds of people of all ages, each with their own painful memories, reach up to touch the cold stone, take a picture of a child next to the name of his or her unseen father, trace the gray inscription of a beloved son, or lay a wreath for a group of old buddies.

Even for this visiting Canadian, who did not know one name on the list, it was impossible to remain unmoved. Some people who came just stood and stared; others broke down and wept. However, all can admit to choking back more than a few tears. Visitors' emotions range from a sense of bereavement, self-pity, and sorrow to shock, but the overwhelming question asked by all who see this monument is, "Why?"

Young boys were taken from loving families and ordered to fight old mens' battles, to protect the private wealth of yet another corrupt Third World leader. They were hampered all the while by the hostility of the people they were supposed to be rescuing and the bureaucratic red tape from their own chain of command.

Fifty thousand of them died, and for no good reason. Fifty thousand deaths is one statistic that lives forever in the minds of all who have touched, and been touched by the Monument.

Fifty thousand is also the number of Americans who are killed by cigarettes every eight weeks.

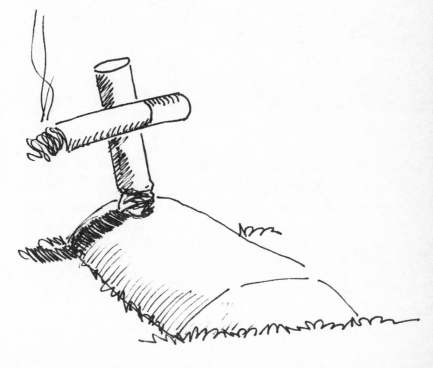

ALCOHOL — WORLD'S MOST ABUSED DRUG

Alcohol is a deadly adversary when taken in excess quantities, although it is safe and even beneficial in small quantities — one or two "standard" drinks per day.

WHAT CONSTITUTES A "STANDARD" DRINK?

One "standard" drink = 0.6 ounces of absolute alcohol
  = 1 ounce of spirits
  = 5 ounces of wine
  = 12 ounces of beer

Because of alcohol's legality, social acceptability, and ready availability, it has been the most abused drug in the world for thousands of years. By the time most children reach the legal drinking age, they have seen tens of thousands of drinks downed on television shows and in advertisements. Such behavior is thus accorded the status of a "normal" response to stress.

The universality of alcohol abuse makes it a problem affecting most of the world's workforce. While the problem is more severe in countries such as Russia, and even more disastrous among some aboriginal groups such as the Australian aborigines or North American Indians, it is in the mainstream of North American life that the best records are kept. In the United States the costs of alcohol abuse are estimated to be about ten billion dollars every month. The fact that the government makes a little short-term tax money on the sale of alcohol may help balance the budget for the benefit of the image of current politicians. But the enormous long-term costs of treating the health problems caused by today's consumption are merely deferred.

In addition to the financial price of alcohol abuse, the human costs are formidable. When the friendly social drinker has even two drinks before driving home, the degree of driver impairment turns the innocent suburban sedan into a potentially lethal, flesh-crushing battering ram. In most traffic deaths, alcohol is involved. Many victims are sober, but are killed by a drunk driver. Thousands of victims who are not killed outright are injured or maimed for life. The majority of traffic deaths do not take place during office hours, when most roads are filled with cars. They take place on Friday and Saturday nights, when too many cars are filled with drunks.

As well as being implicated in this traffic carnage, alcohol is also involved in many domestic disputes. Excessive alcohol unmasks the latent hostility and aggression in many people. As any local police officer can confirm, crimes of violence are much more likely to occur on weekend nights, after one or both parties have been drinking excessively.

PERILS OF PRESCRIPTION DRUGS

Substances that are supposed to be medicinal aids can also be abused. The classic example of this is with strong narcotics that

244 STRESS FOR SUCCESS

are prescribed for severe pain. These include morphine and, in some countries, heroin. Although such substances are useful and even lifesaving for extreme cases of pain or heart failure, they can readily be abused as "street" drugs.

Less powerful derivatives of opium are present in a lot of commonplace, seemingly innocuous medications such as cough syrups and pain pills containing codeine. Many of these are highly addictive even when taken legitimately for chronic or severe pain. With continual use they can cause a paradoxical "rebound" pain when a regular dosage is missed. This perpetuates the pain-pill cycle, turning the patient's body into a chemical battleground.

Sleeping pills and tranquilizers have claimed a following of abusers as well. Once patients get into their minds the fallacy that sleep is impossible without drugs, then the drugs start abusing the abusers. The adverse effects of such medications can be made far more serious when mixed with even modest quantities of alcohol.

Some prescription drugs are sought by addicts who frequent dozens of doctors, each of whom thinks he or she is the only physician consulted and each of whom hands over a prescription for the desired drug. Young doctors have to be especially careful, as experienced addicts can give Academy Award performances to wrench both pity and the prescription out of the naive physician. Sometimes these drugs are overprescribed by a doctor who pays too much attention to the immediate complaint, and too little to the potentially addictive side effects of the medication. Once received by the patient, the drugs are either abused directly or sold at enormous markups on the street.

Tranquilizers, including sleeping pills, are now the most frequently prescribed drugs in the world. Recent figures show 7% of the British population take them regularly, and similar figures have been seen in North America and other countries. Prescriptions for tranquilizers are written by the medical profession (largely male) for their "overstressed" patients (largely female). Patients blame their doctors for being "pushers," and doctors complain that their anxious patients are "pullers." Regardless of where the blame lies, help for stress does not come in pill form.

Although tranquilizers are appropriate for certain psychiatric illnesses, it is frankly appalling that these pills are in such widespread misuse. The new breed of tranquilizers was originally thought to be completely safe. The previous generation of anti-anxiety pills, the phenobarbital family, had lethal side effects when taken in even moderate overdose. Patients who had the mental instabilities that prompted their doctors to prescribe these tranquilizers were naturally at high risk for a lethal overdose, even when only a handful of pills were consumed as a token suicide attempt.

Thus when Valium came along in 1963, doctors were delighted to note that even an overdose of an entire bottle of 50 pills would produce only a deep sleep, following which the patient would recover in a few days. Although today's tranquilizers are relatively safe when prescribed judiciously (unless taken with alcohol or other drugs), patients have become quite addicted to long-term doses of even one pill per day.

Since the demographics of a family doctor's practice indicate that most adult patients are women, this means that the majority of prescription tranquilizer users (and abusers) are women. For years many were afraid to admit or even recognize these addictions themselves. However, a great step forward was made in 1978 when the First Lady of the United States, Betty Ford, courageously announced her admission into a treatment program to overcome her dual addictions to alcohol and pills. (See chapter 15, regarding the Betty Ford Center.)

THE COCAINE CATASTROPHE

Cocaine is an alkaloid derived from the leaves of the coca plant, a bush that grows naturally in Bolivia, Chile, and Peru. Cocaine has a pronounced excitant action on the central nervous system.

In small doses it produces a pleasurable state of well-being associated with relief from fatigue, a reduction of hunger, and increased excitation during intercourse.

With these attributes it is no wonder that cocaine has become so popular among an increasingly "stressed out" workforce that yearns for instant and easy relief from problems. Cocaine is especially popular during working hours because it is more difficult for others to detect than alcohol. Further explaining its appeal, especially to athletes, cocaine temporarily increases mental alertness, energy and physical strength.

If it were as simple as all this, cocaine would be in great favor as a panacea. However, these positive attributes of the drug, which last only a few minutes, are quickly erased when one considers the downside. After the initial positive sensations, the user is left with a sense of depression, leading to a desire for more of the drug. Cocaine is thus highly habit forming and, in greater amounts, becomes an intoxicant that produces mental agitation, confusion, hallucinations, and potentially fatal convulsions. In some individuals it can become physically addictive.

Chronic use of cocaine is associated with severe personality disturbances, insomnia, loss of appetite to the extent of emaciation, an increased tendency towards violence, and antisocial behavior. The latter two of these changes are exacerbated by the user's need for money. A cocaine habit can easily cost thousands of dollars per week. This explains why so many habitués have turned to purse snatching, break-ins, and robberies.

Cocaine's chemical properties can be enhanced by modifications such as free-basing and intravenous injection (instead of "sniffing" the white powder or eating it). A dangerously new derivative called *crack* has become a scourge of our youth because of its low prices and ready availability, often near schoolyards. For further information on this dangerous response to stress, please consult your local doctor, hospital, public health office, or addiction agency.

WRISTBAND OR TOE TAG?

The list of chemicals that can and have been abused is formidable, and beyond the scope of this book. I have touched on some of the more common addictions that I have seen in my practice, and in the emergency wards of hospitals. However, many who are hooked on alcohol, drugs, or other substances never show up in health care centers. Some keep their addictions secret because even their closest friends and coworkers do not suspect the abuse. Others do so because they do not see their habits as real problems.

Unfortunately many who have sought help are put on a long waiting list. They become discouraged by the bureaucracy and never bother to show up. Some stay away because they are too poor to afford treatment (although not too poor to afford the drugs). Others avoid help because they are too rich (and too vain) to risk their reputation. It's the same as the inevitable story of buying on credit: "You can pay in full now, or you can pay a lot more later."

Substance abusers can save their lives by coming in for help now, although, as we will see in the next chapter, the rehabilitation will not be without anguish. Or they can ignore all this advice, and pay later. I have admitted many substance abusers through the doors of our hospital who knew the risks of their abuse, but thought they were personally immune. Unfortunately, for many, the consequences of substance abuse were far harsher than they had anticipated. Instead of being issued with pre-admission wristbands for hospital identification, they were admitted straight to the morgue, with their names — if known — written on a toe tag.

Chapter 15

SUBSTANCE ABUSE — SOME ANSWERS

REASONS FOR SUBSTANCE ABUSE

When any worker who has abused drugs or alcohol seeks help, or is brought in for help, the first question that will probably be asked is, "What sort of addiction does this person have?" My approach is much more profound and much more likely to offer long-term help: "What sort of person does this addiction have? Let's look at the reasons for the addiction."

In cases of drug abuse related to one's job, it becomes critical for the abuser to have the flexibility to change career directions if necessary. If a dentist hates filling teeth but loves some other kind of activity, even a lower paying one, then he or she should consider a career change. One of my middle-aged patients in just such a predicament sold his urban dental practice and has opened a modest marina north of Toronto in cottage country. Although not making as much money, he is at least making waves. His family is together, he no longer needs drugs to face his day, and his health has improved.

Another of my patients was a working mother trapped in a horrible marriage. Although things were bearable during the week, her husband beat her whenever he was drunk, which was most weekends. She could not sleep, and became an abuser of tranquilizers (which she stole from her job as a nursing home attendant). In the past this woman had been admitted to hospital for professional care and placed on a drug abuse program. However, these measures had been unsuccessful. Her initial reasons for taking the pills were still waiting for her at home. The only way she could hope for long-term improvement would be to sever the bad relationship with her husband so that she could get on with her own life again. She benefited from extensive counseling in my office, and with peers and counselors in a therapy group. A number of de-stress options (mentioned in chapter 10) helped her control her sleep patterns without drugs. However, there is little question that she would have been driven back into her former habits if she had not had the courage to finally leave her spouse and rebuild a safer life with her children.

Similar findings are seen in a host of other cases. A middle management clerk, bored out of her mind all day, turns to cocaine to add some adrenaline, excitement, and memories to her otherwise colorless life. Drug programs alone, although helpful initially, will not solve the boring lifestyle, but perhaps a stress-cure (see chapter 11) would help. A young assembly-line worker whose peer group takes drugs may need to consider changing jobs, companies or, if peer pressure is severe, even changing cities, as we have seen in chapter 12.

INTERCEPTION POINTS ALONG THE JOURNEY TO SUBSTANCE ABUSE

There are three chances to stop drug and alcohol abuse. The first chance is prevention before the habit starts. The second chance is rehabilitation after the user has experimented a little. The third and last chance is resuscitation after the addiction has set in. These chances have progressively less possibility of success. Thus, ideally, we should aim to catch all potential drug and alcohol abusers before they start. However, with drug and alcohol abuse on the rise, not just in our young people but in their parents and grandparents, it is obvious that optimism must be tempered with reality.

Although the authorities are working their hardest to prevent illegal substances from ever getting to the public, the interception of drugs is a difficult and frustrating one. Added to that is the ready accessibility of both alcohol and tobacco to minors. Education must begin at home, and be reinforced by daycare workers and teachers.

For the abuser, the journey from a healthy, sober lifestyle through the point of casual use, to the point of no return, and even beyond, is a sad road to self-destruction, as the fight to stop becomes harder to win the farther along the person has traveled.

When you have a friend or loved one who is demonstrating a dependency on artificial substances to allow them to maintain their lives, it is important that you encourage them to face up to their problems and help them to stop their personal abuse.

DRUG COUNSELING AND THE MEDICAL PROFESSION

Many people have the chance to help intercept a friend's journey towards substance abuse, but the medical profession has one of the best opportunities to offer informed counseling on a more massive scale. Despite the fact that counseling will save far more lives than any other single treatment a doctor can use, this most effective weapon is being used less each year. This is not because doctors care less about their patients. The reasons for the decline in medical counseling lie in the realities of modern medical practice. In all health care systems doctors are penalized every time they do any counseling. In a socialistic system, such as the British

National Health System, the penalty is in the form of time. General practitioners are paid a flat annual fee based on the number of patients on their "list." If they spent time doing preventative counseling with a lot of their patients, they wouldn't have time to see the many acutely ill patients who also need their care each day.

In a more capitalistic medical system, such as in the United States, the doctor's penalty for counseling is money. The fee structure determines that the doctor is not paid by the hour, but by the diagnosis. The fee earned for prescribing pills for six alcoholics with hangover headaches is far greater than the fee for spending the same time trying to prevent one of them from abusing alcohol.

The simple fact is that any prevention of disease through lifestyle counseling is basically a volunteer activity on the doctor's part, and thus is vulnerable to being severely restricted by other demands on that doctor's resources.

Partially because preventive counseling seems like such common sense, this simple service is very price-sensitive to both patients and their insurance plans. Yet all concerned readily pay lavish amounts for diseases and injuries that never needed to take place. The frustrating reality is that it costs a lot more to ignore prevention than to pay for it up front. The 42-year-old cocaine abuser who suddenly has a heart attack at the office is never begrudged his expensive stay in the cardiac intensive care unit, but people object to paying for counseling to prevent the addiction from starting, because they feel that such advice is "just common sense."

The public perception is that a few dollars invested in early prevention is a waste of money. Many people adopt the ostrich's posture and assume that nothing will happen to them personally or to their families. Alas, common sense is not very common.

SUBSTANCE ABUSE AND THE ECONOMY

We all care about the future of our economy. Our jobs depend on whether we cay stay competitive with the rest of the world. To ignore substance abuse in the workplace is to invite disasters, both medical and economic. For example, the U.S. is one of the most drug-ridden countries in the world, a fact that many believe is partly responsible for its declining productivity compared with Japan and other countries. However, the rest of the world is hardly drug free, and lessons learned in America will help other countries cope with their own increasing problems.

Public education, with effective role models marketing good choices to the impressionable potential abuser, has been shown to be very effective in preventing substance abuse. We certainly know the power of the opposite approach — the expensively produced campaigns to destroy health. Compared to the carefully targeted lifestyle ads for alcohol and cigarettes, the meager budgets spent on marketing the alternatives seem badly outclassed, but victories are being won. Governments can help by stopping the subsidization of alcohol and tobacco abuse.

The consequences of cigarette smoking — including health care, absenteeism, and accidental fires — cost billions of dollars in North

America annually. Our current practice of having these costs borne by general insurance payments or from general tax revenues means that the nonsmoker is heavily subsidizing the abuser's habit, to the tune of almost two dollars a pack. Although cigarette smokers think they are hard done by with taxes on their habit, the amount they contribute doesn't even pay half their upcoming bill for self-induced ill health. If the generous public subsidization of death were stopped, the users would be much more likely to quit or at least reduce their consumption of cigarettes and other tobacco products.

Workplace use of drugs costs North American industry further billions a year in absenteeism and turnover, as well as untold billions in poor-quality work. Yet, even out of this crisis, can come opportunity. Insurance companies, governments, corporations, and individuals have never had greater financial motivation to work together to help prevent the carnage.

EMPLOYEE ASSISTANCE PLANS — SOME SUCCESS STORIES

rkplace innovations such as Employee Assistance Plans (EAPs) provide excellent examples of effective cooperation for the common good. Companies and government agencies are now realizing that it costs a lot more to do nothing than it does to set up an effective drug and alcohol abuse program. However, during times of recession, EAPs totally funded by management are vulnerable to being cut off.

What seems to best prevent this from happening is having the plan jointly funded by a union or by the workers directly, even if their contribution is only a token 10% or 15% of the costs. Management, even in a recession, is much less likely to cancel a program when it is not footing the entire bill. Some of the money governments waste on post-disaster expenses could be better spent in encouraging EAPs. The benefits in human terms are obvious and, in financial terms, the money all comes from the same taxpayer anyway.

The Duke Power Company in Charlotte, North Carolina, has

recently introduced an EAP program, which has been well received by all. One reason for this is that the company took great care to work with its employees, educating them to the severity of the substance abuse problem and reassuring them that the motives were to help abusers, not further abuse them by ending their careers.

Similarly, MacMillan Bloedel, an international pulp and paper giant based in Vancouver, British Columbia, started a very innovative Employee Assistance Plan with its 15,000 workers, funded by both the union and the company. Raymond Smith, president and chief executive officer, told me of the stresses of his forestry workers: "Each man gets up at six in the morning, and climbs up four hundred feet of densely forested mountain. He then works all day on a steep damp slope with a heavy chainsaw in his hands, and one foot braced high above the other."

The life of forestry workers is hard, and many take early retirement due to physical disability. The reason so few of these forestry workers stayed in good health long enough to enjoy their post-retirement years was explained in one word: booze. With not much to do in a remote logging camp after dark, most men drank prodigiously, making alcohol almost an occupational hazard. Smith was very concerned for his workers and their families, and initiated the company's first Employee Assistance Plan to preempt health failures due to substance abuse. Initially the unions were suspicious of his motives, and only one local voted to give this plan a try.

Right from the beginning, Smith insisted on principles of high ethics; otherwise, he knew the plan would never work. Any counseling undertaken was kept in the strictest confidence. No worker could be fired for admitting an addiction, and no employee's career path could be derailed because of having sought help. Smith had no interest in finding out the names of those he helped, but wanted to expand the service to the rest of his crews. Soon the system flourished.

In British Columbia alone, MacMillan Bloedel has 10,000 employees, and has treated 3,000 in its EAP over the last 10 years. The service has now been expanded to help the families of workers. Smith rightly points out that no worker can be fairly expected to concentrate on the job if a spouse, adolescent child, or parent is on a drunken rampage at home. MacMillan Bloedel's success rate has been impressive, whether measured in financial, moral, humanitarian, or ethical terms. Smith has now expanded the service to provide care and counseling for community members who work for other companies, and even those who are unemployed.

RX FOR SUBSTANCE ABUSE — SOME POSITIVE ACTION STEPS

GET AT THE ROOT CAUSE, BUT REMAIN FLEXIBLE

Once one has correctly identified the real cause of substance abuse, then one must be flexible enough to take whatever remedial action is indicated. On an individual level, as we have seen, this counseling, learning a new trade, getting married, seeking a divorce, leaving home, or even leaving town to get a viable new start.

AVOID PUNISHMENT OF END USERS

Punishment of workers who abuse drugs has been found to be worse than useless. One regional railroad had a longstanding policy of instantly firing any train driver found drunk on the job. For years none was reported by peers, even though drinking on the job was rampant and a number of errors and indeed fatal accidents were later found to be caused by impaired drivers. The company then changed the policy regarding alcohol abuse from firing to help and rehabilitation, with guaranteed anonymity so that no abuser's career could be derailed.

All of a sudden, dozens of cases were turned in. A few even turned themselves in. Once rehabilitated, the ex-alcohol abuser or drug addict often becomes a loyal and productive asset for the company, instead of a potential liability. By preventing even one derailment, crash, or chemical spill due to driver impairment, for example, a company can save millions of dollars, at a relatively low cost.

ENLIST SUPPORT WHEREVER IT CAN BE FOUND

The love and support of friends, family members, and mentors are a critical supplement to any help given by doctors, employers, clergy, support groups, and social agencies. All of these could be thought of as forming ropes in the safety net under a person having a substance abuse problem.

ESTABLISH ALTERNATIVE HIGHS

Most addicts think of rehabilitation as having to give up something. This is a negative, self-defeating thought. Negative motivation usually produces negative results. However, positive motivation can work wonders. For example, instead of the smoker dreading the loss of her nicotine, she should dwell on the positive images of being able to taste her food, smell her perfume, and feel the surge of self-control and confidence when she resists each temptation to light up.

The alcoholic should picture the laughter he will have with his children, their children and even — if he stays fit — the next generation. The cocaine user should think of how much better he or she could perform when no longer in need of the chemical crutch.

ACCEPT THE FACT THAT LIFE HAS LOW POINTS

We all have times when we feel unconfident, inadequate, lonely, or depressed. Without such lows, we probably couldn't appreciate the high points in our lives. Professional chefs tell me they enjoy eating cheap hamburgers and French fries once in a while. Such humble dishes provide a change, helping them appreciate the filet mignon, truffles, and other fine foods with which they usually work.

Media advertising, television shows, and movies all apply subtle pressures for us to feel good at all times. The reality is that this is an unattainable goal. This means that the only way people can hold themselves up to the impossible standard is through artificial means. There is no question that, if a person is depressed, a dose of drugs will make him or her feel better. To counter that, it may help to remind the person that there is nothing wrong with having a "hamburger" of a day. It just means he or she will enjoy tomorrow's "filet mignon" all the more.

AVOID HYPOCRISY

In the 1960s marijuana was much less potent than it is today, and as such was used at least occasionally by a majority of the "flower child" generation. A shocked parent who criticized the kids for needing external stimulants had a credibility problem if he or she had a cigarette in one hand, a large martini in the other, and a couple of tranquilizers and a headache pill floating in his or her stomach.

As a doctor counseling patients, I could hardly get a smoker to quit if I were covered in cigarette ashes and had brown nicotine stains on my fingers. The same applies to anyone espousing abstinence from drug and alcohol abuse.

By the way, alcohol or drug addiction treatment that ignores a patient's addiction to ordinary cigarettes makes as little sense as having the fire department put out the blaze in your kitchen but leave the rest of the house burning. Substance abusers, no matter what the substance, are not exactly keeping their body's best interests in mind, so it is not surprising that a lot of them smoke, and smoke heavily. By not addressing this dependence, the nicotine addiction is being condoned. Furthermore, it is hard to get an addict to concentrate on painful or negative areas of discussion if he or she is getting a "fix" of nicotine during counseling.

Jean Matthews Larsen, executive director of the Health Recovery Center in Minneapolis, noted that 63% of the graduates of this program smoked one to four packs of cigarettes a day when they entered treatment for other addictions. However, because of their total commitment to ridding the body of its daily chemical load, only 8% were smoking at the end of six months. In other words, just because someone is giving up one addiction doesn't preclude their giving up another.

USE FULL STRENGTH REHABILITATION METHODS WHEN NECESSARY

When all else fails, and the patient is in real danger of slipping over the edge, more drastic measures are needed. A showcase of how such measures may be implemented exists in California, at the Betty Ford Center. In 1978 the former First Lady of the United States made a historic impact on closet abusers everywhere when she bravely admitted her drug and alcohol dependency as she was signed into a naval hospital for treatment.

Four years later, she opened the Betty Ford Center for drug and alcohol rehabilitation in Rancho Mirage, California. It operates on the principles of Alcoholics Anonymous and "tough love," approaching addiction as a physical disease with extensive social and psychological consequences. Described by some patients as a cross between a boot camp and a POW camp, the discipline and lifestyle are austere. Living space is shared, as are all household duties, and contact with the outside world is restricted. The idea is to have each patient rebuild the bonding and trust that they have lost, to once again find self-respect. The Center's program is not costly, the majority of the clientele is neither rich nor famous, and it succeeds in almost 75% of its cases.

Inspired by Ford's courage, many other high-profile stars and role models came forth with their own bluntly-stated admissions of abuse. Actress Elizabeth Taylor, instead of following the passive excuse of blaming her problems on pills or the doctors who gave them to her, held her head high, telling *The New York Times* that she was a drunk and a junkie. She added quite correctly, "There's simply not a polite way of saying it." With public admissions like this from people who had so much to lose from potential scandal, ordinary addicts realized that they, too, could make that admission, get the required treatment, and still keep their self-respect.

In Canada, rehabilitation centers have also been very successful in their help to abusers. Information on facilities may be obtained through the Addiction Research Foundation in Toronto.

DRUG TESTING — A CONTROVERSIAL ISSUE

THE ONE TEST YOU CAN'T STUDY FOR

The early detection of drug abuse is an important opportunity to intercept the destructive journey of the abuser, but it is one fraught with complications that are potentially disastrous to both employer and employee. Of course, some cases of addiction are not particularly hidden, and are easy to identify. The alcoholic who is slurring her speech as she weaves down the corridors, the cocaine freak with the glassy eyes and fixed pupils, and the heroin mainliner who has needle marks all over his forearms can all be easily noticed by coworkers.

Some cases are much harder to detect. However, with some drugs, some quantities, and in some individuals, it is possible for the trained observer to detect hidden addiction. The telltale slipping of job performance, coming in late or not at all, and subtle changes in habits of dress can betray a closet addiction. The definitive way is to test for hidden abuse of drugs or alcohol, but this suddenly lands one in volatile controversies over human rights and invasion of privacy.

In my family medical practice, I have treated individual abusers in office, emergency ward, and hospital settings. As a public speaker, having spoken to over 500 corporations, government departments, and associations around the world, I have met literally hundreds of human resource and Employee Assistance Plan managers who are concerned about how to maximize effectiveness. From this information base, I would like to suggest some guidelines that will help to satisfy both the employer's need for a safe, drug-free work environment, and the individual worker's need for protection of human rights, especially privacy.

EXPLAIN REASONS FOR TESTING

Mandatory drug testing is usually accepted by workers if reasonable suspicion is explained, just as a breathalyzer test is for a drunk found driving on the sidewalk. Reasonable suspicion would include:

- Unexplained inability of an individual to concentrate for normal periods of time, to the detriment of a the individual's usual performance.
- A sudden increase in the rate of accidental injuries on the job.
- Unexplained changes in a worker's punctuality or absenteeism rates.
- Observed physical and behavioral changes such as change in pupil dilatation, speed or pattern of speech, unusual mood swings, or even a change in cash flow. In the case of a stu-

dent, a sudden plunge in marks could indicate impairment, providing a reasonable justification for drug testing.

HAVE THE BACKING OF RECOGNIZED AUTHORITY AND BE FAIR

Testing is always easier if the government orders it, not the company. This is one reason why it is no longer a contentious issue that the public can expect astronauts, soldiers, air traffic controllers, airline pilots, and nuclear reactor operators to be subjected to drug tests in just the same way that a tanker-truck driver can be arbitrarily tested by the roadside breathalyzer.

Drug testing is also more palatable if it includes the entire hierarchy, from executive office to rookie clerks. If parttime student employees are expected to let themselves be tested for cocaine or crack use, it is only fair that the boss be tested for alcohol after a business lunch.

TESTS MUST BE ACCURATE AND RELIABLE

Tests must be accurate, done by an accredited lab using strict specimen labeling and standardized calibration of testing machines. Unfortunately, not all labs are equal. Many labs give unreliable results, thus causing more problems than they solve. One of my patients was told by a lab contacted by his company that he had tested positive for amphetamines. My patient's doubts about the validity of the lab's results were even greater when they showed that he was also pregnant. If a positive test is obtained, at least two more corroborative samples should be taken and preferably sent to different labs.

KEEP RESULTS CONFIDENTIAL

In the old days, the navy doctor could get away with announcing a sailor's venereal disease over a bullhorn, but the consequences of such indiscretion in the modern workplace can be disastrous. As Raymond Smith of MacMillan Bloedel said, ''It is none of the company's business who is addicted to what, as long as it is being treated and as long as safety is not jeopardized.'' A positive drug test is not like a positive typhoid test, and thus no one but the individual and his or her Employee Assistance counselor or health professional needs to know.

ALWAYS AIM TO HELP, NOT HARM

The consequence of a positive test must be help, not harm. Although it is perfectly appropriate to have a clear set of corporate guidelines defining what the criteria are for dismissal (such as stealing, gross insubordination, disloyalty, drinking or taking drugs while on the job), it is unfair to use an isolated test result as the basis for immediate dismissal. In all companies where this has been done, the results are exactly the opposite of what the company had hoped for. Usually the response to a sudden dismissal of this kind is that the morale of the remaining workers goes down. Safety and profits decline. Abusers do not step forward to get treatment, and are not referred by their coworkers. Addiction problems continue and employee theft rises.

On the other hand, if drug test results are handled ethically, as part of a comprehensive assistance plan with perhaps a confidential copy sent to the employee's family doctor with the worker's permission, then the first step to a lasting recovery can be taken. Considering the average costs in time and money involved in retraining a replacement worker — if a suitable one can even be found — it is well worth a company's efforts to try to salvage rather than ''discard'' the impaired worker.

The intensity and severity of substance abuse is perhaps one of the most critical challenges we have faced in the history of the workplace, and indeed our society. It will test our capacity to offer workers and their families prevention rather than just cure, and to show addicts compassion rather than hostility. These simple tools represent the best counterattack against the violence of substance abuse.

Chapter 16

STRESS FOR SUCCESS — THE HANSON PRESCRIPTIONS

PRACTICAL EXAMPLES OF GOOD STRESS MANAGEMENT

We have seen how stress works, and we have seen how we can work stress. Let's look at a couple of outstanding examples from two very different work situations.

On the day after the stock market crashed on "Black Monday," October 19, 1987, employees in investment houses were under incredible levels of stress. Phones were ringing off their hooks as a fever of anxiety and even panic spread among the media and the public. On the morning of October 20 the staff at the multi-billion dollar Mackenzie Financial Corporation in Toronto were convened for an emergency meeting.

As company president Jim O'Donnell rose to address his employees, there was, naturally, an atmosphere of apprehension in the room. With a straight face, O'Donnell announced that he brought them good news and bad news. The good news was that they were all fired. The bad news was that there were no other jobs available anywhere else in the world. O'Donnell's timely sense of the ridiculous caused a tremendous catharsis of laughter, and levels of morale throughout the entire audience surged.

O'Donnell then went on to outline a brilliant crisis strategy.

His first concern was that each staff member should remain compassionate with respect to the fears of dealers and customers. Rather than passively reacting as phone calls came in, he suggested that his staff be pro-active. Each was to make the first move, calling his or her dealers to express concern, offer reassurance, and to give dealers the most up-to-the-minute advice to pass on to their own customers.

This strategy would not have been as effective in softening the panic of dealers and customers if O'Donnell's staff had not been able to have had that big laugh when they needed it most. The traditional "textbook" presidential approach would not have been nearly as effective. An interesting postscript to this story is that the strategy worked. Mackenzie Financial went on to dramatically surge past all competitors in post-crash deposits into their funds.

Of quite a different sort is the job of the shoe shiner. This is a job that has no big crises such as those seen in the stock business, but has a chronic steady level of stress that can wear a person down over time. The job is basically repetitive, and many have told me they find it boring after a few years. When working with a group of colleagues along a bank of chairs, some shoe shiners don't even talk to their colleagues, much less their customers.

Many shoe shiners I have encountered who are friendly and still enjoying their work are ones who are relatively new to the job. The negative thinkers leave after a few years, or stay on and feel trapped. These jaded veterans of shoe shining think of the job as an example of stress that the worker cannot help.

There are, of course, outstanding individual exceptions to this attitude, but examples of large groups of consistently positive thinkers are a little harder to find. One such group works at the airport in St. Louis, Missouri. At several locations around the concourse are a remarkable group of shoe shiners of assorted ages and personalities — all having fun at work. The St. Louis shoe shiners are known as the best in the country. Their customers are grinning. Many even bring a few extra pairs of shoes from home because of the superior quality of the shine they receive.

The shoe shiners of the St. Louis airport have built up an enormous loyalty among local people, frequent flyers, and visiting celebrities. It's not just because of the shines they give, but because of the smiles they impart. They kibitz among themselves, make jokes with passers-by, and keep up a running banter with customers in the chairs.

Soon all within earshot are infected with their contagious high spirits, and even the most stonefaced of customers is loosening up. Even those shoe shiners who have been on the job for decades can't wait to get to work each day, not because of the shoes, but because of the people who wear them and the humor that makes it all fun. The same could be true of almost any job, even yours. Why not start passing some good humor around? It's contagious.

HANSON'S TEN TOOLS FOR STRESS AT WORK

In a world cluttered with complications, it is useful to hold on to a few simple tools for handling stress on your job. Here are 10 of the best. They're easy to remember, and they work.

1. MANAGE YOUR PRIORITIES
Don't just write out a list of things to accomplish each day. Write down whether each is a top priority or an optional priority. This way you can start with only the crucial tasks. When interruptions prevent you from finishing your list, it will mean only the optional items need be deferred.

2. MANAGE YOUR TIME
Take 10 minutes each evening to write down the estimated time it will take you to finish each of the items on your list of activities

for the next day. Then add up all the times, and make sure that realistic travel and documentation times are included. If the total list of top-priority tasks adds up to more than 8 hours, or whatever length of time you have to accomplish the day's work, look for shortcuts and/or for ways of eliminating or delaying some tasks.

3. MANAGE DETAILS

When you have an idea you want to remember, stop what you're doing and write it down. Don't write it on a business card or the back of an old envelope, but in your time and priority management binder, which will become a trusted memory bank. In your alphabetical phone index, keep separate sheets for each of the people you frequently deal with (such as clients, buyers, colleagues, accountants, doctors) over the course of a year. Every time you have an idea that should be mentioned the next time you encounter the person, write it down on that person's page. Then, instead of worrying that you'll forget, you can simply refer to the sheet next time you talk to the person face to face or on the phone.

4. COMMIT YOURSELF TO EXERCISE

A standing appointment, no excuses tolerated, for three hours of fun exercise each week will help you keep fit to handle stress better. If you are physically able, try to make a point of taking no escalators ever. If you work in an office tower, never get off an elevator at the right floor. This will allow you to get some stairclimbing into your daily routine. Park your car in the corner of the parking lot that is farthest from your destination. The walk will do you good. If you travel a lot, see chapter 9 for tips on an "away" exercise program.

5. COMMIT YOURSELF TO RELAXATION

Set aside at least 15 to 20 minutes per day, at whatever time will give you the best results, for reenergizing your day. See chapter 10 for a more complete menu of de-stress options.

6. USE ONLY THE BEST FUELS

A race car cannot give its best performance using a low octane fuel, and we cannot do our best work eating a poor diet, or taking in drugs, alcohol, or tobacco. Remember the old GIGO rule in computer programing, "Garbage in = Garbage out." It applies to your body, too.

7. SET GOALS FOR LEFT BRAIN STIMULATION (TO STIMULATE INTELLECT AND MEMORY)

One way is to learn to play a musical instrument. Another way is to take a course, preferably with the stress of an exam at the end to help discipline the learning mode of your left brain.

A third method of left brain stimulation is to try to memorize something each day. Sir John Gielgud memorizes large quantities of Shakespeare as a form of pure mental exercise to ward off disuse atrophy of the brain. Other suggestions might be to memorize new vocabulary in either your own or a new language, or details from historical events that interest you.

8. SET GOALS FOR RIGHT BRAIN STIMULATION (TO STIMULATE CREATIVITY AND IMAGINATION)

One way is to be a storyteller for your kids. Another way is to read a biography of a favorite person, and look for examples of versatility in the person's life story. Few bureaucratic left-brained automatons ever have biographies written of them, so most interesting people you read about in biographies will be good role models for versatility.

If you are musical, try to "noodle" around with new melody or harmony lines to songs, or even try your hand at writing new music.

If you are studying the grammar and vocabulary of a new language with the left side of your brain, then use the right side to string together spontaneous conversations with others who speak the language. This will not only stimulate your right brain, but is, of course, also one of the best ways to learn to use the language.

9. MAKE A STANDING DATE WITH YOUR KIDS

Spend at least a few minutes each day with your kids, and as long a time as possible on weekends or holidays. If business pressures preclude being home when they are awake, then do as I do: take a book of fairytales or other stories in your briefcase or suitcase when you travel. When it's the kids' bedtime in Toronto, I call home from wherever I might be in the world. My wife puts Kimberley, age 7, and Trevor, age 5, on the phones. For the next five minutes I read a story (from the book they have packed for me) as they hoot with laughter. Who says you can't buy anything for a kid for under ten dollars? Try a few moments of your own time.

You can also apply this if you are a parent delayed in evening meetings in your own town or city. No criticism would befall a parent who excused himself or herself for a five-minute break to become even more vulnerable to stress by swilling coffee or smoking a cigarette. Why not take the same five minutes to bolster your stress defence by calling home? The stresses of work won't be any different, but it is obvious that the outcome will be more positive if you choose the better route.

10. MAKE A STANDING DATE WITH YOUR SPOUSE, CONFIDANT, OR BEST FRIEND

Ideally, your spouse should be all three of the above-mentioned people. Book babysitters for set times each week, even if the two of you are only going out for a walk in the park. It will force you to get away from noncommunicative activities such as staring at the television. The average couple spends only about 12 minutes a day talking to each other in private. This lack of communication can only increase the chances of having an unstable relationship. Most people who are remarried have already figured this one out, but it would be ideal if you could put it into practice during your *first* marriage.

HANSON'S THREE PRINCIPLES OF STRESS COMPARTMENTS

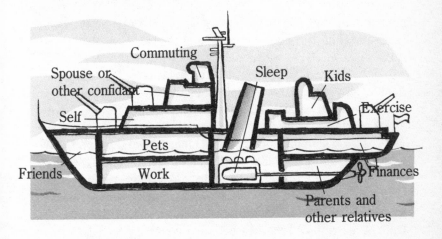

- A good life, like a well-designed battleship, should be made up of many compartments.
- Each compartment can be stressful without fear of endangering performance in the others.
- When stress scores a direct hit, close the hatches by choosing de-stress options and using high-stress cures.

IN CONCLUSION

The poignant tragedy of needless human sacrifice has been well documented by great writers, artists, and film-makers. We are reminded of these senseless wastes every time we pick up a newspaper, listen to the radio, or watch the evening news. And yet together we gallop, heads down, like great herds of lemmings, towards a sheer cliff. We blame the stress for driving us to the brink, and we blame the job for giving us the stress.

The bloodshed when people sail over that cliff is all the more horrific because it never needed to happen at all. For years it has been my mission to try to help stop the carnage. The best way I can do it is to reach out to each of you, point out the cliff towards which you are headed, and hope that you will then save yourself. There are medical geniuses with heroic and courageous constitutions who are waiting to save you after you crash. However, I have seen the results, and I implore you not to test their skills.

Work is indeed full of stress; we all know that. But stress can be full of joy, and that we didn't all know. Recognize your most important job of all, and run your Department of One as if your life depended on it because, in truth, it does. Treat those who work for you with patience and guidance. Treat those who work with you with honesty and commitment. Treat those who love you with more time. And even more importantly, treat yourself with respect, humor, good food, mental and physical exercise, relaxation, adventure, daydreams, and memories. Never retire from at least some kind of work, and never try to hide from a challenge.

I wish you love at home, happiness in your work, and success with your stress.

Appendix A

EXERCISE ROUTINES

One of the body's most important needs when faced with the stresses of the modern workplace is good old-fashioned exercise. Much as we might wish that this aspect of our lives could somehow be delegated to others, or relegated to lesser levels of importance, the exact opposite is true.

Our bodies were built for motion, and yet the modern workplace provides them with virtually none. Thus, it is vital that we face up to the fact that the only way to be fit is to exercise. No plastic surgery, diet pill, exercise contraption that attaches to your doorknobs, or stomach electrodes that do your situps for you will suffice. In spite of all our technology, the fact remains that only work works.

We should all be doing at least three hours of some sort of exercise a week, or about half an hour per day. For those who do, and are pronounced fit by their doctors, it is not absolutely necessary to do more (although greater investments in exercise do still improve fitness, and are thus to be encouraged wherever possible).

For the vast majority of our population who are obese, flabby, or short of breath when climbing a flight of stairs, it is strongly recommended that they first see their doctors before beginning vigorous activities. Next, the out-of-shape should consult a fitness professional for a full assessment (your doctor will probably know of a reputable fitness institute in your area). Many who have ignored this advice simply signed up for a competitive sport that focused all their attention on external objects, such as a ball, a puck, or the pavement over which they were jogging. In the process, simple internal warning signals such as the pulse rate were ignored and, in some tragic cases that I have seen, death while exercising was the result.

For those of you who have not yet been assessed and placed on a measurable exercise routine (either as an end in itself, or as a way to get into shape for the safe pursuit of other activities), I include a simple example of a 30-minute program designed for a "typical" 40-year-old male who wishes to regain his former level of fitness and prevent his muscles from atrophying. In the first example, equipment is used that could be found in most fitness clubs or, increasingly, in the home. In the second example, the program was modified to give the same man some hope of fitness when on the road, and away from such facilities. Here, simple use can be made of ordinary pieces of furniture found in any hotel room. Although there are countless new exercise devices for the traveler, from elastic bands to hollow weights that can be filled with water, these are beyond the scope of this book.

In the third example, our typical man finds himself on a long airplane journey, and wishes to do something to help him feel fit upon arrival. Obviously it is best that he do his full program back on the ground sometime during the day. However, there are also a few simple exercises that can combat the stiffness, bloated abdomen, and swollen ankles that so frequently attend travel in the skies.

While many airlines have published full routines that exercise virtually every muscle in the body through isometrics or slow movements, it is not necessary that the fit traveler include them all. Those taking short trips of less than two hours will probably not need them. However, on longer flights, especially over several time zones, exercise can be very helpful. I have included only those few exercises that are of the most benefit, and the most practical in the circumstances. Obviously it wouldn't be sensible to have 300 passengers all doing windmills with their arms during the in-flight movie.

FULL GYM

2 minutes every pace; then 3 minutes moderate. Get pulse up to 120-132.

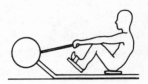

Extend arms, clasp hands. Shrug shoulders forward and drop head slowly. 4 repetitions.

4 slow repetitions, each leg. No bouncing or jerking motions. Do not extend past the point of difficulty. (If stiff, it may take weeks to do it fully. Just aim for improvement each day.)

20 repetitions. Tuck head forward. Exhale as head comes up.

20 repetitions. If necessary initially, anchor feet under edge of weights.

1 minute easy tension and then 8 minutes moderate tension (to target pulse rate of 144-156).

4 slow repetitions each leg. Note that the knee being bent must be behind the straight knee.

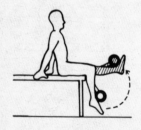

40 pounds tension. 2 × 10 repetitions.

30 pounds. 2 × 10 repetitions.

60 pounds. 2 × 10 repetitions.

80 pounds. 2 × 10 repetitions.

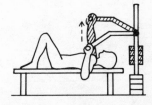

Seated on bench. 20 pounds.
2 × 10 repetitions.

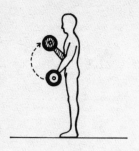

20 pounds each arm. 2 × 10 repetitions.

Bend one elbow and point it towards the ceiling. Use the other hand to slowly pull it in towards head. 4 repetitions each arm.

4 slow repetitions.

PROGRAM FOR AIRPLANE

10 repetitions in each direction.

Can be done with legs stretched under seat ahead of you. 10 slow rotations (against resistance) each way with each leg.

Good for reducing foot and ankle swelling. Ideally done in aisle, but can also be done seated. Straighten legs. Slowly point toes away from you, and then towards you. Resist each movement with the opposing muscles. Repeat 20 × each leg.

3 repetitions each way. Do slowly and do not hyperventilate.

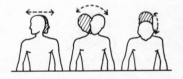

Good for reducing the bloated feeling after prolonged flight. Exhale as you pull in stomach muscles. Pressing palms and knees into each other increases muscle tension in abdomen. Repeat 4 times.

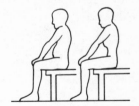

Exhale as you slowly roll down, starting at your first vertebrae and working your way down the spine. Repeat 4 times.

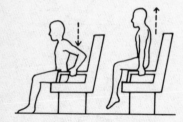

Do in seat of airplane. Repeat 10 times.

EXERCISES FOR THE HOTEL ROOM

20 repetitions each leg (or climb 3 flights of stairs).

20 repetitions. Do not bend knees more than 90°.

20 lunges with each leg.

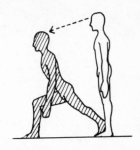

4 slow stretches with each leg. Keep bent knee behind straight knee as shown.

20 repetitions.

Start supine, with arms extended overhead, and one knee bent. Raise yourself to assume illustrated position, and then return. 12 repetitions each leg.

Hands shoulder width apart on bench or foot of bed. Feet on floor, legs straight, hips relaxed. Lower body until elbows bent 90°. 20 repetitions. Can be made even more challenging if feet are placed on a chair (bend knees slightly).

2 × 10 repetitions. Do not bend knees past 90°.

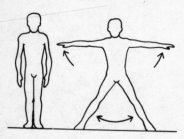

2 × 20.

3 to 5 minutes. Can be done even without skipping rope, but rope can easily be packed. Heart rate no more than 150 per minute.

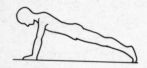

For greater body toning, start with feet up on a chair. 2 × 15 repetitions.

Appendix B

NUTRITION AT WORK

A balanced diet for nutritional fitness at work should include the following categories.

FATS

About 30% of daily calories should be in the form of fats. These can include a small amount (300 mg) of cholesterol — or less if your doctor finds your serum cholesterol to be more than 200 mg.

Studies have shown that only 7% of North Americans, and even fewer people in other countries, know their own cholesterol levels. Well over a quarter of all North American adults exceed recommended levels. Virtually all should have their blood tested for cholesterol at least every five years. If your doctor tells you your blood tests are normal, you can eat some cheese, dairy products, meats, and oils as part of your balanced diet. On the other hand, if your blood levels, body weight, family history, stress levels, lifestyle habits, and/or cardiac findings demonstrate any increased risks for a heart attack, your doctor may recommend significant reductions in saturated fats.

The question of who will have a heart attack is certainly multifactorial. However, one must remember that avoiding whole milk dairy products, eggs, and meats is no guarantee of eliminating saturated fats from one's diet. Surveys show that consumers in North America are eating less red meat than they used to, but have unwittingly doubled their consumption of cheese (which has even more cholesterol) in the last 20 years. Chicken has also become a popular substitute for red meats. Although poultry's white meat is lean, its dark meat and skin are high in saturated fats. Fat levels are even higher when the chicken is fried.

Although dietary cholesterol can be found only in animal products, saturated fats can also be found in many of the cheaper margarine and other vegetable sources of fat, such as palm and coconut oil. For those who are at risk, all of the saturated fats — including animal cholesterol — should be restricted. Because these fats are easily hidden in a variety of products, including "health foods," one should read the fine print on prepared foods to see if they contain surprises. Even many roasted nuts, granola bars, and muffins sold in vegetarian health food stores are high in the very saturated fats that customers think they are avoiding.

For people whose blood levels of cholesterol are elevated, a professional nutritional consultation with the entire family would help greatly to educate everyone with regard to eating habits. Individual pursuit of a radical fat-restricted diet should not be undertaken without medical consultation. Some people can develop poor immune systems as a result of such diets. They thus become vulnerable to severe illnesses, simply from going overboard on fat restrictions.

PROTEIN

Protein should make up about 15% of daily calories. In simpler terms, this means a piece of lean fish or meat about the size of a deck of playing cards. For those who prefer a vegetarian format, protein can easily be taken in the form of egg whites, certain vegetables such as beans, and/or dairy products.

CARBOHYDRATES

Carbohydrates should make up about 50% of daily calories. The carbohydrate category is always popular as it includes desserts. However, 90% of one's carbohydrates should be in the more complex form, such as is found in vegetables, whole grain cereals, and pastas. About 10% or less should be in the form of simple refined sugars, candies, and refined flours.

FIBER

A healthy diet should include 50 grams of fiber a day. Levels of 35 grams are declared sufficient by the American and Canadian Cancer Societies. But most people do not measure fiber precisely, and usually overestimate their consumption. By raising their target to 50 grams, most people will eat at least 35 grams.

Fiber, found only in plant materials and never in animal products such as milk, eggs, or meats, is the inert substance that forms the walls of plant cells. As it essentially never enters the body's bloodstream, dietary fiber has no side effects when taken with a balanced diet. It adds no calories to the daily diet. On the contrary, this level of fiber can carry out up to 150 undigested calories in each bowel movement.

Fiber can easily be obtained from favorite foods such as apples, pasta, peas, and some breakfast cereals. Many restaurants are now offering wholegrain breads instead of the fiberfree white variety. On the whole, however, it takes some vigilance to spot the fiber on many a restaurant menu. The search is well worth the effort, though, in terms of better performance at work, better resistance to stress, and avoidance of the "expense account paunch."

WATER

You should drink eight glasses of water a day. If local tap water is tasty enough to past muster, then it would be perfectly suited to the task. On the other hand, if — as in many cities — the office water supply is a little distasteful in such large quantities, then bottled or filtered water would be a good investment.

In some restaurants, an order of water all around will be greeted with minimal enthusiasm by the waitress or waiter who would rather see expensive drinks inflating the final tip. However, in some areas, tap water may be in short supply at certain times of the year, and water may not be served unless you ask for it.

If the tap water is potable, I usually ask the waiter for a whole jug for the table. If the local water tastes offensive, then I ask for a large quart- or liter-sized bottle, which is still less expensive than most alcoholic alternatives. Waiters have no financial incentive for attentively refilling water glasses, as they would if you were drinking a vintage wine. Thus my volume order of a supply for the table is usually appreciated.

In a buffet style presentation, I usually take three glasses and fill them with water, to avoid having to get up and hunt for replacement supplies when a glass runs dry. If you eat lunch at your desk, then try to keep a couple of bottles of your favorite brand of spring water within reach. Besides being necessary for health, water also makes an ideal substitute for caffeine to sip on during thirsty moments.

APPROPRIATE VITAMINS AND MINERALS

Consult your doctor to see if you have any signs of vitamin or mineral deficiencies. While it is true that a healthy body can usually find a full complement of vitamins and minerals from fresh natural foods, some supplementation is needed at times. In the winter, when foods are less fresh, and during periods of illness or stress, extra vitamin C can be helpful. However, I would suggest you take this with your doctor's knowledge. Although Dr. Linus Pauling feels vitamin C is safe in huge doses, there may be mitigating circumstances, such as kidney stones or metabolic acidosis, that would limit the safe levels for an individual.

Some cancers and precancerous conditions can be helped by taking vitamin E (in the case of cancers of the bowel), and others by taking large doses of the B vitamins.

It seems that what Norman Cousins and Linus Pauling have been saying all along — that vitamin supplements can offer some improvements in health — has now been proven true. It has been accepted even by the medical establishment, which had long had a distrust of such claims in the past. To be sure, there are certainly many charlatans touting vitamins in much the same way as snake-oil was marketed in the past. If one has a particular medical problem, one should get a diagnosis before starting self medication with vitamins, and then do so only with one's doctor's knowledge. For further specific information, I suggest you contact your local public health office or registered nutrition professional for additional reading.

LET THE SUPPLEMENT BUYER BEWARE

Great caution is required in buying dietary supplements because many "natural" vitamins store badly, and have lost their value before they are even taken. Although this is not a problem with most reputable brands, this is particularly true of the unfamiliar generic varieties. Many unqualified "experts" have convinced people to spend ridiculous sums of money for vitamins they didn't need. The effect may even be to delay medical investigation.

Some vitamins, such as vitamin A, can be lethal in high doses. Thus such pills should never be taken on a whim, like candy or peanuts from a bowl. Your doctor or nutrition professional will be able to put you on a sensible regime of supplementation appropriate for your personal needs, often with very little expense.

HOW MUCH TO EAT AT A TIME

The number of calories taken at each meal or snack is a matter of personal preference, as well as a matter of the requirements of the job. A manual laborer will have to eat differently from a sedentary computer operator. People who work in extremely hot environments will need more fluids and more salts than workers who have air-conditioned offices.

Those who wake up with their stomachs still full of partly un-digested food from from the night before may not feel up to any breakfast at all, and will be able to eat larger lunches and dinners than most. Some feel sluggish after big meals, and prefer to divide their calories into smaller snacks for parts of their schedules. Shift workers, especially those who have to swing between day and night shifts every couple of weeks, may need to go on a modified Jet Lag diet (see chapter 9).

ABOUT THE AUTHOR

Peter Hanson was born in Vancouver, B.C. He graduated from the University of Toronto medical school in 1971, and at 24 was appointed as the team doctor of the Toronto Argonaut football club, making him the youngest team doctor for any professional sports organization in North America.

After leaving the Argonaut organization, Dr. Hanson worked at a number of Toronto-area hospitals. He spent two years doing full-time emergency-room work before opening his own practice in Newmarket, Ontario, which soon grew to have more than 4,000 patients.

His work in the field of stress and stress-management developed into his first, self-published book, *The Joy of Stress*, which remained on the national bestseller list for 69 consecutive weeks. *The Joy of Stress*, since its introduction in Canada, has been subsequently published in the United States, United Kingdom, France, Australia and New Zealand.

Although Dr. Hanson has left his practice of 15 years, his mission to spread the message of preventative health is still intact. Whether he is speaking to an audience of 5,000, or is engaged on a radio talk show in Perth, Australia, or Perth, Scotland, the questions he is asked are the same as those that were asked by his patients in his office. By reaching so many millions through *The Joy of Stress*, and now with *Stress for Success*, Dr. Hanson continues to deliver his message, and far from quitting his practice, he has enlarged it, at least by a little bit.

Dr. Hanson is available for speaking engagements and seminars.

In Canada, contact: Hanson Stress Management
Organization, Inc.
5 Thornbury Crescent
Islington, Ontario
M9A 2M1

Telephone   (416) 232-0687
Fax number (416) 234-1891

In the U.S., contact: National Speakers Bureau
222 Wisconsin Avenue
Lake Forest, Illinois 60045

Telephone (800) 323-9442 or
(312) 295-1122

In the U.K., contact: Prime Performers
The Studio, 5 Kiddipore Avenue
London NW3 7SX

Telephone (01) 431-0211

In Australia, contact: Celebrity Speakers
P.O. Box 50
St. Leonard's, NSW 2065

Telephone   (02) 439-3255
Fax number (02) 439-3679

For *Stress for Success* tapes, contact:

The Book Fiend
P.O. Box 596R
Toronto, Ontario, Canada
M4G 4E1

ACKNOWLEDGMENTS

Mountaineers have a technique of climbing in which the lead climber holds his or her body steady over a difficult break in the rockface, and the next climbers use his or her back as a ladder to more easily continue the ascent. This technique, known as *court echelle* (literally, "short ladder"), is not restricted to mountain climbing, but is found in the teamwork of most endeavors. In climbing my own mountains to complete this book, therefore, I am forever grateful to the many others who figuratively or literally joined my rope.

For role models, I could have asked for none better than Sir Edmund Hillary, K.B.E., conqueror of Everest; Ken Blanchard; Norman Vincent Peale; futurist John Naisbitt; columnist Art Buchwald; and, from his earliest days as a stand-up comedian, Bob Newhart. For parents, I couldn't have chosen better. I am grateful to George and Donna Hanson for making so many personal sacrifices in their youth to see that my sister Penny and I were able to have the best possible education and opportunities.

For colleagues, I have been blessed with many, such as Jim O'Donnell, Glenn Miller, Chris Ansley, Laurie Skreslet, and Joe MacInnis who have helped me in concrete ways with their input into their business worlds, as well as in supportive ways, when I just needed their friendship.

I would like to thank the whole terrific team at Collins Canada for their enthusiasm, support and invaluable contributions throughout the process of creating this book; the talented people at Doubleday U.S.A. (David Gernert and Nancy Evans), and Pan Books (Hilary Davies and Sally Strange) of the U.K., Australia and New Zealand, for their support and confidence in this project, and for listening to my feedback from the "field." I am delighted to have had the opportunity to reunite the same team that made it possible for the self-published book, *The Joy of Stress*, to have been such a record-breaking success. Freelance editor Elma Schemenauer was, as she was in *The Joy of Stress*, a pleasure to work with. Peter Kovalik did his usual fine job of witty artwork to liven up the text.

Many others are new to the team, but no less important in their contributions. Diana Redegeld, my phenomenal researcher, kept my fax machine hot with detailed materials from computer databases, printed articles, and television shows. My rookie literary agent, the legendary publisher Jack McClelland, did a superb job of advising and representing me; I am forever grateful for his ongoing counsel and friendship.

In addition to meeting people in audiences all over the world, one of the added advantages to being a public speaker is the opportunity to forge strong friendships among clients and fellow speakers. It was in this capacity that I met Bob Marbut, president and CEO of Harte-Hanks Communications, Inc.; Michael Brickell, president and COO of Holt Renfrew and Co., Limited; Blanton Belk, president and founder of Up With People; Charles Garfield, author of *Peak Performers*; Tom Connellan, author of *How to Grow People into Self-Starters*; underwater diving and human performance expert, Dr. Joe MacInnis; and Everest summiteer Laurie Skreslet.

I am also grateful to the following: Bill Wilkerson and Larry Stout, partners in Fraser Kelly Corpworld Group, Inc.; Ron Charles, Chris Thomas, and Doug Caldwell of the Caldwell Partners International; Dr. Kerry Crofton, Ph.D., for her insights into the healthy "Type A"; Ray Smith of MacMillan Bloedel; Les McPhail of Consumer's Distributors; John Palmer, Phemmis Anno, and Laura Ferrier. I am also grateful to Keith Silverberg of Suntastic Holidays for coordinating my byzantine travel arrangements, and Marc Doubois of Fitnessland for helping me stay fit at home. For all their important feedback I would like to thank Nancy Ansley, Gail Palermo, Joan Brickell, and Cathy Grieve; Michael Kane, Director of Regulatory Affairs, U.S.G. Corp; David Rosenboom for his bio-feedback; and others too numerous to name.

BIBLIOGRAPHY AND RECOMMENDED READING

Allen, Steve, and Wollman, Jane. *How to Be Funny*. New York: McGraw-Hill, 1987.

Belson, David. *What to Say and How to Say It: For All Occasions*. Secaucus: Citadel Press, 1961.

Bensen, Herbert, and Klipper, Miriam Z. *The Relaxation Response*. New York: Avon, 1976.

Blanchard, Kenneth, and Peale, Norman Vincent. *The Power of Ethical Management*. New York: Morrow.

Bolles, Richard N. *What Color is Your Parachute?* updated ed. Berkeley: Ten Speed Press, 1987.

Brod, Craig and St. John, Wes. *Technostress: The Human Cost of the Computer Revolution*. Toronto: Addison-Wesley.

Campbell, Jeremy. *Winston Churchill's Afternoon Nap: A Wide-Awake Inquiry into the Human Nature of Time*. New York: Simon & Schuster, 1987.

Connellan, Thomas K. *How to Grow People into Self Starters*. Ann Arbor: The Achievement Institute, 1980.

Cousins, Norman. *Anatomy of an Illness As Perceived by the Patient*. New York: Bantam, 1981.

Cousins, Norman. *The Healing Heart*. New York: Avon, 1984.

De Bono, Edward. *Lateral Thinking*. New York: Harper & Row.

De Bono, Edward. *The Use of Lateral Thinking*. New York: Penguin.

Dienhart, Ligita, and Pinsel, E. Melvin. *Power Lunching*. Chicago: Turnbull and Willoughby, 1985.

Drucker, Peter F. *The Changing World of the Executive*. New York: Times Books, 1982.

Ehret, Charles F., and Scanlon, Lynne Waller. *Overcoming Jet Lag*. New York: Berkley, 1986.

Fletcher, Leon. *How to Speak Like a Pro*. New York: Ballantine, 1983.

Ford, Betty, and Chase, Chris. *Betty: A Glad Awakening*. New York: Doubleday, 1987.

Garfield, Charles. *Peak Performers: The New Heroes of American Business*. New York: Avon, 1987.

Grothe, Marcey and Wylie, Peter. *Problem Bosses: Who They Are and How to Deal with Them*. New York: Fawcett, 1988.

Harvey-Jones, John. *Make It Happen: Reflections on Leadership*. London: William Collins and Sons.

Hochheiser, Robert M. *How to Work For a Jerk: Your Success is the Best Revenge*. New York: Vintage.

Humes, James C. *Instant Eloquence*. New York: Stein & Day, 1980.

King, Patricia. *Never Work for a Jerk!* Danbury: Watts, 1987.

Levering, Robert; Moskowitz, Milton, and Katz, Michael. *The 100 Best Companies to Work for in America*. New York: Signet, 1987.

Lieberman, Gerald F. *3,500 Good Quotes for Speakers*. New York: Doubleday, 1985.

MacInnis, Joe. *Underwater Man*. Van Nuys: Panorama.

Mackay, Charles. *Extraordinary Popular Delusions and the Madness of Crowds*. Fort Lauderdale: Templeton, 1985.

Mackay, Harvey. *Swim With the Sharks, Without Being Eaten Alive*. New York: Morrow, 1988.

Meyers, Gerald C., and Holusha, John. *When It Hits the Fan: Managing the Nine Crises of Business*. Boston: Houghton Mifflin, 1986.

Naisbitt, John. *Megatrends: Ten New Directions Transforming Our Lives*. 6th ed. New York: Warner, 1983.

Naisbitt, John, and Aburdene, Patricia. *Re-inventing the Corporation: Transforming Your Job and Your Company for the New Information Society*. New York: Warner, 1985.

O'Hara, Bruce. *Put Work in Its Place*. Work Well.

Oncken, William, Jr. *Managing Management Time: Who's Got the Monkey?* Englewood Cliffs: Prentice-Hall, 1984.

Peck, M. Scott. *The Road Less Traveled*. New York: Touchstone, 1980.

Pendleton, Winston K. *Speaker's Handbook of Successful Openers and Closers*. Englewood Cliffs: Prentice-Hall, 1984.

Peters, Thomas, and Austin, Nancy. *A Passion for Excellence: The Leadership Difference*. New York: Random, 1985.

Peters, Tom. *Thriving on Chaos: A Revolutionary Agenda for Today's Manager*. New York: Knopf, 1987.

Roskies, Ethel. *Stress Management for the Healthy Type A: Theory and Practice*. New York: Guilford Press, 1987.

Secretan, Lance H.K. *Managerial Moxie: A Basic Strategy for the Corporate Trenches*. Toronto: Holt, 1986.

Secretan, Lance H.K. *The Masterclass*. New York: Stoddart.

Shaevitz, Marjorie Helen. *The Superwoman Syndrome*. New York: Warner, 1985.

Siegel, Bernie S. *Love Medicine and Miracles: Lessons Learned about Self-Healing from a Surgeon's Experience with Exceptional Patients*. New York: Harper and Row, 1988.

Spicer, Keith. *Think on Your Feet: The Winging It Handbook*. Toronto: Doubleday, 1985.

Spicer, Keith. *The Winging It Logic System*. Toronto: Doubleday, 1984.

Taylor, Harold L. *Delegate: The Key to Successful Management*. New York: Beaufort, 1984.

Taylor, Harold L. *Making Time Work for You: A Guidebook to Effective and Productive Time Management*. New York: Beaufort, 1982.

Valenti, Jack. *Speak Up With Confidence: How to Prepare, Learn and Deliver Effective Speeches*. New York: Morrow, 1983.

Veninga, Robert L., and Spradley, James P. *The Work-Stress Connection: How to Cope with Job Burnout*. New York: Ballantine, 1982.

Villiers, Alan and others. *Men, Ships and the Sea-Captain*. New York: National Geographic Society.

BIBLIOGRAPHY AND RECOMMENDED READING 295

Waitley, Dennis. *The Double Win*. New York: Berkley, 1986.
Waitley, Dennis. *The Psychology of Winning*. New York: Berkley, 1984.
Waitley, Dennis. *The Seeds of Greatness: The Ten Best Kept Secrets of Total Success*. New York: Pocket, 1988.
Waitley, Dennis. *The Winner's Edge*. New York: Berkley, 1984.
Waitley, Dennis, and Witt, Reni. *The Joy of Working: The 30 Day System to Success, Wealth and Happiness on the Job*. New York: Ballantine, 1986.
Waterman, Robert H., Jr. *The Renewal Factor: How the Best Get and Keep the Competitive Edge*. New York: Bantam, 1987.
Watson, Thomas J. *A Business and Its Beliefs: The Ideas That Helped Build IBM*. New York: McGraw-Hill.
Wells, Joel. *Coping in the Eighties: Eliminating Needless Stress and Guilt*. Thomas More, 1986.
Witkin-Lanoil, Georgia. *The Male Stress Syndrome: How to Recognize and Live With It*. New York: Newmarket Press, 1986.
Wohlmuth, Ed. *The Overnight Guide to Public Speaking*. Philadelphia: Running Press, 1983.
Ziglar, Zig. *Top Performance: How to Develop Excellence in Yourself and Others*. New York: Berkley, 1987.

MAGAZINES AND PERIODICALS:

The British Medical Journal
The Canadian Medical Association Journal
Financial Post
Financial Times
Fortune
Globe and Mail (Report on Business)
Journal of the American Medical Association
Journal of Stress
The Lancet
Maclean's
New England Journal of Medicine
Newsweek
Time
U.S. News and World Report
The Wall Street Journal

NEWSLETTERS:

Harvard Medical School Health Letter
John Naisbitt's Trend Letter
Mayo Clinic Health Letter

OTHER REFERENCE SOURCES:

Dialog Information Services — Medline (Medical Journals)
                                       The Newspaper Index
                                       The Popular Magazine Index

INDEX